THE FRANCHISE FRAUD

THE FRANCHISE FRAUD

How to Protect Yourself before and after You Invest

ROBERT L. PURVIN, JR.

Chairman, Board of Trustees
American Association of Franchisees and Dealers

JOHN WILEY & SONS, INC.

New York • Chichester • Brisbane • Toronto • Singapore

This text is printed on acid-free paper.

Copyright © 1994 by Robert L. Purvin, Jr.
Published by John Wiley & Sons, Inc.

This publication is designed to provide accurate and
authoritative information in regard to the subject
matter covered. It is sold with the understanding that
the publisher is not engaged in rendering legal, accounting,
or other professional services. If legal advice or other
expert assistance is required, the services of a competent
professional person should be sought. *From a Declaration
of Principles jointly adopted by a Committee of the
American Bar Association and a Committee of Publishers.*

Library of Congress Cataloging in Publication Data:

Purvin, Robert L., Jr.
The franchise fraud : how to protect yourself
before and after you invest / Robert L. Purvin
    p.   cm.
Includes index.
ISBN 0-471-59947-6

Printed in the United States of America

10 9 8 7 6 5 4 3 2 1

To my franchisee clients whose tribulations unfortunately mandated this effort.

To the memory of my mother, Lois Davis Hirshberg, whose sense of fairness, justice, and equality is behind every word.

To my secretary Kim whose dedication and efficiency kept me focused and on schedule.

And especially to my good friend Dandy; may this book provide you the ammunition to lead a successful crusade against franchise fraud and abuse in the United States.

Foreword

The franchise industry has come a long way and many individuals have come together in the struggle for truth in franchising.

But let me first go back a number of years. In the mid-80s, I, as a freshly minted MBA with solid years of experience in the business world behind me, decided to become an entrepreneur. Not having limitless financial resources, I started to investigate what type of business I should consider and what I could afford. After reading all of the available literature and having many discussions with bankers, accountants, consultants, friends, and relatives, I kept being pointed toward franchising. Mind you, not a particular franchise, just franchising. Published articles and discussions always brought up that often quoted (as well as misquoted) study: 95 percent of franchises succeed versus 20 percent of independents, and so on.

A friend introduced me to a couple who were franchisors in the pizza industry who had sold about 70 franchises and were going strong. We met and I was anxious to sign on the bottom line and start the money rolling in. Early in the process, my common sense warning system should have gone on alert, but I got caught up in the passion of the moment. I won't bore you with all the gory details, but one early example will suffice: the highly proclaimed "locational analysis." I lived in the south part of the city, so I wanted my business to be close to home (so much for market research). One of the franchisors, the vice president for franchise sales, and I drove around the neighborhood one morning looking at empty storefronts and rental prices. Relying upon looks and intuition, one was chosen and I was left to negotiate with the landlord (an item not covered in MBA school and in years to come, an item I proved to be not good at). In addition, this location proved to be on the border of three zip codes, making direct mail, which is the lifeblood of advertising for pizza parlors, prohibitive.

In short, through the next three years as a franchisee I became more and more aware of the fact that I might not have known how to make a pizza, but I knew more about business practices than the franchisor. In the end, I was never able to overcome the locational problems and lack of vision and support from the franchisor, and I got out. A short time later the pizza market went south due to over-saturation, most of the franchises, and my particular franchisor went bankrupt.

Since that time, I have been providing consulting services to the business community. I continue to follow the world of franchising but more from a knowledgeable position. I was amazed that the public, the government, bankers, and other professionals were not seeing through the hype and understanding what was really going on. Many had fallen for The Franchise Fraud. I grew increasingly concerned about the media hype and misinformation that was circulating on the advantages of becoming a franchisee. Most of the information available based the advantages upon benefits considered by the franchisors in marketing their particular franchises rather than actual benefits as the potential franchisee.

"Sure fire success," "low failure rate," "be your own boss," "control your own destiny" were phrases that I continually heard or read. After long hours of meetings, discussions, and research with potential franchisees, current franchisees, ex-franchisees, independent entrepreneurs, and other professionals, I became convinced that the above phrases were not true across the broad spectrum called "franchising," but may be true under very specific circumstances, all coming together and dictating success.

My interest in educating the potential and existing franchisee was further strengthened by a startling statistic that I came upon in *Franchising in the Economy,* published by the International Franchise Association Educational Foundation. Roughly translated, this publication's research showed that 73 percent of all franchising sales dollars were attributed to sales of franchise units in the areas of car dealerships, gas stations, and soft drink bottlers. Keeping this statistic in mind, consider that 87 percent of all franchises being opened today belong to all other categories, excluding the three just mentioned. My question then became why is this very important detail not mentioned in the writings expounding the glories of franchising.

My mission during these last years has been to inform. Is all franchising bad? Certainly not! I have conducted numerous seminars and training events through organizations nationwide as well as through the National Association of Small Business Development Centers, of which I am a member. My message is clear. Let us walk through the hype and high profile success stories and get to the basics of business. A strong business plan developed in response to good solid marketing research that tells you, *the entrepreneur,* that there is a sufficient and steady demand for your product or service in a particular geographic location is a critical factor in business success. Once you have completed that plan, you must decide through further intense research whether an additional crucial factor of success is that you be a franchisee. If the answer is yes, then you must investigate and compare all franchisors that offer the product/service in which you are interested in order to make the best choice.

In the beginning, the above approach was not well received. I was deemed a doomsayer, a negative personality. It was with great joy that I met Robert Purvin and learned of his long struggle to gain truth in franchising. I recognized early that Bob was not out for personal gain or glory, but was out there with the minority opinion because he truly believed that wrongs were being wrought on an unsuspecting public. Bob worked with, represented, and defended those that thought they had bought the "American Dream" only to see it shattered before their eyes.

During the last two years, the tide has started to turn. Many legislators on the federal and state levels have begun to pay attention to the rising voices. Franchisees have also begun to pay attention and to try to curb abuses by unethical, uncaring, and greedy franchisors who are giving all of franchising a bad name, just as the good name in year's past was claimed by all.

This book is long past due. Robert Purvin tells the story of franchising that comes from years of experience, observation, and research. Understanding the information provided in this book is a starting point. Only by understanding the truth can we fully develop, promote, and benefit from the potential that strong franchise systems have to offer.

Anne Dugan
Director of Small
Business Development Center,
University of Pittsburgh

Preface

Twenty-five years ago Americans were in love with the Corvair, a cute, affordable, and economical little car that seemed to be America's answer to the European compact economy cars like the Volkswagen. Induced by an unprecedented advertising campaign by General Motors, millions of Corvairs were sold in the few years following its introduction. Then Ralph Nader wrote a book called *Unsafe at Any Speed* which exposed the Corvair as a dangerous and deadly accident waiting to happen. Nader accused General Motors of knowingly marketing a dangerous vehicle to the American public.

The Corvair's popularity screeched to a halt and the line was ultimately discontinued. More importantly, consumers were informed about possible safety hazards in cars and began to demand better built, safer automobiles. In essence, the concept of consumer protection was born and a spate of new laws and regulations were spawned assuring that safety is built into American products.

Twenty-five years earlier, during the Great Depression, a similar scenario played out when the serious risks of the U.S. securities industry and the banking industry were exposed. As a result, new securities and banking laws and regulations were designed to protect naive American investors from tragic misfortune in reliance on industries that promoted themselves as safe and secure institutions for achieving financial independence, profit, and security.

A quarter-century after Ralph Nader exposed the safety hazards of the Corvair, the American public has a new love—commercial retail franchising. The franchising industry has successfully promoted the sale of franchised businesses as a safe and proven path to achieving the American dream of business ownership. Moreover, the franchising industry has marketed itself as a benevolent and protective order. The current slogan of the International

Franchise Association, the powerful trade association of franchisors, is "In business for yourself, but not by yourself!"

This book demonstrates that the franchising industry has portrayed a seriously false and fraudulent image. Although thousands of Americans have had successful experiences owning a franchise, an unacceptable number—also numbering in the thousands—have lost their life savings believing that franchising was the "safe path" to business ownership. Thousands more have become entrapped or enslaved by their franchise systems, discovering they are more owned than owners.

It must be remembered that there were thousands, even millions, of satisfied Corvair owners, and certainly the vast majority of Americans were not injured during the collapse of the banking system during the Depression. These consumer "scandals" shocked our conscience because we expected safety and security from our automobiles and banks. Similarly, the franchising industry portrays itself as a Mecca for achieving business ownership with the security of a proven business system and a caring franchisor protecting its franchisees from the uncertainties and pitfalls of commerce.

In truth, as often as not, franchising provides neither safety *nor business ownership;* sometimes the franchisor is the enemy instead of the protector.

This is a book that had to be written; it reveals a side of franchising, the dark side, that has rarely been told. How unproven franchisors' bask in the glory of the successes of a relative few blue chip companies. How the franchising industry has exploited questionable statistics to drive the franchise boom. Stated simply, *The Franchise Fraud* is the false representation by the franchising industry that franchising *per se* is a safe and secure means of owning a business.

There now exists a runaway market of franchised businesses. Some 3,000 to 5,000 franchisors are marketing their businesses through franchising, and willing buyers gobble up franchise opportunities without hesitation or basic understanding of the pitfalls of the industry. Because of an eager buying public, the modern franchise product is a poor imitation of franchises of 50 years ago. Most franchisors promise nothing but a trademark license of frequently dubious value. In many franchise systems, the franchisee never owns a business, never has the right to be in business apart from the franchise "license."

Indeed, most franchisees discover that the termination of their franchise also terminates their right to earn a living in their chosen profession—or to ply the trade they have spent thousands of dollars to learn.

The manuscript that follows intends to expose to grave perils of owning a franchise—without denying that a demanding, careful franchisee can yet achieve successful business ownership through franchising. More importantly, this work is a demonstration of how to capture the promise of franchising—rather than be captured and entrapped by the modern tricks of the franchisor's trade.

Most importantly, this book exposes the perils of the franchise marketplace—and demonstrates how prospective franchisees can demand a fair deal in the market—and demand and obtain a franchise that includes a fair and just opportunity to own a business of value for the mutual benefit of franchisor and franchisee.

This book is as much about solutions and market corrections as it is about revelation and education. If the ills of franchising are explained by the maxim, "Power corrupts," the path to safe franchising is found in the old adage about strength in numbers. This book represents an urgent call for franchisees throughout the United States to join together to demand and bargain for fair and equitable franchise relationships.

The Franchise Fraud exists because the consuming public has failed to demand quality and equitable franchise relationships. With education and direction, a discerning public will not allow The Franchise Fraud to continue. Existing and prospective franchisees can use the tools presented in these pages to join together to demand that the promise of franchising be delivered. As autos have been made much safer, and our savings deposits are now insured, The Franchise Fraud can be beaten—read on!

Acknowledgments

Having never written a book before, I didn't appreciate the importance of the author's acknowledgments. I now understand their significance because I, too, am experiencing the compelling drive to recognize those people who helped or supported me, or on whose shoulders I have emotionally and/or intellectually stood to take command of my subject.

Scores of clients over a 20-year law practice have been my inspiration. Most of the franchisees I have represented through the years believed and trusted, and were burned. They are regular folks who bought into the American dream of business ownership, and bought into The Franchise Fraud, hook, line, and sinker. Their stories simply need to be told.

This book is not about the criminal element that is present in any industry. Although I have met my share of blackhearted franchisors (and also some blackhearted franchisees), the basic premise of *The Franchise Fraud* is that the problem emanates from a natural order dictating inevitable corruption when there is a critical imbalance in economic power.

It has been the many franchisors I have dealt with, respected, and liked as individuals who have led me to conclude that the ills in the franchising industry are more *systemic* than based on evil intentions. If we can somehow fix the system, balance the industry, all the players will be better for it.

I am indebted to many scholars, tacticians, negotiators, and warriors whose brilliance and courage educated me and led me to this place. Harold Brown, the patriarch and philosopher of franchisee rights, has preached long and loud for years. Harold endured ridicule from the franchising industry when he stood alone and called for the recognition of a fiduciary relationship in franchising. Timothy Fine, who unfortunately was taken from us far too soon, was among the first to actively organize franchisees and press for legislative solutions to industry injustices. Andy Selden, of Minneapolis, has been a leader in organizing franchisee trade associations. Mike Dady should be singled out for an excellent track record in actually winning battles in court.

Franchisees have had their champions in government, only not enough of them. Craig Tregillus at the Federal Trade Commission, John Hayden in California, and others have performed their level best to work for fairness in franchising. As long as 25 years ago, Congressman Abner Mikva led an unsuccessful effort to pass a federal franchise law.

All these stalwarts worked to frame and protect franchisee rights and interests without any vocal constituency backing their efforts—or providing the grass roots support that might have corrected many problems before they got out of hand.

Recently, Congressman John LaFalce of New York has taken up the banner and is testing the political currents to determine if there is enough franchisee support to seek a legislative solution to franchising problems. Dean Sagar is the congressional staffer who has served as Congressman's LaFalce's eyes, ears, and advisor over the past few years. I take personal pride in having encouraged Mr. Sagar to refocus his substantial professional talents to the injustices in franchising (he had served as a legislative expert and aide regarding issues relating to banking, housing finance, and issues affecting senior citizens). LaFalce and Sagar fortuitously found one another, and the combination appears to have benefited the interests of franchisees all over the country.

Beyond inspiration, there is practical support. There are those special people in my life who, but for their support, confidence, and assistance, I never could have achieved the production of more than 3,000 pages for 8 progressive drafts culminating in a 400-page manuscript. There were my colleagues at the American Association of Franchisees and Dealers (AAFD), Mark McDonald, Bob Kline, Paul D'Heilly, Bill Stone, and Mark Zuckerman, who have taken up the slack, often without compensation, so I could find the time to research and write. My secretary Kim, blessed with a willing nature and flying fingers, found the time and stamina to somehow keep up with my verbosity.

Too often, we have this thing about saving the best for last, when rightfully the "best" should be at the top of the list. In my case, I must acknowledge my personal *Big 3:* My daughter Jorie and my very special friends Julie and Dean. At the ripe age of 15, my daughter has been my taskmaster and an amazing source of support. My friend Julie defines best friend; in fact, she simply defines "best."

And were it not for my friend Dean, and a pact we made some years ago to bring fairness and justice to the franchising industry, neither this book nor the American Association of Franchisees and Dealers, nor the surging crusade against franchise fraud and abuse in the United States, would have happened. When all is said and done, my good friend may be the catalyst for the very real possibility that we will reclaim the American Dream of business ownership in the foreseeable future.

And through it all, I have learned that partnerships, friendships, associations, and unions make us all so much greater than the sum of our parts. Many years ago, I toasted Dean and his lovely wife Ruth on the occasion of their marriage. My toast for them might well be my wish for the franchising community:

> Each to the other
> As each would from the other
> With love, devotion, trust,
>   and mutual respect;
> And together,
> A better life for us both.
> We make this marriage contract.

Contents

Contents

Contents

THE FRANCHISE FRAUD

Chapter 1

The Plunder of an American Dream: A Basic Primer to Franchise Fraud

It is a major component of the American Dream—owning your own business—looking forward to that day when you polish the counter, place a boutonniere in your coat lapel, and open your front door to your very own business enterprise. You are going to provide service with a smile, stand behind your products, work long but satisfying hours, and be your own boss. More importantly, because you bought a franchise, you know your product is already accepted, and your trademark is well-known. You believe your franchisor is in your corner to support your success, and you expect a helpful hand if you find yourself in trouble or meet unexpected barriers.

Roberta Y. and Gary E. were among 12 entrepreneurs who believed the promise of franchising when they each purchased a fast-food chicken franchise. Having left stable jobs, they bought into the American dream of business ownership. Although the franchisor was unknown, and its principals had little prior restaurant experience, the product was excellent and the franchisor's original location was a great success. Less than a year later, all the franchisees were headed on their way out of business, each having lost a lifetime's savings in the process. The franchisor simply did not know how to select and train its franchisees and could not clone its initial success.

Edgar & Ellen T., Mary and Greg S., Melanie H., Sharon S., Don B., and Stan M. were among hundreds of purchasers of private post office and business services franchises from several "leading" companies. Each believed franchisor (and industry) claims that 95 percent of all franchisees are still in business after five years, compared to a reported 60 percent failure rate for nonfranchised new businesses. They bought the promise of franchising only to learn that the franchising industry only counts closed stores as failures—holding on without any income, or selling at a loss, or abandoning a financial drain to the franchisor is never included in the store failure statistics.

Tom F. retired from the Air Force after a 20-year career. Jim M. and Stan W. each gave up lucrative middle management careers. John S. inherited $200,000 when his parents died, and Al F. had owned several successful small businesses. All these folks bought various kinds of automotive service franchises in "proven" systems.

Tom and Stan suffered a complete lack of promised training and support. Stan sold out at a loss. Tom held on and finally the franchisor went bankrupt. After several years of learning the hard way, Tom's transmission shop earns him a decent living. Jim M. bought a tune-up business from a major franchisor who failed to research the local market and recommended a high rent location that was saturated with competition. Jim lost $300,000 within a few months. After he closed down, Jim's franchisor sued to recover past due royalties and forced Jim into bankruptcy.

Al's tire business did well until his franchisor opened another nearby location—just outside the 3-mile protected territory, but in the middle of Al's market. Bill S. just bought a "dog" oil and lube shop that had been taken over by the franchisor from the previous franchise owner. The franchisor sold the shop to Bill "cheap" to get out from under an expensive lease. Bill has been losing $3,000 to $4,000 per month for 9 months, and has run through his entire inheritance.

Joyce and Martin M.'s premium brand ice cream shop could not compete with their own brand which was available in every supermarket and convenience store. And where are all of those yogurt shop owners that dotted every strip shopping center just a few years ago?

Mike and Sue D., Dale and Carole K., George and Debbie D., Diane S., Bill S. and hundreds like them may be the biggest victims for believing the promise of franchising. They were all successful independent business persons who joined an "established" temporary employment services franchise to grow their business and gain the security of a national chain. At the behest of their franchisor, each opened multiple offices. While some of the new offices succeeded, most predictably failed, and the failures forced all of these trusting franchisees out of business. The successful operations are now owned and operated by the franchisor—as company owned offices!

★　★　★　★

Franchising has been called the future of American commerce, an ideal means of extending the dream of business ownership to millions of Americans. Franchising is recognized as a magnificent vehicle for capital formation and rapid business expansion. Franchising is also lauded as an excellent mechanism for job training (or retraining) necessary to a vibrant economy.

Business franchising is fundamentally a mechanism of product or service distribution. Typically, any manufacturing or service business must build a system of distribution to develop a market for its products. Building an internal distribution system of company-owned stores or offices requires enormous capital and substantial risk. Moreover, internal growth usually takes many years. Through franchising, the owner of a business or product (the "franchisor") grants rights to others (the "franchisees") to engage in the business of distributing the franchisor's products and/or services using the franchisors' trademarks, trade names, and marketing system. In theory, a franchisee acquires the right to own a business representing or selling a proven product line or service, a respected trademark, and an established operating system that has been fully "debugged" to achieve maximum profit.

To corporate management, franchising has the added benefits of attracting dedicated and motivated middle management with little or no salary commitments, and an "own-your-own-business" attitude from retail-level managers. To the prospective franchisee, acquiring a franchise to operate a business can mean buying into an established business system, a recognized trademark, proven experience, and valuable training. Indeed, buying into a strong franchise system can cover a multitude of sins, and make up for many small catastrophes.

Franchising has the potential to provide all of the preceding benefits, and more. On the other hand, buying into a franchise system with an unproven product, an unknown trademark, and/or an untested operating system may constitute the only "catastrophe" necessary to cause you to lose your entire life savings. Moreover, investing in a franchise enterprise that provides little support but takes much in the way of royalties, fees, and other charges can ensure failure rather than success.

Unfortunately, many, if not most, of the 3,500 franchise opportunities being offered today in the United States are not well established and fail to provide market strength or any significant support for their franchisees. Too often, franchising is a fraud.

Through franchising, as many dollars have been bilked from an unsuspecting public as have been made when the industry fulfills its enormous promise. Believing themselves protected by federal and state laws, unwary

3

investors have gobbled up hundreds of thousands of franchises across virtu-ally every conceivable sector of the U.S. economy. Bedazzled by Department of Commerce statistics "alleged" to verify that 95 percent of all franchisees are successful, would-be entrepreneurs grab for the brass ring of business ownership through franchising.

THE LURE OF FRANCHISING

Franchisors, those who grant or sell franchises, paint a magical picture for franchising. The lure of franchising is the promise of business ownership and *success*. If the word *promise* is too strong, at the very least the lure of franchising is the representation that the vast majority of franchised businesses are success-ful. Franchising also represents the promise of training, support, guidance, and the immediate goodwill associated with the franchisor's trademark.

Pick up any directory of franchise opportunities (and there are several to choose from), or any of the several business publications directed at prospec-tive entrepreneurs, and you will find story after story, and advertisement after advertisement, proclaiming franchising as the surest, safest path to achieving the American Dream of business ownership.[1] It is not uncommon to see such slogans as the "McDonald's® of the maid service business," or "Ace Windshield Repair—The Next McDonald's.®"

More prevalent (and far worse) than identifying all franchises with the ob-vious industry leaders are ever-present suggestions that franchising *per se* is a surefire path to success in business. Over the past 10 years, more than 270 articles have been published in major magazines and journals (not to mention hundreds more in newspapers across the country) chronicling the explosive growth of the franchising industry. Here are two examples:

> There is an economic recession going on, but you wouldn't know to look at the franchise industry. Although not without its own road hazards, fran-chising continues to be one of the most popular ways to start a business. In 1990, it brought in $615.1 billion, or about 34 percent of all U.S. retail sales. Pioneered by household names like McDonald's, Kentucky Fried Chicken, and Baskin-Robbins, franchisees capitalize on name recognition and the consumer's perception of product quality.

From a franchisee's point of view, there are a number of advantages attached to owning a franchised business. The security of having a parent company behind you, with its marketing and advertising muscle, is appealing. So, too, is the assistance you receive with site selection, store design and sometimes even financing. The entrepreneur with little or no business experience faces a tough situation on his own; as a franchisee, he receives valuable business training at company headquarters, the franchising location . . . or both.[2]

And from a recent newspaper article syndicated across the United States:[3]

It's the American Dream. Owning your own business. Being the boss. Calling the shots. Making as much money as you want.

But for many wannabe entrepreneurs who have seen the mortality rate of small-business ownership, the franchise strategy has proved to be rewarding.

The advantages that franchises offer can be tremendous: name recognition, national advertising support and a track record.

The simple truth is that franchising is sold, predominantly, on the premise that the purchase of a franchise is the guarantee of success. And it is franchising "generally" that is touted, not particular franchisors within the industry.

Most established franchisors belong to the International Franchise Association (the IFA), a powerful trade association and self proclaimed "voice" of the franchising industry. The IFA annually produces the International Franchise Expo, the nation's largest annual franchising trade show. Full-page advertisements that appeared in many publications promoting the 1993 Franchise Expo, proclaimed:

Whatever your reasons for wanting a successful business of your own, take a close look at the franchise option:

—Almost 3,000 separate franchise opportunities to choose from . . .

—Only a handful require any previous experience . . .

—70 different industry sectors . . .

—Start-up costs from under $10,000 to $1 million plus . . .

Many independent business start-ups fail because of obstacles that could have been avoided. With a franchise, you'll be trained in avoiding those obstacles AND in getting maximum potential from your business. You'll be in business *FOR* yourself, but not *BY* yourself.[4]

The clear implication is that the "franchise option" of business ownership, *standing on its own,* greatly enhances the odds of business success.

In reality, the odds in favor of success are not nearly as rosy as the franchising industry maintains, and the risks of business ownership are substantial for franchised businesses. Indeed, in some respects, such as buying into an already troubled franchise system, risk of failure in franchising may be even greater than starting a business from scratch.

While it may be appropriate to identify McDonald's with success, the same cannot be said of Fotomat, Orange Julius, Gibralter Transmissions, Minnie Pearl, Computerland, Burger Chef, Mary Poppins Maid Service, First World Travel, or Penguins Frozen Yogurt, among many well-known systems that have suffered substantial unit failures. Moreover, many hundreds of unremembered fly-by-night franchises have failed—whole systems have simply gone out of business and disappeared.

THE FRANCHISE MODEL VERSUS REALITY

The universal image of a franchisee is of a business person striving to share in the American Dream of business ownership—driven by an entrepreneurial spirit, but cautious enough to buy a franchised business to ensure success of the enterprise.

The model franchise conjures up an image of the franchisor and franchisee working hand-in-hand to achieve financial success. The franchisor has been described as a partner, a mentor, a big brother, a coach in your corner—all images of a benevolent, experienced, knowledgeable support center and resource who is ready, willing, and able to nurture, support, and protect the franchisees of the system for the good of all.[5]

The franchising model describes the very essence of why people look to the franchising form of business ownership—the desire to have a strong, recognized product and system behind them to drastically reduce the long odds against starting a successful business enterprise from scratch.

While the franchise model of business ownership may often work as designed, many claimed attributes of franchising can best be described as *myths* when applied to the industry generally. Franchise promoters have succeeded in attributing almost mystical powers to franchising to lure thousands of would-be entrepreneurs to take the plunge into franchised business ownership. A few of the more notable myths about franchising follow.

Myth 1. Franchising Is a Safe Investment

Franchising is heralded as the safe path to business ownership. Franchisors cite statistics that up to 95 percent of all franchise businesses are successful, compared with an 80 percent failure rate for independently owned businesses.

As is closely examined in Chapter 4, there are only a few blue chip franchise opportunities. Many, if not most, franchises are unproven and unrecognized systems whose value is suspect. Thousands of franchisees fail every year. A recent 1992 study by Les Rager of Rubinoff Rager Incorporated, observed, "The popular perception that only 5 percent of franchises fail after five years is not only incorrect, but is used by many franchisors as a marketing statement even when their own company has much larger franchisee attrition."[6]

Myth 2. Franchisees Are in Business for Themselves, But Supported by Their Franchisors

Franchise agreements generally require strict adherence to an operating system, but offer little or no support to the franchisee. Most franchise agreements provide that the franchisee derives no goodwill (no ownership equity) from the ongoing business "ownership." Moreover, typical franchisees have less control over their own operation and destiny than do most employees. Modern franchise agreements frequently exceed 50 pages of minute detail and are supplemented by volumes of operating manuals that exert complete control over the franchise relationship.

While the conventional wisdom talks about the protective relationship of a franchisor to its franchisees, virtually every court case decided in the United States has ruled that a franchisor has no fiduciary obligations to its franchisees. Instead, U.S. courts have agreed with franchisors that franchise agreements are "arm's length" business transactions.

In their selling efforts franchisors claim to be partners and mentors in the franchisee's corner. In the franchise agreement, however, the story changes; franchisors invariably deny any binding protective duties to their franchisees.[7] Once in court, franchisors argue they are merely sellers of goods and services owing no special duties of care or support to their franchisees.

Myth 3. Franchisees Own Their Franchised Businesses

A franchisee who has paid for the right to own a business has fewer legal rights than most employees. For example, a franchisee who is terminated usually is restrained from staying in business in competition with the former franchisor. By comparison, a terminated employee (who never "owned" any interest in his or her employer's business) can go to work for any competitor and cannot be stopped from working in his other chosen profession.

Although franchise agreements invariably provide that the franchisee is an "independent contractor"—and not the agent, employee, servant, or partner of the franchisor—there is very little "independence" permitted in most franchise relationships. Franchisor standard operating procedures manuals usually dictate every minute detail of the business operations—from the size and color of the signs to the method of wiping the tables or the proper way to wear a uniform. The franchisee agrees, in advance (by signing the franchise agreement), to permit the franchisor to unilaterally amend the operations manual at any time. Effectively, the franchisor is free to modify and dictate system operations at any time and without any consultation or approval from the franchisees in the field.

Myth 4. The Franchisee Gains a Valuable Asset in the Trade Name and Trademarks of the Typical Franchise

Trademark strength is a reality with only a small fraction of the most successful franchising companies. Frequently, franchisors fail to protect their trademarks or the uniformity of their systems. Indeed, most of the estimated 3,500 franchisors in the United States have trademarks that are little recognized. You can perform a very simple test of this assertion. Pick up any of the many franchise directories—the *Franchise Annual,* published by INFO Franchise News, has the most entries (over 5,000 U.S. and Canadian franchisors were listed in 1993)—and check a few pages at random. Simply compare how many names you recognize in comparison with companies you have never heard of. If you recognized more than 5 percent of the companies listed you have done very well. But next, count how many companies you respect for quality and service from the list you recognize; for most of us, the list of well-regarded trademarks is small indeed.

Myth 5. Franchising Promises a "Proven" Business System

One of the most frequently cited reasons for buying a franchise is the opportunity to own and operate an established and proven business. A franchised business is represented to have worked out all the operational and marketing bugs that make businesses risky. All the franchisee need do is follow the franchisor's rules to avoid all the trial-and-error mistakes faced by most novice business people.

Many proven franchise systems have mastered such operational challenges as site selection, outlet design and construction, trademark protection, purchasing and cost controls, and advertising and marketing strategies. Unfortunately, there are many more franchisors who have never developed a proven success formula. Too frequently, companies launch into franchising without adequate preparation or an established track record. Often franchising is used as a growth method in lieu of planned growth. Franchising as a concept does not promise *proven performance*—rather, buying a franchise from a proven performer is a script for success.

Myth 6. Franchising Creates a Critical Mass of Market Penetration

Although it is true that a successful franchisor can rapidly achieve market penetration through franchising, the fact that a company sells franchises does not equate to the achievement of market penetration. Market penetration means that a chain embraces enough units to enjoy a broad customer base and economies in purchasing, distribution, and advertising. Only the cream of franchise opportunities can accurately substantiate claims of market penetration. For example, the 500th company to make *Entrepreneur* magazine's 1993 Franchise 500® had a total of eight units (only 6 of which are franchised) nationwide!

THE FRANCHISE FRAUD

The franchising industry suffers from something I call "systemic fraud." It is the industrywide representation, supported by questionable Department of Commerce statistics, that a franchised business is built on a foundation of gold (or "Golden Arches") and that franchising is a sure way for an entrepreneur to own a business. The many myths about franchising have been spawned and spread by the franchising industry. Make no mistake, when a myth is represented as truth, and relied on by unknowing investors to their detriment, the result is fraud.

THE REPRESENTATION BY THE FRANCHISING INDUSTRY THAT BUYING *ANY* FRANCHISE IS A GUARANTEE OF BUSINESS SUCCESS IS FALSE AND IRRESPONSIBLE. IT IS *THE FRANCHISE FRAUD.*

The Franchise Fraud is more than the representation that franchising is a foolproof, risk-free way of achieving the American dream of business ownership. It is the representation that franchising *is* synonymous with Budweiser or McDonald's. The Franchise Fraud is the industrywide representation that franchising per se *automatically* promises success, rather than the strength of the particular franchise system.

I cannot begin to recount the number of prospective franchisees who have come to me seeking approval of some little-known hamburger stand franchise. When I ask why the choice of an unknown brand, the response is usually, "Well I wanted a McDonald's, but I couldn't afford it." To these would-be franchisees, owning a franchise, *any franchise* (rather than the name and reputation of McDonald's or Budweiser), is the only factor on which they rely for the success of their business.

I recently encountered a franchise salesman who disputed my definition of franchising as a mechanism of product distribution. "Franchising is a method of cloning business success!" said the salesman, who was not bothered by the fact that the chain of franchised transmission shops he represented had lost 20 percent of its franchises the previous year, or that I had never heard of the company—to him franchising was synonymous with success.

In "buying a franchise," most franchisees actually acquire no equity in the franchised business, pay exorbitant fees for their own training, and are not entitled to such employee benefits as paid vacations, medical insurance, worker's compensation, paid holidays, or even *minimum wage.*

Moreover, an employee who quits a job cannot be restrained from getting a new one. To the contrary, franchisees in most states can be restrained from operating in competition with their former franchisor for periods of two years or more, and are thus precluded from engaging in their trade or profession unless they leave town (and sometimes not even then!).

This is *not* an indictment of all franchise opportunities. There are many solid business opportunities available through franchising to those who can afford them, but there are rarely any free rides. Indeed, even the most solid franchise opportunities, like McDonald's, have significant drawbacks for would-be entrepreneurs. The typical McDonald's licensee rents his or her restaurant from McDonalds, and the franchise agreement is tied to the lease. Terminating a franchise with McDonald's means terminating the business. There is no taking down the sign and going independent, unless McDonald's wants the sign down.

The Franchise Fraud also represents that franchisees are protected by federal and state law, and therefore franchisees can buy with confidence from franchisors who have complied with various laws. The plain truth is the franchise laws, allegedly designed to protect investors, really protect the franchisors whose powerful lobbies have turned the structure and interpretation of franchise legislation to their own benefit.

In fact, most laws "regulating" the offer and sale of franchises merely require a franchisor to disclose all the details of the franchise "opportunity"— sometimes lurid details indeed. When the prospective purchaser signs the

11

franchise agreement, all claims of fraud and abuse are commonly forfeited, because the franchisor has technically "disclosed" the policy in question in the fine print of the legally mandated disclosure statements.

It is very common for substantial rights to be forfeited in the franchise agreement. Usually, as long as the forfeitures are described in the disclosure statement (which typically has never been discussed in the sales process), the contract will be honored. Even if the franchisee read the offering circular cover to cover, provisions which effectively confiscate important rights would not be recognized by most franchise purchasers. Indeed, attorneys who are not specifically schooled in franchise law often would not recognize the risks "disclosed" in the typical franchise offering. Nevertheless, most court cases have held that the existence of disclosure precludes the franchisee from claiming that he or she did not know or understand the kinds of jeopardy explained in legalese in the franchise offering circular.

Without exception, so-called franchise investment laws lack important protections that are usually present in statutes designed to protect investors and consumers. For example, there are no minimum standards that franchisors must meet to qualify to sell a franchise. Nor are there any investor suitability requirements to be met by prospective franchisees that might prevent the offer of speculative ventures to unwary or unsophisticated investors. Minimum investment requirements have been basic investor protections in federal and state securities laws for almost 60 years. No such laws protect franchisees.

The IFA has developed substantial economic muscle to promote the franchising industry and to influence the legislative and judicial processes. As a result of the industry's enormous influence, laws governing franchising are as one-sided as the franchise agreements drafted to franchisors' specifications. Since there is no organized voice for franchisees in the United States, legislation tends to insulate and protect franchisors.

Questionable Failure Rate Statistics

As detailed in Chapter 4, the franchising industry, and publications produced or encouraged by the industry, have claimed for years that 95 percent of all franchisees are still in business after 5 years. The claim has been attributed to a Department of Commerce study called *Franchising in the U.S. Economy*

1981–1983. The study is several years old, but is still frequently quoted and uniformly used by the industry to promote franchising.[8]

More recently, the industry has pointed to an IFA-sponsored "Gallop Poll" that purported to reach similar conclusions.[9]

Until recently, there had never been any critical examination or audit of the franchising statistics relied on by the industry for the past 10 to 20 years. Those of us who have experienced the "dark side" of franchising on a daily basis (and have witnessed the failure of enormous numbers of franchisees and entire franchise systems) have known, instinctively, that the franchising industry statistics could not be accurate. Recently, study after study has openly questioned the veracity of industry claims. Commentators are just now beginning to understand that franchising statistics have been drawn from improper premises and false assumptions.

Franchisors can be very creative in defining a franchise failure. The Popeye's Fried Chicken franchise for San Diego County has been in existence since 1980. In the past 11 years, no less than 5 individual franchisees have owned the San Diego Popeye's franchise, and each of them have lost their entire investment. Five businesses have gone under, but the "franchise" still exists 11 years after it was started! When the subtle statistic is mentioned to the general public, Popeye's can accurately claim the franchise has continued to exist for 11 years. The public understands the claim to mean that the original franchisee has succeeded.

McDonald's claims only a 3 percent attrition rate, but McDonald's counts only closed stores. In other words, if a store is transferred to a new owner, even though the selling franchisee has lost virtually everything, the franchise does not become a part of attrition statistics because the business still exists!

Recent studies demonstrate that franchise failure rates are similar to, *or worse than,* failure rates of all business start-ups.[10] Moreover, other recent studies suggest the failure rate of *entire franchise systems* (let alone individual franchisees) is dramatically higher than previously believed. Franchisor failure rates are staggering when the stable blue chip franchisors are removed from the calculations. One such study found that 69 percent of the 1,100 franchise companies rated by *Entrepreneur* magazine in 1987 were no longer listed in the ratings for 1992.[11] Spot checking of the 700+ companies who had fallen out of *Entrepreneur's* ratings reveals that most of these companies have gone out of business. This is not an indication of the failure of individual franchises; the study chronicles the failure of entire franchise systems over a 5-year period. If 69 percent of the franchising companies have failed over the past 5 years, what must be the percentage of individual unit failures? A similar study in 1992 by the *Info Franchise Newsletter* reported that 852 franchising companies had disappeared from Info's *1993 Franchise Annual,* a directory of franchisors, "We just couldn't find them, so we assume they've gone out of business."[12]

It may be that more franchise businesses succeed than do independent businesses, but the margin of success is certainly not as impressive as the franchising industry claims. An accurate study would reveal that new franchises, like all new businesses, cannot claim to be anything but speculative business opportunities. Many franchise systems which would be regarded as *majors,* have had a significant number of failures in their franchisee ranks. Snelling & Snelling, Dunhill Personnel Systems, and Western Temporary Services, all leaders in the employment services industry, have had substantial attrition in their franchise systems in the past 5 years.

Many commentators believe the claim that 95 percent of all franchises still exist after 5 years is really no more than a subtle half-truth that amounts to a blatant lie as related to the general public.[13] At a 1992 congressional hearing, franchise attorney Rupert Barkoff, then Chairman of the American Bar Association's Forum on Franchising, testified that failure rates of 30 percent to 40 percent and as high as 50 percent would not be surprising.

The franchising industry generally, and most franchisors individually, routinely rely on such questionable and suspicious Department of Commerce statistics in touting franchising. Because the statistics exist, however unreliable, individual franchisors are not responsible for the accuracy of the statistics. In effect, the franchising industry has been able to embrace these staggering statistics, without being responsible for them. This is one aspect of a "systemic fraud."

FRANCHISEE *ABUSE* IS A BIGGER PROBLEM THAN FRAUD

However deceiving the commonly exalted franchise statistics, a far more devastating aspect of the systemic nature of *The Franchise Fraud* is the complete misrepresentation of the franchise relationship. Indeed, more troubling than fraud in the inducement of the sale of a franchise is the way most franchises are treated once in business. Individual franchisees usually lack bargaining power, and consequently accept one-sided contracts which provide little benefit to the franchisee. Although a popular trademark and proven operating system can present a substantial opportunity, the vast majority of franchises are unknown, unproven, and unlikely to justify required franchise fees and royalties.

Look closely at this passage by Erica Kotite, which was quoted earlier in the chapter:

> From a franchisee's point of view, there are a number of advantages attached to owning a franchised business. The security of having a parent company behind you, with its marketing and advertising muscle, is appealing. So, too, is the assistance you receive with site selection, store design, and sometimes even financing. The entrepreneur with little or no business experience faces a tough situation on his own; as a franchisee, he receives valuable business training at company headquarters, the franchising location . . . or both.

Although the typical franchise agreement states the franchisee is an independent contractor, (in essence, in business for him or herself), most franchisees have fewer rights than employees, and may more closely resemble indentured servants. (See Chapter 5.) The most common complaint of franchisees is that they are given no support from their franchisors, nor are they allowed to operate independently.

It is an unfortunate truth that for most franchisors "franchising" is their product, rather than *the means to sell* their products or services. To stay in business, franchisors must continue selling franchises. All too often, franchisors saturate their markets. Where a franchisee has an exclusive territory, the only way a franchisor can earn additional fees is by getting the existing franchisees to sell out.

Another common abuse occurs when a franchisor intentionally exploits its franchise network to pave the way for company-owned offices. Typically, the franchisor encourages investors to open several units knowing some will succeed and some will fail. The franchisor actually hopes the franchisee will be overextended and will give up the good units in order to escape the failed ones. Effectively, the franchisor retains the successful offices and abandons the losers—all with the franchisee's capital at risk.

Other times, a franchisor will open company offices in the best markets, and only sell franchises in markets the company has decided to pass by. The president of a major fast-food franchisor in California recently announced a major corporate expansion plan at the company's annual shareholders meeting. The president reported that the company had identified 300 new sites—the best 100 were targeted to be company-owned stores, and the rest were reserved for franchises. Although it may be a backhanded compliment, most franchisors are not so "public" about such practices.

Some franchise systems actually churn their franchises; that is, force a franchisee out of business so the same franchise can be resold over and over again for additional franchise fees. Churning in the stock market has been illegal since the depression, but many *major* franchisors thrive on the practice. Although the saddest experiences encountered in my law practice have involved multiple business failures (when whole franchise systems came crashing down). I have had unique experiences involving some of the most highly regarded franchise opportunities.

The most brutal manifestation of *The Franchise Fraud,* however, occurs on a franchisee's termination, or attempted termination, of the franchise relationship. Only when a franchisee tries to go independent or change brands is it discovered how "indentured" (rather than "free") the relationship really is. Many franchise agreements claim to own the business on termination, or claim the right to buy the business for a price substantially under market value. Modern franchise agreements provide that the franchisor owns all the goodwill[14] of the business by association with the franchisor's trade name and trademarks. The franchisor is only required to pay for the hard assets and fixtures.

As noted earlier, many franchisors control the franchisee's site, and the franchisee literally must move to a new location. Even if the franchisee could afford to relocate, invariably the franchise agreement contains a clause prohibiting the franchisee from competing with the franchisor on termination.

Even when the franchise agreement appears to support the franchisee's rights to go independent, few franchisors will allow a franchisee to leave without an expensive fight. If franchisees can successfully break away, more may try. Franchisors believe they must discourage franchisees from leaving.

Consequently, in the marketplace or the courtroom, franchisors can be depended on to be formidable antagonists when a franchisee tries to go independent.

Combating Systemic Fraud

I have called The Franchise Fraud "systemic fraud." This means the serious misrepresentations in franchising are purported by the industry, and relied on by individual franchisees. In some instances, systemic fraud arises from the franchising industry making obviously false claims as to the generic virtues of franchising. In other instances, the fraud is inherent in the franchise relationship and is represented by a failure to disclose those aspects of franchising that make owning a franchise undesirable.

Curiously, the indictment of the franchising industry is not an indictment of individual franchisors. Indeed, the large majority of franchisors comply with the laws and regulations governing their franchise operations. The problem is that the laws applicable to franchising allow, even support, the abuse of franchisees.

I have great difficulty faulting a franchisor for taking advantage of its market power and assuming every benefit allowed by law. Such is the essence of a free market economy. Unfortunately, the free market can be brutal when there is substantial imbalance of economic and negotiating power. Franchisees, lacking any kind of collective voice, are no match for the economic power and authority of franchisors.

The promise of franchising can be most alluring. When the principles of franchising are ethically applied, enormous potential can be realized. But in the hands of unscrupulous promoters, or inept corporate managers, franchising can become an outright fraud upon those would-be entrepreneurs coming in at the retail level. For many franchisors, franchising *is* their business, rather than a vehicle *to grow* their business.

Most of the chapters in this book describe and analyze various manifestations of The Franchise Fraud. The Franchise Fraud does not appear in exactly the same way in any franchise system. But in all its manifestations, there is one important common element: The Franchise Fraud exists because franchisees lack sufficient market power, economic power, or political power to stop it. In the absence of countervailing market power for franchisees, franchisors are able to wield enormous control over their franchise systems. Until franchisee market power is developed, The Franchise Fraud will continue unabated.

I do not mean to overstate the case. Franchisors have good and valid reasons for contractual restrictions in the structure of their franchise relationships. Historically, franchisors have had the negotiating leverage to drive very hard bargains with franchisees. That is the nature of our free market economy. The major thrust of this book is to address what franchisees can do to improve their negotiating leverage with franchisors and to gain market balance.

The Franchise Fraud is less an indictment of what franchising delivers *as it is of what franchising promises.* In today's economy and marketplace, the *promise* of franchising is tragically false. Franchising is not the safe, secure investment it is portrayed to be. Indeed, franchising represents risk management for the franchisor, not the franchisee. The franchisees, like foot soldiers assaulting a hill, frequently bear heavy casualties while establishing markets for franchisors. Worse, franchisees are more often exploited than supported.

Many thriving franchise systems do work basically as advertised. But for every successful reputable franchisor, probably a hundred don't make the grade. The franchising industry has done such an excellent job of marketing itself, that the chaff is sold as the wheat. More importantly, the industry lacks any type of countervailing force to test its claims and hold franchise abuses in check.

The result is the franchising industry, as a whole, is in terrific jeopardy. More and more, franchise abuses are recognized, and the industry's reputation is further tarnished. Still, franchisors exercise more and more power, and the exercise of power is largely unchecked because individual franchisees usually lack political or economic clout.

Once franchisees understand the importance of a unified voice, achievement of a balance in the franchising marketplace (and therefore the franchising industry) can occur in a heartbeat. A collective and cohesive effort by franchisees can bring economic, political, and judicial forces to an immediate turn.

Much of what is wrong with franchising can be corrected. Much of franchising's potential and promise can be realized and delivered. But first the problems must be identified and exposed. Most importantly, franchisees must understand and achieve sufficient market power to negotiate fair and equitable franchise agreements. For franchising to achieve its enormous potential, franchisees must effectively organize so that natural market forces can be allowed to work. Only in a balanced market will franchising's full capacity as a win-win method of business distribution be fully achieved.

The coalescing of the franchisee power base is inevitable and eminent. The following chapters chronicle all that franchising can be, and all that franchising has become. More importantly, this book portrays the plunder of an American dream and sets forth the blueprint for making the dream real once again.

Chapter 2

The Promise of Franchising

The potential of franchising is very real. Franchising has a unique capacity for rapid capital development and business expansion for franchisors. At the same time, would-be franchisees have the potential to achieve reduced risk business ownership. With a strong trademark and quality products and services, the combined strengths of the franchisor and franchisee can create a truly formidable profit center. The chapter examines key examples of successful franchise systems.

In the seminars I give on franchising, I tell the story this way:

> I am frequently reminded of my client, Joe, who had started his new business two short years ago and was brimming with confidence in his business future. Joe was one of those guys who pumped himself up in the morning and headed off to work under a full head of steam, ready to find new customers, make new sales, and move his business another two notches ahead.
>
> One typical morning Joe arrived at work ready to make that first sales call. As was his habit, he first listened to his voice mail. His first message was from the wife of Joe's star sales manager, reporting that her husband had just turned himself in to the Betty Ford Clinic for alcohol rehabilitation—he was history for at least the next six weeks. Disturbed, but undaunted, Joe went to his administrative assistant's office to discuss how to cover in his sales manager's absence.
>
> Joe's administrative assistant was a middle-aged woman who had become the glue of his company since its inception. Such was her ability to counsel and soothe, that the employees all referred to her as Mom, including Joe. I guess she took the nickname to heart, because that very morning the administrative assistant informed Joe she had decided to go back home to be a full-time mother to her three teenage children. She would work until the end of the month, and then be available on an on-call basis for a short period of time.

Joe was shaken by the immediate loss of his two key employees. He didn't know it, but he was about to be deserted again—this time by his trusted secretary of several years, who literally organized and managed Joe's professional life. She was invaluable because she was a very bright woman whose skills and intelligence far exceeded the requirements of a typical secretarial position. This she apparently understood because she announced she had enrolled full time in college to finish her degree.

It was now just 9:00 A.M. in the morning, Joe had only been in his office for an hour, but his day was complete. The wind was fully knocked out of his sails, and Joe's hard-charging demeanor was destroyed.

Back in his office, Joe flopped himself into his high-back executive chair, leaned back, closed his eyes, and put his hands to his forehead.

After a deep sigh, Joe looked to the heavens and whispered softly, but audibly, "Thank God I Own a Budweiser Franchise."

My story always makes its point. The more tragic the tale, the more impactful the ending and more obvious the moral. An established franchise system with a reputation for quality products and services, and a strong trademark, can offset numerous business setbacks. No doubt about it, owning a franchise in a proven system can be the ticket to business success.

The tragedy of the Franchise Fraud is that the enormous potential of modern franchising *can be* very real. Given negotiating balance between sellers and buyers of franchises, franchising can truly be a win-win situation. Franchising has a unique capacity for rapid capital development and business expansion for franchisors. For would-be franchisees, *enlightened* franchise systems provide a reduced risk opportunity for business ownership.

Assuming a strong trademark and an underlying quality product or service, the combined strengths of the franchisor and franchisee can create a truly formidable profit center. To succeed, a franchisor and franchisee need only recognize the *interdependency* of each to the other, or at the very least, have a healthy respect for each other's rights and duties within the franchise relationship.

THE FRANCHISOR'S PERSPECTIVE

From the franchisor's perspective, a franchise system of product and service distribution seems almost too good to be true. Franchising promises to provide all the following business benefits:

1. There is rapid business expansion.

2. Capital formation comes from franchisees who provide the capital for their own operations.

3. The typical franchisor receives a percentage of gross revenues and does not incur risk for the profit or loss of the franchise locations.

4. Franchisees provide self-motivated branch management with a vested interest in the success of the franchise.

5. The franchisee pays for training, and management training actually becomes a profit center for the franchisor.

6. The franchising of the company product or service makes actual system expansion a profit center.

7. The capital formation from franchising is "off-balance sheet." In other words, since the franchisor is not borrowing the capital to build the branch operation, no liability hits the balance sheet, and consequently, franchise businesses frequently have very positive debt/equity ratios.

8. The ultimate benefit is that the franchisor, who usually receives a percentage of gross revenue, instead of a percentage of profit, can be profitable even when the branches are losing money!

Quite simply, franchising represents the entrepreneur's dream. Through franchising, it is legal (even desirable) to raise large sums of money from individual investors who could not legally qualify to make even a modest purchase of stock in the franchisor. As is discussed in Chapter 4, federal and state securities laws would likely prohibit the sale of stock by most franchising companies to the vast majority of franchisees. In other words, a franchisor can extract an investment of several hundred thousand dollars from a franchisee who could not qualify for even a modest investment if the franchisor was selling stock in its company. This means that franchising opens entirely new capital sources unavailable from traditional capital markets.

THE FRANCHISEE'S PERSPECTIVE

As attractive as franchising is to potential franchisors, a franchise system that follows the franchise model can be equally attractive to the would-be entrepreneur who wants to own his own small business. Along with owning a home, business ownership is commonly recognized as part of the American Dream. However, unlike home ownership, which has long been available to most middle-class citizens, business ownership has traditionally been outside the reach of most Americans.

Business ownership is difficult to achieve for two primary reasons:

1. The high cost of getting started and trained.
2. The substantial risk of failure, which makes financing a new business venture almost impossible.

In theory, a franchised business system takes direct aim at both obstacles to business ownership without eliminating either. Franchising promises training and start-up expertise. Although start-up costs are not eliminated and the franchisee pays for training, most franchise systems provide start-up assistance and training to new franchisees.

Potentially, the franchise model of business ownership can provide significant opportunities, advantages, and protections that, with judicious application, can and should dramatically improve a business owner's chances of success. Read the previous sentence very carefully. The franchise model of business ownership is a theory *that should work, if all the assumptions attendant to the theory are present and accurate.* Use of the theory requires "judicious application" to make sure a particular business opportunity meets the requisite assumptions of the franchising model, and that the business opportunity under consideration takes maximum advantage of the theoretical model.

In other words, buying a franchise is not a slam dunk for business success. On the other hand, starting a business that meets the attributes of the franchise business model can provide important advantages and protections. The list of potential attributes that can be derived by the franchisee through franchising is impressive:

1. A proven product or service with an established market.
2. An established recognized trademark.
3. The availability of training and expertise of the franchisor.
4. The availability of marketing and operational assistance.

5. Franchisor support, including site evaluation, start-up assistance, and ongoing operational support.

6. The availability of financing and financial support by virtue of the success of the franchise system.

An Established Product and Market

Above all else, the franchise model of business ownership presupposes a quality product or service with an already established market. All of franchising's promises to reduce business failures are based on the assumption of product and service acceptance in the marketplace. In fact, the ingredient of an established and recognized product and service is so important to the franchise model I have made it a cardinal rule in selecting a franchise opportunity. The purchase of a Budweiser distributorship, or a McDonald's restaurant, effectively assures product acceptance for the franchise owner.

Truly, more than anything else, *product and market acceptance defines the lure of franchising.* The same cannot be said of hundreds of "opportunities" to purchase unknown beer distributorships and unrecognized hamburger restaurant franchises. The point to understand is that most franchisees look to franchising to establish their markets for them. Franchising has an enormous capacity to accomplish this purpose, provided the franchise opportunity, has, in fact, an established market for quality products and services.

An Established Trademark and Marketing System

Going hand in hand with the quality of the product and the acceptance of the product in the marketplace, the franchise model involves an established trademark that acts like a magnet to draw customers to the franchised business. Again, franchising has proven time and again that a recognized and respected trademark is a dramatic impetus to a high-volume business.

Again, the caution. The vast majority of franchise opportunities for sale in the United States today *do not involve* established trademarks. Indeed, of the 3,000–plus franchise businesses estimated to be operating today, probably fewer than 300 would meet the franchise model attribute of having a recognized and respected trademark. Like beauty, the quality of a trademark is in the eye of the beholder. Generally speaking, only systems that have posted attractive sales volumes over an extended time can be regarded as established.

Franchisor's Training and Expertise

Another major attribute of the franchise model is the promise of the franchisor's expertise and training to be made available to franchisees. In fact, it is the job-training aspects of franchising that have endeared the industry to the Small Business Administration and the Department of Commerce. As government is ever eager to provide continuing job training and business opportunities to the citizenry, an industry that promises job training will naturally be extolled by our government as a boon to the U.S. economy.

The franchise model of business ownership is a marvelous mechanism for successful job training *when the franchisor possesses the promised expertise and provides comprehensive training to its franchisees.* Although virtually every franchisor claims to provide training, too often franchisee training is wholly inadequate. Quality franchise opportunities have well designed and implemented training programs to thoroughly prepare new franchisees in every aspect of the franchised business.

Several major franchisors have permanent training centers, like McDonald's Hamburger University, where their new franchisees learn the franchised business from top to bottom. The good training programs will all provide complete training in general business operations as well as the unique features of the franchisor's system. At a minimum, training should include:

- Site selection guidelines and processes.
- How to develop a budget and business plan for the franchised business.
- Complete orientation to business operations in all phases, including review of the company's standard operating procedures manuals.
- Training in how to fill out all reports and to keep books for the business.
- *Perhaps most important, how to market and sell the franchisor's products and services.*

- Complete orientation to the services and help that are available from the franchisor.

Marketing and Operating Assistance

A prime attraction to a franchise business is buying into an established marketing network for a particular trademarked product or service. Without exception, franchisees expect and anticipate substantial operating and marketing assistance from their franchisors.

Truly, the amalgamation of numerous franchised outlets, combined with the economic strength of the parent franchisor, can facilitate and enhance efforts to establish an effective buying, marketing, and operational cooperative. A franchised distribution system can be an enormous marketing advantage.

When the advantages of the franchise business model are put to effective use, the power of a franchise business is unequaled in the history of commerce. Such examples as General Motors, Coca-Cola, Pepsi-Cola, McDonald's, Budweiser, 7-Eleven, and Century 21 all suggest marketing successes that have been unsurpassed among commercial enterprises. And when the attributes of a powerful buying and marketing network are present, a franchisee can be advantaged and protected by the economic strength of the entire franchise system.

Initially, the quality of the franchisor's marketing system is readily apparent from the presence of the company in the marketplace. Ideally, the franchisor has built an impressive marketing and advertising department to aggregate the advertising fees and contributions made by all the franchisees in the system.

A major advantage of franchising is the potential of a system of independent businesses to pool resources to effectively penetrate a market with concentrated advertising. A strong franchisor will deliver the promise of franchising by demonstrating marketing leadership, by the development of advertising programs and campaigns, by matching the financial funds contributed by the franchisees in the system, by developing advertising cooperatives for the franchisees in local markets, and by providing ongoing marketing support and assistance to address unique problems in local markets.

Franchisor Ongoing Support

When it works as advertised, franchising is an effective system of product and service distribution involving a distribution network eager and receptive to the marketing and sales leadership of the franchisor. In any "company-owned" chain store operation, ongoing operational support and direction flows continuously from corporate management down to retail outlets. If there is poor performance at the retail level, the corporation as a whole suffers the loss, and corporate management must take responsibility for solving the problems at the retail level.

On the other hand, in a franchising system, the corporate headquarters is shielded from the impact of the operating losses at the retail level. The franchisor typically gets a percentage of gross revenues and is therefore insulated from losses. Nevertheless, to prosper, it should be incumbent on corporate management to enhance the profitability at the retail level.

Notwithstanding the franchise industry promises of guidance and support, the lack of ongoing support from the franchisor is the most common complaint of disgruntled franchisees. Franchisees expect franchisors to provide a helping hand in the form of marketing and economic support as an obvious incident of franchising. Franchisees assume franchisors will assist and allow some leeway in building the franchisees' market. When problems arise, franchisees look to their franchisors for solutions and assistance in implementing solutions.

Franchisor support can come in many forms. At the very least, a franchisor would be expected to provide guidance and advice to address any problem. Usually, however, franchisees expect some form of financial assistance—either by direct loans or advances or by relaxing requirements for franchisees to pay fees. Unfortunately, financial assistance is the rare exception, rather than the rule, in franchising. More likely, the franchisor will provide advice, but not money—and, at best, a payment plan to "catch up" with past-due royalties and fees owed the franchisor.

Most successful franchisors develop advertising cooperatives (or co-ops) that assist in providing funding and planning for local marketing efforts. Co-ops are also used to create buying power at the local or regional level—buying co-ops are able to achieve volume discounts and drive better bargains from system suppliers.

Some franchisors have long had policies of matching the marketing dollars invested by their franchisees' advertising co-ops to encourage franchisees to invest heavily in local marketing efforts, or to prompt franchisees to participate in company-initiated marketing campaigns. Many franchising companies have recognized the importance of their franchise networks and have supported them economically both on a systemwide and individual basis.

Given the enormous benefits accruing to franchisors from the franchising business model, I am constantly baffled when franchising companies are unwilling to provide support and enhance resources in the hands of their franchisees. Invariably, however, the most successful franchise systems involve the franchisor investing heavily in its franchises and going the extra mile to enhance the success of their franchise networks.

In choosing a franchise opportunity, the evaluation of the potential franchisor's track record in supporting its franchisees is of critical importance. Does the franchisor make an ongoing investment in the improvement of the franchise system? Does the franchisor have a history of granting relief and financial assistance to distressed franchisees? Has the franchisor developed a reputation for attempting to foster and preserve good franchisee relations as opposed to exhibiting oppressive behavior to the franchisee network?

The *promise* of ongoing franchisor support is most prevalent in the franchising industry. When the promise is *delivered*, franchising usually works as advertised.

Availability of Financing

Although most franchisees believe buying a franchise will open the door to finding start-up capital, this is rarely the case. To the contrary, *franchisors have turned to franchising to provide capital for their own business expansion.* Very few franchisors provide hard capital to their franchisees, although some franchisors do provide "soft capital" in the form of inventory credit or by financing a portion of franchise fees.

Although not intended to help franchisees finance their businesses, a trend is developing where the franchisor acquires the real property location of the franchise establishment and sublets the premises to the franchisee. Franchisors are frequently able to negotiate better leasing terms with landlords than would be extended to financially less attractive franchisees. The franchisor's purpose is to control the location in the event the franchisee is terminated (*this practice has become a major mechanism of the Franchise Fraud*). As a practical matter, however, the franchisee may get better leasing terms as a result of the franchisor's efforts.[1]

Ultimately, the franchisor's control of the real estate premises frequently deprives the franchisee of any leverage whatsoever if problems develop in the franchise relationship. The franchisor can evict the franchisee on termination and effectively deny the franchisee any equity in the franchised business. Nevertheless, when a franchisor provides the real estate, affordability of the franchise business may be enhanced.

Because franchises are sometimes perceived to be safer investments by banks and other commercial lenders, financing for a franchised enterprise may be more readily available than for nonfranchised business opportunities. Consequently, ownership of a franchised business may be easier to achieve for more Americans than independent business start-ups.

For the most part, however, franchisees must provide the capital for their licensed businesses through their own resources and based on their own credit potential. Although franchising does not automatically provide capital, franchising does appear to facilitate access to capital markets. The Small Business Administration (which offers loan guarantee programs for businesses) generally tends to steer away from business start-ups. Franchise start-ups, on the other hand, are often able to borrow money from traditional lenders based on the proven success of their franchise networks. It should be noted that many lenders, including SBA program lenders, are taking a new cautious look at the safety of lending to franchise start-ups. Recently, many lenders have claimed to have been burned by false assumptions that a franchise business is a safer investment than other business enterprises.

The promise of a well-conceived and budgeted marketing and business plan for the franchise units is a claimed attribute of franchising that will indirectly help in obtaining start-up capital. If franchisees enjoy a superior success rate over independent business start-ups, the reason is quite probably that franchise start-ups are based on sound and proven budgeting models contained in franchise offering circulars and required by the franchisors. The truly blue chip franchisors are very selective in their franchise candidates, choosing only investors with a substantial net worth and ample business experience, and requiring sound and competent budgets and capital reserves to ensure the franchise business takes hold and prospers. Lenders and investors put great reliance on well-developed business plans in deciding to provide capital. Presumably, the franchisor's business plan has been developed over repeated experience and will indicate a sound credit or investment risk.

On the other hand, and another caution to prospective franchise purchasors, hungry franchisors are apt to be careless in their selection of franchisees. Rather than qualify franchisees for their ability to survive in business, most franchising companies qualify their franchisees for their ability to pay the up-front franchise fees, which represent a large portion of many franchisors' profits.

SOME EXAMPLES OF FRANCHISE SUCCESSES

The best way to appreciate the mutual benefits to franchisor and franchisee is to look at some interesting examples. We can start with an inventor and enterprising entrepreneur named Isaac Singer.

Singer is well known as the inventor of the sewing machine. As the story goes, Singer needed capital to start his sewing machine business. The inventor figured out that to sell his new invention he would have to teach his customers how to use his machines, and this could be an expensive process. Singer's solution was to license the right for individuals to open Singer Sewing Centers throughout the country, establishing retail outlets for his sewing machines, but also providing sewing classes and other services relating to his product line. Most historians mark the establishment of Singer Sewing Centers as the first modern-day business format franchise.

In 1850, Singer sold individual franchises for as much as $5,000. The franchisee received complete training in how to use the Singer sewing machine and was also trained on how to operate a sewing center—to give classes and provide tips on sewing.

Singer's network of sewing centers provided distribution outlets for his products. Not only did he gain significant capital from his franchisees but the existence of his distribution network, together with his capital base, made financing of his manufacturing enterprise a viable proposition. In addition to capital, and immediate rapid expansion of his distribution centers, Singer also gained sewing center managers—who were dedicated to the company by virtue of the fact they claimed equity in the business venture.

Singer's franchisees fared well. They gained a ground-floor opportunity with modest investment in an industry brimming with potential and connected with a trademark and trade name that said "leader in the industry." All the elements were present for a successful franchise system, and the company still prospers today.

Singer built his franchise system around an important new invention. But many franchises (recently, maybe most) are built around a marketing system and image rather than a tangible product. Suppose Singer hadn't invented a great new product that was capable of creating an industry onto itself. Rather, suppose he was merely an accomplished salesman trying to increase the market for his product.

In the early 1950s, an enterprising salesman represented a line of ice cream milkshake mixing machines he wanted to sell to various hamburger and ice cream stands throughout the country. This particular milkshake machine's biggest virtue was its ability to blend four or five milkshakes at one time, thus its name, the Multi-Mixer. The Multi-Mixer was of unique value to high-volume restaurants. On the other hand, most restaurants doing lower volume didn't require the expense of the machine's capabilities and advanced design.

The enterprising salesman was Ray Kroc, and he was able to parlay his desire to sell his Multi-Mixer machines into the world's largest franchised operation, and the standard by which all franchise systems are judged—McDonald's. Kroc was the consummate salesman if he was anything. He was known for making sales by solving his customers' problems, and creating sales opportunities by creating new opportunities for his customers. Kroc recognized that by helping his customers increase their sales volume they would need his shake mixer.

It so happened a little hamburger stand in San Bernardino, California, owned by the MacDonald brothers[2] was one of Kroc's biggest customers. Kroc was intrigued by the MacDonalds' success, and he studied their system, which involved the sale of 15-cent hamburgers and shakes in huge quantities. Kroc realized that if he could replicate the MacDonalds' system, he would be creating a substantial market for his Multi-Mixer shake machines. In fact, in the early years of McDonald's, Kroc earned more personal profit from the sale of Multi-Mixers than from franchises.

The franchised restaurant system developed by Kroc is a classic example of the benefits of franchising to the franchisor. Neither Kroc nor the MacDonald brothers had the capital to create a chain of hamburger stands. Franchising provided the capital and the capitalists to finance the rapid growth of the McDonald's systems in the 1950s and 1960s. Lending capital wasn't available, nor were the traditional securities markets. What financed McDonald's were individual entrepreneurs who saw in McDonald's an opportunity to own a business with a proven track record and a substantial opportunity for success.

But the biggest lesson to be learned from the McDonald's experience, and the lesson that is invariably repeated in successful franchising enterprises, is the singular dedication and purpose of McDonald's to sell hamburgers, fries, and shakes to a consuming public, and a concomitant dedication to its franchisees as its primary network for product and service distribution. Although in the 1970s, McDonald's experimented with alternate methods of distribution, the company has come to dedicate itself to its franchises and to require dedication from its franchises. The success of the McDonald's system cannot be disputed and is boasted on thousands of signs across the United States—"Billions and Billions Served"!

Another fascinating example of franchising success is the Century 21 Real Estate Network. Like Singer and McDonald's, Century 21 is a franchising pioneer, having developed a concept that today is called "conversion franchising." In some ways, this concept seems to defy one of my fundamental requirements for a recommended franchise opportunity: *A franchisor is in the business of distributing quality goods and services to the consuming public as opposed to being in business for the main purpose of selling franchises.*

In truth, Century 21 merely represents a variation on the theme, because Century 21 developed a masterful franchise concept that enabled successful locally owned independent real estate offices to dramatically improve their individual abilities to market quality services to the consuming public.

Conversion franchising allows a successful independent business to "convert" its name and trade style to that of a large marketing network. The founders of Century 21, Art Bartlett and Marsh Fischer, recognized the enormous marketing power of national chains. They targeted established well run independently owned real estate offices to join the Century 21 national network.

Century 21 franchisees pay an initial franchise fee and an ongoing royalty in exchange for the use of the Century 21 name and trade style, a national referral network, and an increased opportunity to market Century 21 services on a nationwide basis.

Although Century 21 sells products and services to the franchisees (rather than ultimate consumers) in exchange for franchise fees, Century 21 franchises are effectively able to improve the quality and services available to their customers by virtue of their participating in a nationwide network of independent real estate agents.

Since 1971, Century 21 has grown to be the largest network of locally owned and operated real estate agents. However, following the Century 21 example, the real estate industry has become a model for the concept of conversion franchising for such successful operations as Realty World, ERA, and Re-Max. Other household names such as Better Homes and Gardens and Prudential have entered into conversion franchising and successfully capitalized on trade names that were built in other industries altogether.

In judging conversion franchise opportunities, prospective franchisees should measure the level of services available from the franchisor that will allow the franchisee to improve the quality and competitiveness of the services that can be offered to ultimate consumers.

An interesting difference between *converted* franchisees and other forms of franchising is that a "conversion franchise" represents the merger of an already successful business with a developed franchise network. Most people think of franchise opportunities as business start-ups requiring a substantial level of training and business expertise to be imparted by the franchisor to the franchisee. Most conversion franchises, on the other hand, result from the process of the franchisor and the franchisee each selecting the other as a result of the proven track records of existing businesses.

Conversion franchising also has some unique *hazards* in comparison with other franchise opportunities in that previously independent business owners may unintentionally surrender their independence, and even their business ownership. I recently represented an independent motel in Coral Gables, Florida, that converted to a franchise of a major motel chain hoping to expand its business by being on the nationwide reservation network.

My clients were displeased by the performance of the franchisor in comparison with the expense of joining the network. However, when my clients attempted to terminate their franchise, they discovered their franchise agreement claimed to transfer ownership of their business to franchisor. If the contract was enforceable according to its terms, my clients had purportedly sold their entire motel for the privilege of the use of a national reservation network!

Similarly, I am currently representing clients who have been in the employment agency business for 25 years. Fifteen years ago, they decided to provide temporary employment services to their company, and they became franchisees of a national temp agency. Over time, my clients became dissatisfied with their franchise relationship (and lack of perceived benefit) and decided to go independent. They are now in an expensive legal battle with their franchisor who claims to own the agency, the temporary employees, and the customers of the business. The franchisor further denies my clients the right to continue in business after a quarter century of service in their community.

Notwithstanding the important caution about the unique risks of converting an existing business to a franchise operation, to me the most important lesson to be learned from conversion franchising, and the ultimate solution for the woes of franchisees in today's franchising marketplace, is the powerful market dynamics to be gained through a nationwide network of common businesses pooling resources for the good of the network. Every businessperson who has bought into conversion franchising has expected to gain market power by virtue of association with a larger system. This very same logic must inevitably ring true for the collective good of franchisees throughout the United States. The collective negotiating, political, and market power of franchisees increases in direct proportion to the ability of franchisees to effectively organize as a cohesive whole.

In the model business format franchise, all the positive attributes of franchising are assumed to exist and provide distinct advantages for an entrepreneur wishing to start a new business. *However, few if any of these attributes are found in the vast majority of franchise "opportunities" on the market today.* Since it is not my purpose to add to the illusion that franchising per se is a foolproof method of business ownership, I need to stress this caveat over and over again. This chapter extols *"the promise"* of franchising, by praising what the franchise model can accomplish if *judiciously applied to a proper opportunity.*

I am inevitably drawn to analogize franchising to a powerful prescription wonder drug. We commonly hear the admonition to use strong drugs only under the direction of a physician, with the further warning that all drugs have a potential for abuse and should be kept out of the reach of small children. Similarly, franchising can be powerful medicine when used judiciously and not abused. This text is dedicated to identifying the many methods of franchise abuse, and to careful evaluation of how to be sure franchising works so that it can live up to its enormous promise.

The Swing of the Pendulum: A Perspective on the History of Franchising

The roots of franchising can be traced to feudal times. The first franchises may have been granted by the Pope providing the right to collect tithes. Most of the 13 American colonies were business franchises granted by the King of England. Modern franchising has culminated in the explosive growth of franchising over the past 40 years.

I find the history of franchising to be enthralling. As a history buff, I have always been fascinated by the evolution of human thought and practices, and how history often seems to repeat itself in spite of the enormous lessons humankind could gain by heeding the admonitions of historians.

This book is not the proper format for a thorough and researched analysis of the historical underpinnings of franchising into modern times. No one has ever completely undertaken the project, though it would certainly be an enterprising task. A recent book, *The Roadside Empires,* which traces the modern history of some of the United States' great franchising chains, has only touched the tip of the franchising iceberg.[1] The 3,500 franchisors estimated to be operating in the United States are involved in hundreds of industries that far exceed the scope of restaurants and hotels. It has been my long held suspicion any business concept can be franchised. This belief was confirmed when I heard of a concern out of Texas that had franchised a "Rent-a-Judge" service.

It is helpful to examine the economic ancestors of the franchising business model to appreciate the enormous economic force franchising has become.

More importantly, a historical perspective of franchising will be helpful in understanding both the potential for franchise fraud and abuse as well as the positive mechanisms for tapping and controlling franchising's potential. As we will see, the essence of the history of franchising has been captured in the maxim, "Power corrupts; absolute power corrupts absolutely!" Franchisors have enjoyed ever increasing power and dominance over their franchise systems, and have effectively created a power vacuum, increasingly sucking valuable rights from franchised businesses.

The lessons of history teach us that power in a vacuum has disastrous results. On the other hand, one person's power against another's equal countervailing power can create circumstances of equity, progress, and some of the most notable achievements in the history of mankind. Our entire economic system of capitalism is based on the expectation that a willing buyer and willing seller, each with equal bargaining power, will come together to make mutually advantageous contracts. From such agreements come prosperity and growth. On the other hand, when mutuality of bargaining power is missing, the common result is tyranny and abuse of power. The history of franchising is susceptible to the analysis of these very economic dynamics.

Historically and legally, a franchise arises when the owner of a trademarked product or service licenses another person to engage in the business of selling products and services under the licensor's trade name and trademark for a fee. A business format franchise describes the licensing of a business or trade style, as opposed to the right to sell a particular product. In other words, the licensor grants the right to engage in the use of a "business format."

As noted in Chapter 2, Isaac Singer is generally regarded as the creator of the business format franchise in the early 1850s. The licensing of product distribution rights was already common in Singer's time, thus commercial franchising was hardly a new concept. Singer's wrinkle was in expanding the franchise to include more than the right to distribute a manufacturer's product; Singer franchised the entire look and feel of his business operation. Singer granted the right to operate a "sewing center business" that comprised a complete business format of Singer Sewing Centers, not simply the right to sell Singer Sewing Machines.

Product franchises, dealerships, and distributorships have probably existed since the beginning of commerce. Even today, with the explosive growth of business format franchising, three times as much sales volume is generated from product franchises than from business format franchises. Bottling companies, beer distributorships, petroleum dealerships, automotive dealerships, and hundreds of single line or primary line brand-name retail outlets are all best described as product franchises, as opposed to business format franchises.

The distinction between a business format franchise and a product franchise is not always clear. Indeed, legally there is no distinction. All commercial franchises look and behave the same in that they involve the right to engage in a certain business pursuant to a license connected to a specific trademark.

However, the distinction between business format and product franchises is very important in comparing the potential for franchise fraud and abuse. A product manufacturer must develop a distribution network to sell products to the ultimate consumer. With a product franchise, the quality of the product, its availability, and its value are fairly apparent and readily ascertained. More important, the product franchisor has a vested interest in system sales.

Business format franchisors, on the other hand, are marketing a style of doing business, and do not have inventories of goods and products that must be moved out and sold on an ongoing basis. For the business format franchisor, the business being sold *is* the inventory and the quality is much more subjective. The value of the business format is based on a combination of factors:

1. The quality of the trademark.

2. The value of the franchisor's reputation for quality and service.

3. The quality and strength of the franchisor's business system.

4. The quality of the training and support provided by the franchisor.

5. The amount of royalties and other fees charged by the franchisor.

It is becoming more and more difficult to distinguish between a product franchise and a business format franchise. Fifty years ago, a product franchise, such as a car dealership, had no common theme other than the brand of cars being sold. Consequently, Ford dealers competed with each other as well as competing brands. Today, most car dealers of an individual brand look and feel much alike—they have a common business format. Gasoline service stations, which years ago were purely product franchises, today provide a full business format for most franchisees. In other words, most service stations have a common theme and appearance. In some cases, such as Arco AM/PM Mini Markets, the sale of petroleum products is incidental to the total business concept or format.

I'll return to business format franchising, and its modern history, later. First, however, let's look back at the historical development of franchising.

TRACING TO FEUDAL TIMES

Although Isaac Singer may have developed the first business format franchise, the commercial concepts involved in franchising have existed at least since the Middle Ages.

If Singer is to be credited with any enhancement on the model, it is the linkage of the right to engage in business for a fee with the right to use a trademark. Singer licensed the right to utilize a trademark in connection with the operation of a trade or business and in exchange for the payment of franchise fees and royalties. The model had been used for hundreds of years, but other property rights were substituted for the right to the trademark.

The franchise model can be traced at least as far back as feudal times. In reviewing the history of Europe from the fifth to the twelfth century, we are hard pressed to assign responsibility for the invention of the model.

Early on, the Roman Catholic Church developed a practice of granting local clergy the right to collect tithes (essentially church taxes) in exchange for the requirement of passing a portion of those tithes on to Rome. Many years ago, I read about the tithing rights granted by the church. In my recent research for this book (which was certainly not exhaustive), I was unable to uncover any historical discussion of the practice, including the references I recalled from my youth. Perhaps when the history of franchising is finally written, the church's role in the development of the franchise model can be fully explored.[2]

At the same time the Catholic Church was franchising the right to run a parish in the name of the pope, the feudal or "manorial" system of commerce was developing throughout Europe.

Between the fifth and the twelfth centuries, socioeconomic and political systems developed in England and throughout Europe based on the establishment of large estates or manors. Kings and noblemen owned or controlled the land and the peasants who worked and farmed the land. The manorial political and economic system that developed through the Middle Ages is commonly called feudalism. These feudal or manorial systems developed with slight differences throughout Europe. Generally, however, the economics of feudalism were similar throughout the continent.

Feudal kings and noblemen were the only land owners and therefore controlled the land. Peasants for the most part were either slaves or indentured servants of the noblemen. Over the centuries, as the peasant populations worked hard to increase the product and income of the manor, the peasants, or serfs as they were known in England, began to demand more and more rights and privileges from the lords of the manor.

Over time, many enterprising and productive serfs were rewarded with additional rights and privileges with respect to the land they worked. In England, some serfs received special rights and privileges, including rights to the profits from the land subject to fees or taxes paid to the king or noble, as the case may have been. These fees were called Royal Tithes and were the etymological roots to modern commercial "royalties." Serfs so honored were granted a special status called "freemen."

In France, the process of granting additional rights to a peasant or a serf was called *francis,* literally meaning to grant rights or power to a peasant or serf. The french root word *francis* became the English term *to enfranchise,* again meaning "to empower or to grant rights to one who had none." Thus, a peasant or person who was granted citizenship, Freeman status, or the right to vote, was said to have gained the franchise, or to be enfranchised.

Commercial franchising is built on the feudal model. Granting a franchise is the granting of rights for a fee or fees—usually the modern-day descendant of the Royal Tithe—the royalty. And just as in feudal times, the modern royalty is a percentage of the proceeds gained by use of the right by the franchisee.

With the perspective of several hundred years of history, we can see the so-called freemen enjoyed very few meaningful advantages over serfs. Freemen and serfs alike were subservient to the lords of the manors. Freemen had no independent ownership of the land they worked, although freemen were granted the right to work a particular parcel of land for their own benefit, subject to the royal taxes or *mesne* profits that were paid to the lord and king. Serfs also benefited from the land they tilled, although they were indentured to the lord of the manor.

The study of the feudal or manorial economic systems of the Middle Ages is fascinating for its similarity to the franchise business model. Indeed, the very purpose of the manorial system was to grow the manor without risk or financial commitment of the lord of the manor, just as franchisors seek to grow their systems with the labor and risk capital of the franchisees.

In many ways, freemen were at greater risk than the serfs. The manorial lords had a vested interest in their peasant population. The loss of a serf was, in effect, the loss of a property interest. Lords had no such interest in freemen, and no incentive to protect them.

Similarly, employers have a vested interest and investment in their employees, whereas franchisors have much less incentive to protect a franchisee. On the other hand, freemen obtained their status by virtue of their hard work and production. By their enterprise, freemen made themselves valuable to the manor lords. Nevertheless, freemen came to recognize there were few true privileges to their status. Freemen were still subject to the will of the manor lords and were exploited by the harsh taxation.

I have long held the perspective that all of history, and certainly all of economic history, can be understood in light of people's continuing struggle to balance the drive for economic and political security against the urge for greater independence and freedom. Feudalism is a classic example of this struggle. Serfs were effectively slaves of the manor but were protected, housed, and fed by the manorial economic system. So-called freemen relinquished the security of the manorial system for greater freedom and the opportunity for greater prosperity. Serfs and freemen alike were peasants within the feudal system. There was no middle class of any note until late in the nineteenth century when a mercantile and industrial system of economics had supplanted and replaced the manorial system of the Middle Ages.

Franchising also exemplifies the struggle between the individual's often conflicting desire for freedom and security, and a balance between the two. The typical franchisee is seeking a degree of entrepreneurial independence, but the security of a developed and proven system to temper the risks of unlimited freedom.

The evolution of freeman status within the feudal economic system has continually mirrored the development of commercial franchising within the United States. Early in the thirteenth century, a struggle developed as freemen

41

began to realize their rights and privileges were far below the political, socio-logical, and economic rights they thought they had and deserved.

Today, franchisees are beginning to recognize their own enfranchisement is substantially less meaningful than represented at the outset of the franchise relationship. Franchisees are beginning to openly object to perceived exploitation by franchisors. Franchisees increasingly see themselves as indentured and captive in their franchise systems, rather than independent businesspeople who are benevolently protected by the wisdom and strength of their franchisors.

A landmark date in English history was 1215, the year of the signing of the Magna Carta. The Magna Carta is considered to be the cornerstone of the English Constitution. In fact, the Magna Carta represents the result of a great political and economic struggle between the "franchisees" of the day and the ultimate franchisor, the king of England.

Banding together in a political and economic power play, freemen de-manded and won from the king such important rights as the right to own property, the right to representation as part of the compact with the monarchy, and many other political and economic rights that have become the foundation of our free market economy and democratic political system.

I am constantly fascinated by the similarity of modern franchising to the feudal economic system, as well as the trend of franchising toward a time when franchisees will demand of their franchisors the economic and political rights and privileges that indicate the true ownership and equity in the franchised business. As that day approaches, franchising in the United States will emerge from its Dark Ages and into a truly golden era of entrepreneurial management.

COLONIAL FRANCHISES

Jumping forward a few centuries, we find the franchise model still thriving, but with a new name and style. The feudal system of individual enfranchise-ment of the twelfth century became the model for the enfranchisement of whole communities in the sixteenth through the eighteenth centuries—the granting of colonies.

Colonialism was the mechanism that financed and propelled European ex-pansion throughout the world, and colonialism was completely grounded in the traditions of feudalism. For the most part, European monarchs granted "franchisees" to commercial ventures that agreed to establish colonies under the authority and protection of the monarch and in exchange for the payment "royalties" and taxes.

By colonial times, the concept of franchising was well established. Indeed, each of the 13 American colonies—as well as the many colonies established throughout the world—were commercial franchises designed to extend the realm of a sovereign by granting rights to others in exchange for taxes and fees.

Typically colonies were promoted and established by people (the colonists) who were seeking new freedom and independence while still being protected by the authority of the sovereign. Like modern commercial franchisees, colonists respected both their independence and their allegiance to their franchisor, the king. Also like modern franchisees, colonists believed themselves to be exploited by their sovereigns and *ultimately* demanded respect, fairness, and representation from their "franchisor." Monarchies that failed to respect their colonies ultimately lost them—such was the plight of colonialism in America.

The American colonial experience has many lessons for students of franchising. These lessons are explored in detail in Chapter 13. Ultimately, however, the resolve of the American colonists to achieve representation, fairness, or independence must underscore every page of this work, because the historical perspective is only meaningful if it can help us to understand *today,* to avoid the mistakes of the past, and to benefit by repeating yesterday's successes. The colonial experience can serve the franchising industry well—both franchisors and franchisees—if it is carefully studied, and if its lessons are well applied.

MODERN HISTORY

Returning to business format franchising, we again trace our steps from Isaac Singer. As you may have already figured out, the Singer Sewing Center was really a hybrid, having some elements of the product franchise (the selling of Singer sewing machines) and other elements of a service business operated as specified by Singer (the Sewing Center). Hybrid enterprises continue to exist, such as Arco AM/PM Mini-Markets or A&W Restaurants, which are built around the famous root beer. Weight Watchers and Jenny Craig Diet Centers, although falling into the business format franchise categorization, have a whole line of products that are sold to the general public through franchised diet centers, and also through other outlets. (For example, Weight Watchers, which is owned by Heinz, sells products in supermarkets.)

Today, business format franchising has evolved to the point where many franchise opportunities incorporate no true product at all. For example, H&R Block Income Tax Services, Century 21 Real Estate Services, Uniglobe Travel, and many many other franchisors associate their trademark and marketing system with a *style of doing business,* and not a particular product manufactured by the franchisor and distributed through the franchise system.

By contrast, almost all early franchise systems were designed for the ultimate purpose of product distribution, whether it be sewing machines, soft drinks, automobiles, gasoline, or ice cream.

Early franchisees were granted a license to utilize the franchisor's service mark and operating system as well as an exclusive territory in return for the payment of a royalty to the franchisor. On the other hand, early franchisors generally did not require a commitment to adhere to the operational structure of the franchised system; that is, the typical franchise did not involve or dictate a business format.

In essence, early franchising was product driven: Brand names were more important than trade names. The emphasis was on selling products, and manufacturers needed their distribution networks to keep inventories moving. Although having a franchise for a well-known brand was a valuable right, franchises were generally terminable at will (on very short notice, e.g., 30 days). If either party failed to perform, the other party could end the relationship. Franchisors had to remain competitive, or their franchisees might change brands; franchisees who failed to market their brands aggressively found themselves without a product to sell.

The relationship benefited both the franchisor and franchisee by creating market penetration and sales volume through joint efforts to market the franchised "brand." The capital generated by franchised expansion fostered enormous system growth with unprecedented speed. By 1930, there were literally thousands of gasoline franchises, and everything from automobiles to farm equipment, beer and distilled spirits to soft drinks, and insurance agencies to brands of paint were marketed through dealer networks.

The franchising equation produced a startling impact on the distribution of products and services within the United States. Following Singer's early example, automobile manufacturers, soft drink companies, and breweries developed national distribution networks by franchising local dealers, bottlers, and distributors. In effect, franchisees were local investors who provided capital and assumed the risk of the distribution effort in local markets.

THE RISE OF THE BUSINESS FORMAT FRANCHISE

In the 1930s, franchising began to take root as a successful method for cloning a business format that did not evolve around a specific product or brand. Such diverse chains as Western Auto Supply, Rexall, and Ben Franklin brought franchising to general retailing with dramatic success.

In 1924, A&W Root Beer founded an early version of the fast food chain—initially building an entire drive-in business around a soft drink product. An early A&W franchisee was J. Willard Marriott who left A&W to franchise Hot Shoppes restaurants on the way to becoming the Marriott Corporation and a major force in franchising restaurants and hotels.

These early successes of business format franchisors ignited a franchising boom for chains hungry for rapid growth and the enormous capacity of franchising to create capital and local management. In 1935, Howard Johnson started what is believed to be the first franchised restaurant chain. At the same time Travelodge was dotting the United States with hundreds of motels owned by local "mom and pop" operators.

Where brand names distinguished product franchises, business format franchises were built around the franchisor's trade name and distinguishing symbols (the trademarks). A chain's popularity could spread rapidly in an increasingly mobile society.

In the 1940s the first megafranchises came into existence: Dairy Queen had established 2,500 units by 1948, and was followed closely by rival Tastee Freeze (1,500 units by the mid-1950s). One author has marked Dairy Queen as launching the "food franchising race."[3] In truth, the race was just getting started, because the explosion of franchise growth did not even begin until the 1950s.

Dairy Queen (and A&W before it) had launched the drive-in as the new *fast* way for Americans to eat. The drive-in was copied extensively, by independents as well as by chains, but it was the franchisors who capitalized most on the model. Bob's Big Boy, Scotts, White Castle, Carvel Ice Cream, Chicken Delight, and Baskin-Robbins were already big names when the fast-food explosion really occurred.

The lure of franchising was to give a mom-and-pop operation an identification with a national chain, the recognition of a trademark, and high-volume buying power. And the model worked, creating a powerful "partnership" between big business and independent entrepreneurs. The mom-and-pop enterprises, whether it be convenience stores, hamburger stands, service stations, or budget motels, developed into highly profitable small business enterprises achieving enormous profit and growth for the parent franchisors.

The key ingredients in the first phase of the business format franchise explosion were fairly consistent in all systems:

1. High-volume/low-cost (economical) products.
2. Big emphasis on convenience foods.
3. Businesses that traditionally had been independent mom-and-pop operations.

And yet, something important was missing—uniformity and consistency. Because customers did not receive a predictable experience when patronizing a franchised business, franchised systems remained one step below company-owned chains, which were able to maintain consistent quality throughout their systems.

The evolution of franchising met a critical crossroads when franchisors began to stress the importance of system uniformity. Much of franchising's enormous success, and much of what is wrong in the industry, can be traced directly to the success of franchisors in demanding system uniformity and consistency. For in order to invoke uniformity, franchisors needed power and authority over their franchisees. First franchisors had to change American law.

Americans, as a nationality, were born of political revolution. Our founding fathers rejected the authority of a monarch, and built a country founded on the principles of independence and the free determination of people. A little more than a century later, our nation rejected the tyrannical control of our country's industries by powerful robber barons. Beating back the coercion of the monopolies and cartels at the beginning of this century, the United States established strong antitrust laws designed to preserve competition and the viability of small independent businesses.

Although product franchises were welcomed by American commerce with open arms, the efforts of franchisors to control the quality of their systems were only successful after many difficult legal battles. The new breed of business format franchisors recognized they could only compete effectively if they could enforce uniform quality standards throughout their franchised networks. Although many other franchisees recognized the benefits to be gained from uniform quality standards, many franchisees feared the ultimate control that could be exercised by franchisors, and the resulting loss of independence at the franchisee level.

Stated simply, American antitrust law is designed to enhance and promote competition and equality in the marketplace. Our commercial law is built on the premise that a free (and uncontrolled) economy will develop fair and balanced commercial relationships. Too much power in one party's hand usually means coercive and unfair business practices. Competition is seen in U.S. law as the great keeper of the peace and commercial tranquility.

Consequently, U.S. law in the 1930s, 1940s, and 1950s would not permit a franchisor to control the quality, services, products, or style of its franchisees. A franchisor could not dictate prices, was not allowed to require franchisees to carry certain brands, or even to dictate the look and feel of the franchised business. Franchisors wanted to tie the right to use the franchisor's trade name to the requirement of following a uniform system.

Fearing the loss of autonomy and important franchise rights, many franchisees and consumers resisted the efforts of franchisors to amalgamate commercial power through franchising. Franchisees could never provide a negotiating balance against the power of the franchisor. In the end, the fears of the franchisees who fought against franchise controls have been proven right.

In the late 1950s and early 1960s, franchisors' economic muscle began to bear fruit in the courtroom. Courts began to buy the franchisor's claims that uniform systems would breed better competitors, and courts began allowing a franchisor to develop strong marketing systems. The enforcement of uniform systems was seen to be procompetitive rather than anticompetitive.

Following several important court cases, franchisors gained some very important commercial powers. For the first time, franchisors were allowed to dictate a franchisee's style of doing business, the products the franchisee sells, from whom the franchisee buys, and the way products are prepared and/or dressed. Franchisors were allowed to set prices, to establish and dictate site locations, color schemes, advertising—literally anything germane to the franchisor's business operation—provided solely that the franchisor could justify the intended practice as tied to the quality represented by the trade name. First and foremost, the franchisor could protect the viability of the trade name.

The franchisor's success in gaining control of the franchised system, in fact, finally allowed franchising companies to compete (and even outperform) company-owned chain stores. The franchisor's success also meant the loss of freedom and self-determination for franchisees. Without the protection of the United States' antitrust laws, franchisees lost critical leverage to require franchisors to negotiate contractual concessions rather than impose them without compromise or *quid pro quo*.

THE FRANCHISE EXPLOSION

Armed with new power to control franchised systems, business format franchising began to explode in the United States in the late 1950s. The huge success of franchising was attributable in part to the ability of franchisors to control their quality and consistency. The franchise explosion also was ignited by a new industry that combined with franchising to revolutionize the way Americans eat. Indeed, for many franchising is synonymous with fast food.

Because virtually any business format is franchiseable given the proper system development, it is difficult to understand why fast-food restaurants have become the standard of the public's perception of franchising. For whatever reason, the fast-food industry has set the standard for business format franchising. Mom-and-pop ice cream and hamburger stands have blended with franchising to reshape the American diet. My personal view is that happenstance matched the fast-food industry with the franchising mechanism for business growth, and the comfortable combination caused an explosion. Much like bacteria in a receptive petri dish, the resulting rapid growth was most predictable. Whatever the reason, fast food and franchising went very well together.

McDonald's, Burger King, Burger Chef, Hardee's, Jack-in-the-Box, Kentucky Fried Chicken, Arby's, Roy Rogers, and Denny's, followed later by other fast-food giants such as Wendy's, Pizza Hut, Sonic, Little Caesar's, Domino's, Subway—the fast-food avalanche has literally dominated the way Americans eat. To best appreciate the enormity of the fast-food sales volume, it has been reported that McDonald's *alone* purchases 7.5 percent of the U.S. potato crop annually. The fast-food industry was an estimated $45-billion-dollar industry in 1985. By 1995, the industry will grow to over $80 billion.[4]

In the 1950s and 1960s, fast food so dominated franchising that the two terms were almost synonymous. In the past 30 years, however, the franchise model has proven to be an exceptional vehicle for business expansion across the broad spectrum of the U.S. economy. Franchising has made its impact in real estate (with such giants as Century 21, Re-Max, Better Homes and Gardens, ERA, Prudential, and many others), in the employment services industry (Manpower, Snelling & Snelling, Adia, Western Temp, Norrell), lodging (Travelodge was followed by such giants as Holiday Inn, Ramada Inn, Howard Johnson, and Marriott as well as Hilton, Sheraton, and literally scores of other notables), car rentals, janitorial services, hardware stores, and retail markets. Franchising has touched virtually every sector of American retail and service industries.

The business format franchise model is an economic invention whose impact rivals the industrial revolution, the transportation revolution, even the invention of the wheel. In the opinion of John Naisbitt, author of the best-selling book *Megatrends,* "Franchising is the single most successful marketing concept ever."

Various franchise directories regularly list 2,500 to 4,000 franchised business opportunities annually. The Department of Commerce has estimated that approximately 480,000 franchised business outlets exist in the United States, and the number is expected to exceed 500,000 in the 1990s. The franchise industry is said to be responsible for a third to half of all retail sales in the United States, and this enormous growth has been accomplished largely in the span of the past 40 years.

A unique method of capital formation and product and service distribution (with the fortunate "side-effect" of capturing quality middle-level management), the franchising format is perhaps unrivaled in the history of business. When it works right, the franchise model is free enterprise at its very best. Franchising can marry the entrepreneurial spirit with a proven business system and experienced management and training. When the model works as advertised, the franchisor gains capital and dedicated management, and the franchisee has an investment in an established business with substantially increased odds of success.

And while the history of the mom-and-pop business is impressive, some franchised businesses were not limited to the commerce generated at a specific location. Thus, the really profitable franchised businesses have proven to be distributors who were able to extend their businesses through a large market area. Consequently, automobile dealerships have been better business opportunities than hamburger stands and service stations, because they could draw customers from a much larger territory. The giant business successes for franchising have been the beverage distributors, both soft drinks and beer and wine, and other distribution companies that have engineered the franchise model to achieve very profitable businesses.

With the huge success of the franchise business model came enormous profits and power to the franchisors. The industry was labeled with success, and the label of success created a rush to buy franchises. Given the incredible demand for franchised businesses, franchisors found it unnecessary to give away as many rights in order to sell their licensed businesses.

As franchising has evolved since the 1960s, and to the present, the image of franchising has created an avalanche of available franchise opportunities. Under close scrutiny, however, these franchise opportunities bear little resemblance to the business enterprises that proved so successful in the 1950s and 1960s.

Gone are exclusive territories. In fact, gone is the promise of any territorial rights in most franchise systems. Gone, too, is any semblance of a true equity in the franchise business. Sophisticated modern franchisors control the real estate, territory, product, customers, and all other aspects of the franchise business. Today, most franchisees are simply managers without a salary and without a guaranteed job.

Although an investment in an established franchisor is a mere shell of the opportunity it once was, the purchase of a blue chip franchise is a gold mine compared with most of the franchising product available to Americans in the United States. In addressing my personal concerns with abuse in the franchising industry, I am displeased by the erosion of the value of franchise opportunities among the blue chip franchisors. More importantly, too many franchise opportunities are veritable frauds.

Of the 3,500 companies estimated to be selling franchises today, probably less than 300 have recognizable trademarks or proven operating systems. The remaining 3,200 "opportunities" are with little-known companies that have slight or no operating experience. As new data becomes available, they suggest that most franchise opportunities are no more safe or secure than starting an independent new business from scratch.

The historical perspective of modern-day franchising as a foolproof path to success helped to spawn the avalanche of franchising in the United States. It is the glamour of the industry that has helped to create The Franchise Fraud, and open the door to potential economic disaster for millions of Americans.

Understand, there is nothing wrong with the franchise business model. The magnificent mechanism of product and service distribution that we call franchising, like any other human system, must be subjected to a cybernetic balance to maintain its vitality within acceptable parameters (see Chapter 10). Over the past 15 to 20 years, the United States has suffered from runaway franchising, much as it suffered runaway inflation in the 1960s and 1970s. Today, franchising is out of control because franchisees, and those who represent franchisees, have been unable to harness the energy of franchising by bridling the power of the franchisors through balanced negotiation and franchisee protection.

Fortunately, the history of franchising, if it continues to mirror the history of political enfranchisement, suggests the population of franchisees will ultimately come together and demand the rights and freedoms promised by the franchise model.

Chapter 4

Stealing from the Middle Class

The inducement to sell franchises based on false promises of the industry is the most commonly recognized form of The Franchise Fraud. Serious flaws in government statistics give a false impression of franchising as being virtually risk free. More importantly, franchising acts as a major fraud on middle-class Americans, allowing companies lacking access to securities markets to entice investments of an individual's entire net worth without meeting any standards of suitability or fairness. This chapter also examines some amazing statistics that indicate very few franchising companies have any proven track record even by industry standards.

The franchising industry has systematically represented franchising as the proven path to reversing the odds against business failure for entrepreneurs. The International Franchise Association (IFA) has described franchising as "a convenient and economic means for the filling of a drive or desire (for independent business ownership) *with a minimum of risk and investment and maximum opportunities for success* through the utilization of a proven product or service and marketing method [*emphasis added*]."[1]

Typically, the franchisor will make the following claims in its published materials and oral sales pitch:

> Franchising is clearly the wave of the future. According to the Department of Commerce, by the year 2000, 50 percent of all retail sales will be made from franchised outlets. More importantly, the Department of Commerce has reported that although 80 percent of all new businesses fail within 2

years, franchising statistics indicate that 95 percent of all franchisees are still in business after 5 years.

Although there is risk in any new business start-up, franchising has proven itself to dramatically increase the odds of business success.

In the typical scenario, the franchisor touts franchising first, and then goes on to sing the praises of its own enterprise and franchise system. But the message to the general public is clear—*buying any franchise turns a high-risk investment into a much safer one.*

Examples abound. Chick's Natural, a relatively new fast food chicken franchisor, produced a brochure in its first year of existence which exemplifies the practice of trading on the "reputation" of franchising.[2] The brochure begins with the following "Question and Answer":

1. Why purchase a franchise?

According to a U.S. Commerce Department survey on businesses still operating after the first year, after five years and after ten years indicates that franchises operating after the first year compared to independent businesses—is 97% to 62%. After five years the figure is 92% to 23% and after ten years—90% to 18%.

For most Americans, the conventional wisdom holds that franchising is synonymous with success. The *Chick's Natural* brochure took advantage of this conventional wisdom.

The founders of Chick's Natural had very little restaurant experience when they began franchising. Although the founders' original restaurant was successful, the franchisor could not replicate the success, and all the original nine franchisees lost substantial sums. In fact eight of the nine went out of business. The one remaining franchisee was very well financed and ultimately bought out the original franchisor and has continued operating.

The Chick's example is particularly telling, because all the original franchisees agree that Chick's natural style rotisserie chicken is an excellent product. But the company certainly had not developed a recognized and respected trade name, or established a market for its products, *or developed a proven system of restaurant design and operation.*

To tie the success of franchising to the Chick's Natural concept was simply false. Nevertheless the practice is common in the industry. Indeed, the sale of franchises based on the mystique of franchising has become industry standard.

THE FRANCHISE FRAUD AND THE GOVERNMENT

The most chilling aspect of the Franchise Fraud is that the United States Department of Commerce (DOC) is invariably used as the foundation for claims that franchising ensures success. Franchising statistics *always* begin with a reference to a Department of Commerce study that touted franchising as a mechanism to cut the number of business failures in the United States. By citing government authority, accuracy seems assured. Moreover, franchisors arguably cannot be faulted for relying on government statistics in their marketing efforts.

In 1986, the Department of Commerce published a report "Franchising in the Economy 1984–1986." The publication reported the findings and conclusions of a survey conducted by the Department of Commerce on the growth of franchising, and the success rates of franchisees.

The Department of Commerce report documented the phenomenal growth of franchising over the previous 20 years and further projected that franchising would account for 50 percent of all retail sales by the year 2000. It was reported that the incidence of franchise "discontinuance" was less than 1 percent per year, a number the report described as "insignificant." Franchisors, and the franchising industry, have used the Department of Commerce report to suggest that more than 95 percent of all franchisees remain in business after 5 years.

The apparent astronomical rate of success for franchised businesses are frequently compared with a *purported* Small Business Administration study that "allegedly" concluded 80 percent of all independent businesses fail within two years of start-up. The trouble is the alleged study does not exist. However, in March and April of 1978 the House Committee on Small Business conducted hearings in connection with its oversight review of the Small Business Administration on *The Future of Small Business in America*. Testimony given at these hearings quoted a Dun and Bradstreet survey that concluded *55 percent of businesses that fail* do so within five years of start-up.[3] The statistic suggested by the 1977 congressional survey is a far cry from a prediction of the failure rate of *all* businesses.

In December 1993, a new study was released by the Entrepreneurial Growth and Investment Institute in Washington, DC, which raises serious doubt about the accuracy of the failure rate statistics in the DOC report.[4] The study, which was conducted by Dr. Timothy Bates, compared the U.S. Bureau of the Census' Characteristics of Business Owners (CBO) data between 1987 and 1991. During the period analyzed, Dr. Bates found that 34.9 percent of young franchised businesses (less than 4 years old) had failed as compared to only 28 percent of nonfranchised young firms.[5] Dr. Bates' conclusion is staggering in comparison to the DOC survey of 10 years ago, "The message forthcoming in the Census Bureau data is clear: franchising promotes failure in the overall universe of very young firms."[6]

Even putting the contradictory findings of recent studies aside, the Department of Commerce survey of franchising companies had serious flaws. The study was based upon a voluntary questionnaire circulated among some 3,000 franchising companies; 1,942 responded. Of the franchisors who responded, a substantial number were members of the IFA, which encouraged its members to participate in the survey.[7] There was no effort to identify failed franchisors.

The Department of Commerce report was primarily flawed because it was a voluntary survey. The Department of Commerce merely compiled the data provided by franchisors. No audit procedure was conducted, not even spot checking to determine the accuracy of the information reported by franchisors. In essence, the Department of Commerce reported the claims of franchisors as gospel truth.

With voluntary reporting by mainly well established companies, the DOC report was severely biased. Indeed, the report acknowledged more than 1,000 franchising companies in the United States did not participate. There was little or no incentive for a poor performing franchisor to participate and air unfavorable statistics. Moreover, there was no effort to identify failed franchisors, whose failure rates would have drastically altered the study's ultimate conclusions.

A recent study by the American Association of Franchisees and Dealers compared the franchisors listed by *Entrepreneur* magazine in 1987 to

Entrepreneur's rankings for 1992. The study found that almost 70 percent of the franchisors listed and ranked by *Entrepreneur* magazine in 1987 were no longer listed in 1992. A 14 percent annual failure rate of whole franchise systems that were left out of the DOC survey would surely have skewed the report's finding of "insignificant" unit failures.

But the most *deceptive* aspect of the Department of Commerce report was the failure of the report to correctly define a *franchise failure*. Indeed, the term has been much debated, and there is little consensus on what constitutes the failure of a franchise. Logically, most people think of losing money and going out of business as a business failure. On the other hand, what if the business is sold at a loss and a new owner takes over operation of the business; or if the owner hangs on for years, but never earns even an average salary for a manager of a similar business.

A corporation would describe a branch office or store as successful if it earns a suitable profit after paying all expenses. If the branch exactly paid its expenses (and earned no profit), we would likely call it a "break-even" office. If the local office failed to gross sufficient revenues to pay all local expenses, cover the depreciation of the local office assets, *and cover at least the local manager's salary,* the office would operate at a loss, and would be closed after a time. Similarly, should we not define a franchise failure as any franchised business that is unable to pay its owner a fair wage?

The Bates' study previously discussed is the first to compare the profitability of franchised and nonfranchised business. Again the results are startling. In his analysis of some 7,270 businesses over his test period, Dr. Bates found that startup capital for a franchised business averaged $85,293 as compared to average startup capital for a nonfranchised business of only $30,156. Notwithstanding the greater investment, in 1987 nonfranchised businesses reported average pre-tax net income of $19,744 as compared to only (a negative) **−$1,548** for franchised businesses. Dr. Bates concluded, "Despite their larger revenues, much greater capitalization, and their supposed advantages of affiliation with a franchisor parent firm, the franchisees lag behind cohort young firms in profitability and rates of survival."[8]

Anthony De Sio, the CEO of Mail Boxes, Etc. (MBE), a major franchisor (2000 plus units) of private post office and business services franchises, recently defended his company's claim of a 97 percent success rate:

As you all know, MBE calculates the failure rate of its Franchisees by dividing the cumulative total number of store closures by the cumulative number of store openings as of any specific date. This simple method of calculating failure rate is standard for the franchise industry.[9]

The DOC survey followed this industry definition of counting only closed stores as failures and reported the incidence of franchise "discontinuance" to be less than 1 percent per year. The DOC concluded franchise failures over five years were insignificant. You and I read this claim to mean less than 1 percent of individual franchisees fail each year.

The claim, even as we reasonably understand it, is most suspect. Even a cursory review of some of the reporting companies in the DOC review suggests the claim cannot be true, because they report substantial turnover of their franchisees. And if a franchisor experiences substantial turnover of its franchisees, how can it claim a 95 percent franchisee success rate without telling a blatant and bald-faced lie?

The answer is quite simple. Like Mail Boxes, Etc., most franchisors only report a unit failure if the unit completely goes out of business and ceases to exist. If the franchise is taken over by the franchisor, or is resold (over and over), there is no recorded failure. Carried to its logical extreme, there is no franchise failure unless and until the franchise (the mere right to engage in business) is "discontinued" at the franchise location.

Even the best statistics can be deceptive, but this particular claim takes on the identity of fraud because it so clearly deceives the public as to the safety of a franchised enterprise.

If a franchisor sells a franchise for St. Louis, Missouri, that franchise will never go away as long as the franchisor keeps the franchised business in operation. The franchised business may change hands 3, 4, or 100 times, but the franchise still exists.

Other recent studies have revealed that franchisors use several methods to hide evidence of franchise failures.[10] Franchisors simply ignore franchisees who leave the system because they have suffered monetary losses. Most frequently, a "failed" franchise is not closed; rather, the franchise is transferred to a new operator or returned to the franchisor. Unless the franchised outlet actually closes, the business does not show up in "discontinuance" statistics.

Take the example of a national employment services franchisor. As recently as 1986, this company was ranked as the number one fastest growing franchisor in the United States. The company claimed more than 500 franchises and its growth rate was truly phenomenal. The company had long been a leading member of the IFA, and could have been a reporting company in the DOC report.

But a closer inspection of the figures revealed a far different picture. At the same time as the company was growing to 500 units, scores of franchises went out of business or changed hands. In San Diego County alone, there were more than 15 franchises between 1975 and 1990. Only 1 exists today. However, until 1990, the company continued to grow in numbers, and it could (correctly, but not honestly) claim most of its franchises still existed.

In truth, many franchisees lost their investments even while the company claimed few of its franchises had failed. In effect, the company was able to parlay the failures of its franchisees, combined with its reputation as a fast-growing franchisor, to churn the sale of franchises into substantial profits.

Even had the DOC report accurately depicted the franchise success rates of the companies that participated in the survey, the failure to make adjustments for non-reporting companies substantially biased the report's findings. The bulk of franchising companies are not well known, and are not IFA members. The least-known franchisors are most likely to experience business failures, including entire system failures. These undistinguished franchisors that never made the DOC report perhaps best exemplify The Franchise Fraud in the classic sense.

Notwithstanding its questionable findings, the Department of Commerce study represented a bold claim that franchising actually reverses the odds of a new business succeeding. As a result of the Department of Commerce study, the DOC and other agencies of the U.S. government commenced a strong campaign to sell Americans on franchising. Since 1966, the government has published the *Franchise Opportunities Handbook* and other publications and reports aimed at promoting franchising to an American populace ever captivated with an entrepreneurial spirit. Undoubtedly, the government's promotion of franchising stems from the perception of success suggested by the DOC's franchising survey.

There is the famous story of the presidential poll conducted by *Time* magazine in 1948, which reported Thomas Dewey would defeat Harry

Truman in a landslide. When Truman won in an upset, a study was undertaken to determine why the poll had proven so incorrect. The investigators discovered that *Time* readers were predominantly Republicans. Had this factor been recognized, Dewey's weakness would have been apparent, because the poll actually demonstrated Truman had substantial strength among Republicans.

The 1948 *Time* presidential poll is regarded as a benchmark for the public opinion polling industry. We have since learned that if a polling sample is not statistically balanced, substantial bias results. From the embarrassment of the 1948 presidential polls, the polling industry has refined its techniques to keep their margins for error to under 3 percent when necessary.

Like the presidential polls of 1948, the Department of Commerce report paints a grossly inaccurate picture of franchising. Based on the voluntary reporting of the most successful franchising companies, and without any testing or audit, the DOC survey suggested buying a franchise was buying a virtually foolproof ticket to success in business.

Even today, the DOC report is frequently quoted and rarely challenged.[11] It is still relied on as accurate by every franchisor, most reporters and commentators, and even the U.S. government. But franchisees, and those who represent franchisees, know the DOC statistics cannot be accurate.

THE TRUTH BEHIND THE STATISTICS

The conventional claim and implication about franchise statistics is that franchisees uniformly benefit from having an established market for their products and services. Buying a franchise is equated with buying into a well-established trade name, market, and proven successful enterprise. In truth, perhaps less than 10 percent of the franchisors in the United States have recognizable trademarks. If the lure of franchising is buying a proven successful system, few franchisors can substantiate such claims until they are well known and respected in the marketplace.

In 1992, the 100 largest franchisors (by the number of franchised units) accounted for just over 154,000 franchised units.[12] This means that 34 percent of the estimated 540,000 franchises in the United States were granted by less than 3 percent of the franchising companies in business. Only 369 franchising companies (or less than 11 percent) have 100 or more franchised units in business, and that number still may not suggest a well-known name. Although my professional life is immersed in franchising, of the first 20 franchisors ranked by *Entrepreneur* in 1993[13] as having between 100 and 125 units in business, I had never heard of 13 of them:

1. T-Shirts Plus
2. Tuffy Auto Service Centers
3. Practical Rent-A-Car
4. Mr. Transmission
5. SpeeDee Oil Change and Tune-Up
6. Sensible Car Rental Inc.
7. Affordable Used Car Rental System Inc.
8. Mighty Distrib. System of America
9. We Care Hair
10. First Choice Haircutters
11. Super Coups
12. Signs Now
13. UniShippers Association

I recognized 2 of the 20 for negative reasons. Ugly Duckling Car Rental Systems had recently been in bankruptcy and Speedy Sign-A-Rama has been under investigation by the Federal Trade Commission for making false earning's claims and making false statements about the success of its system. In essence, 15 of the first 20 franchisors listed had not established positive name recognition with me.

The fact is that 80 percent to 90 percent of the all franchising companies have little or no track record of success. Hundreds of franchisors never get off the ground, and there are numerous examples of entire systems failing. Worse, scores of franchisors are successful because they are able to sell franchises, not because their franchise concept or business format breeds an inherently successful business enterprise.

Going back to a previous example, the "top ranked" employment services company was an excellent seller of franchises. The company was profitable, not because of its placement of employees, but because it was able to sell franchises and resell those franchises who went out of business to new purchasers.

Even McDonald's, which is admittedly a strong business opportunity for any entrepreneur, has been accused by franchisees of encroaching existing franchisees' territories so it can continue to sell a high volume of franchises. McDonald's franchises, like all franchises, are, in fact, a "product" for sale by the franchisor. The larger the inventory a franchisor has to sell, the more profit the franchisor can make.

Many prospective franchisees are deceived by the apparent profitability of their franchisor. The fact that the franchisor has sold lots of franchises does not mean success for the franchisee. Unless the franchisor is profitable because of the sale of goods and services to the consuming public, the perception that the franchisor's success will be replicated by the franchisee may be false. The franchisee of a widget manufacturer needs to know his or her franchisor sells lots of widgets, because the franchisee will make a living on widget sales and not the sale of franchises. The key statistic is widgets sold—or Big Macs, shakes, and fries—not the number of franchised units.

In my own law practice, I represent a steady stream of franchisees whose businesses have failed. In good times and bad times, I consult an ever-growing class of businesspeople who believe they have been defrauded by their franchisors. Most of my clients terminate their franchises, or at the very least, appeal to their franchisors for substantial reductions in franchise fees and other concessions so they may stay in business.

In my own experience alone I have represented clients of many franchise systems that have failed: Gibraltar Transmissions, Contacts Influential, Minnie Pearl Fried Chicken, InfoPlan, First World Travel, and recently, Nutri-Systems.[14] Additionally, there have been major unit losses in many high-profile systems such as Popeye's and Church's Fried Chicken, The Diet Center, Jack-in-the-Box, Fast Frame, Shakey's Pizza, Ugly Duckling Car Rental, Dunhill Employment Services, and Western Temporary Service, to name only a few.

In counseling my clients, I always caution them to make sure the franchisor is mainly interested in its franchise system as a mechanism of distribution of its retail products to consumers. Is the franchisor dedicated to and dependent on its franchisees, or does it use multiple methods of distribution (company-owned stores or sales through supermarkets)? And does the franchisor recommend a fair markup on its products (a sure sign the franchisor is on the franchisee's side)?

SELLING A LIE

It may be The Franchise Fraud has its roots in misleading government statistics. But these statistics have been fanned feverishly by the franchising industry, which has milked the Department of Commerce study for all it is worth.

Historically, the International Franchise Association has been the only successful lobby in the franchising industry. Representing franchisors, and well financed, the IFA has vigorously promoted the virtues of franchising to the Department of Commerce and has lobbied strongly for the DOC to continue publishing profranchising studies. Largely through the efforts of the IFA, franchisors are able to bask in the glow of the government studies and deftly avoid responsibility for deceptive statistics by merely citing the Department of Commerce as the source.

Franchisors all across the United States have been able to parlay Department of Commerce statistics into the sale of millions of franchise businesses over the past 20 years. Keep in mind, if there are 500,000 franchisees in business today (as these same suspect Department of Commerce statistics claim), then what multiple of businesspeople have bought and sold, or closed, their franchises over the past 20 years? No statistics are available, but if you assume that 2 million franchisees have paid an average of $100,000 in franchise fees and royalties, more than $200 trillion have been spent on franchise fees paid by franchisees to their franchisors. If the existing franchised businesses pay royalties averaging 6 percent of gross sales, the industry generates $45 billion annually in royalty income alone. In other words, it is simply good business to promote the sale of franchising.

Most sources estimate there are between 3,000 to 4,000 franchising companies in the United States. There are several published franchise source books and directories that routinely list 2,000 to 3,000 franchising companies on an annual basis. So there is plenty of product. But how many of these "franchise opportunities" represent acceptable investment risks and suitable business opportunities?

By my definition (which we will focus on in Chapter 9), a suitable franchise opportunity meets eight important tests:

1. The franchising company is primarily interested in distributing quality goods and services to ultimate consumers.

2. The franchising company is dedicated to a franchise system as its *primary* mechanism of product and service distribution.

3. The franchising company, in fact, produces and markets quality goods and services for which there is an established market demand.

4. The franchising company enjoys a substantial reputation and acceptance (this is frequently identified with favorable trademark recognition).

5. The franchisor has an established, well-designed marketing and business plan and offers prospective franchisees substantial and complete training.

6. The franchisor has developed good relations with its franchisees, and the franchisees have a strong franchisee organization that has negotiating leverage with the franchising company.

7. The franchisor has a history of attractive earnings by its franchisees. *Only invest in a franchisor that provides meaningful disclosure of the earnings history and potential of the franchise opportunity being offered.* Anything less is buying a pig in a poke. Like any investment, the franchise opportunity must project sufficient economic benefit to justify the cost of buying the franchise and starting the business. In other words, the economic rewards must justify the price.

8. Finally, is the franchisor respectful of certain fundamental rights of business ownership? Over time, I have developed a special "Franchisee Bill of Rights" that is described in detail in Chapter 13.

With a diligent investigation of various franchise opportunities, you will find that a very small percentage of the more than 3,000 franchise opportunities can meet the eight tests of a recommended franchise system. Only a handful of franchisors earn respect as blue chip franchise opportunities.

A large chunk of franchising companies are more interested in selling franchises than in reaching markets of ultimate customers. Many companies who seek to reach ultimate consumers may not be dedicated to their franchise systems, and franchisees may find themselves in competition with their own brands.

As already noted, most franchising companies cannot claim to have developed substantial market acceptance. However, a franchisor with an exceptional product and a well-designed business and marketing plan may prove to be a solid ground-floor opportunity. Just remember that *ground-floor* opportunities present much higher risks of failure, which should be reflected in the purchase price of the franchise.

The first five criteria for choosing a franchise will usually eliminate hundreds of "opportunities." But the last three criteria really provide the litmus test of proving a franchise opportunity. Very few franchising companies are willing to make earnings claims. More importantly, less than 5 percent of active franchising companies have independent and *recognized* franchisee associations. The ability of franchisees to collectively bargain their franchise relationships and have meaningful access to the franchisor's management may be the single most important protection and criterion, so an independent franchisee association is essential.

The notion of a Franchisee Bill of Rights is new.[15] As of this writing no franchisor has embraced the notion that franchisees should have any "inalienable" rights. More importantly, few franchisors are willing to grant any rights to franchisees beyond the right to use the franchisor's trade name, trademarks and products.

Notwithstanding the difficulty of passing my 8 criteria of franchise selection, the franchising industry spends millions of dollars annually to paint franchising as the safe and secure path to proven business success. But look closely at the industry's own claims and statistics—many of the industry's warts can be seen. For example, of the estimated 540,000 franchised businesses in the United States in 1992, 430,000, or 80 percent, are business format franchises. Business format franchises accounted for only $232.2 billion of the $757.8 billion in retail sales from franchising—only 31 percent of sales came from 80 percent of the franchised businesses. Product franchisors—those companies that manufacture products and have a vested interest in distribution to ultimate consumers—represent only 20 percent of the franchising companies in the United States but accounted for 69 percent of retail sales, a whopping $525.6 billion![16]

Entrepreneur publishes an annual survey it calls the "Franchise 500®." In January 1992, the magazine published its 13th annual survey, grading over 1,300 American franchisors, with industrial rankings for what the magazine considers to be the top 500 franchisors. Note that *Entrepreneur* only lists franchisors who are actively selling franchises at the date of publication, so frequently major companies like Taco Bell, Coca-Cola, and Manpower Employment Services may not even be listed.

In preparing the Franchise 500®, *Entrepreneur* grades each company for numerous objective factors designed to provide quantifiable measures of a "franchise operation." Each franchise system receives a grade of 1 to 5,000.[17] The franchisor with the highest score is ranked number 1. Only the top 500 franchisors attain an industrial ranking that places them on the list of *Entrepreneur's* Franchise 500®.

Simply stated, *Entrepreneur* attempts to grade the top 1,300 franchises (out of the 3,500-plus franchising companies) in the United States. Of these companies, the magazine attempts to rank the very top 500.[18]

The casual reader identifies the Franchise 500® with the Fortune 500® list of the largest U.S. companies. The obvious assumption is that the top 500 franchises would constitute the blue chip franchise opportunities. But a more careful reading of the Franchise 500® industrial ranking system provides startling results.

On *Entrepreneur's* grading scale of 1 to 5,000, McDonald's received the highest weighted rating in 1992 of 4,347.25. Several companies however, received objective ratings as low as 10. Indeed, the lowest ranked company to make the Franchise 500® was the "well-known" Pyravision, Inc., which provides electronic voice mail services in my hometown of San Diego, California. The company achieved a weighted ranking of *68.50* on a scale of 5,000. This is a company I have never heard of, but it was ranked in the top 18 percent of franchisors in the United States by *Entrepreneur* magazine in 1992. Pyravision does not appear at all in *Entrepreneur's* 1993 rankings![19]

Further investigation reveals astounding statistics. For example, on the entire list of 1,300 franchisors, only 40 companies achieved a score of 1,000 or better, and only 203 companies scored better than 250 points on the 5,000-point scale. In other words, the bottom 300 of the Franchise 500® scored 250 points or less, as compared with McDonald's 4,347.[20]

If we look at the scores another way, by lumping the tested companies into classes or grades by 1,000-point increments, we find the following results:

Grade	Score	Number of Companies
A	4,000+	2
B	3,000 to 3,999	1
C	2,000 to 2,999	19
D	1,000 to 1,999	18
F	0 to 999	1260

However you look at the industrial rankings, the list of blue chip franchises is a very short one. Nevertheless, the casual reader of the Franchise 500® would not appreciate the steep decline in the quality of franchise opportunities.

TARGETING THE MIDDLE CLASS

Based on the astounding dollars that flow from the payment of franchise fees, The Franchise Fraud may be the greatest fraud ever perpetrated on the American public. The target of The Franchise Fraud is the middle class. Franchising targets that great body of working Americans who have managed to accumulate $25,000 to $500,000, and long to own their own business. In 1993, *Entrepreneur* reported that the average franchisee "has a net worth of $329,704 before investing in a franchise."[21]

Having challenged available data on franchising, I am a little embarrassed now to rely on government statistics. Alas, they are all we have. According to the 1988 United States Statistical Abstract, approximately 58 million American households have a net worth of between $25,000 and $1,000,000, or approximately 55 percent of American families. Although this may seem a very wide range in net worth, this range represents the population we call the middle class. This is the segment of the American public targeted as most likely to buy a franchise opportunity.

Above a million-dollar net worth, most individuals likely have the expertise and financial resources to start an independent business enterprise from scratch, or to purchase an existing established business. At the very least, individuals or families with a net worth above $500,000 can command the safest, most secure, and proven business opportunities.

So the great bulk of unproven franchise opportunities are left to the buying public with the skimpiest net worth. Although the 8.8 percent of American families who have accumulated between $250,000 and $500,000 can usually afford competent legal and accounting advice and are also able to investigate and secure viable business opportunities, in my experience this group is frequently victimized by The Franchise Fraud. In some ways, these middle Americans are the most vulnerable, because they have the available capital for which most franchisors hunger.

In my law practice, I am frequently posed a tragically telling question by prospective franchisees: "What financing is available to start a new franchise?" These prospective franchisees have entirely missed the point. Franchisees provide the franchisor's financing, not the reverse.

Franchising companies look at their franchise systems as their primary capital market. Franchisors expect their franchisees to develop the real estate, build the store, fund the inventory, pay the employees, and pay all the other expenses relating to the franchise business. In fact, franchisors usually rake their royalty off the top and really do not have any vested interest in their franchisees' achieving a profit. Indeed, a franchisor that is intent on churning franchises may *prefer* to have its franchisees lose money and go out of business so the franchise opportunity can be resold.

But even for ethical franchisors, the franchisee is the source of capital for building the franchisor's business. Therefore, it is the *franchisee's* capital that is invested into the business and provides the funding for business growth. In essence, franchising companies rely on middle-class Americans as their capital market. This fact bears an amazing impact on The Franchise Fraud.

You see, if a young franchising company were to go to traditional capital markets to sell stock or borrow money, most middle-class Americans would be forbidden territory. For the past 50 to 60 years, start-up and emerging companies—until they have achieved certain performance criteria—have been denied access to small investors.

McDonald's is perhaps the best (and most shocking) example of a company being able to raise hundreds of thousands of dollars by selling franchises, but not being able to gain access to public securities markets. Notwithstanding McDonald's phenomenal growth in the 1950s and early 1960s, the company had a very difficult time qualifying to go public in 1965.[22]

Even though McDonald's was the runaway leader in franchising, with more than 700 restaurants open, it had trouble meeting the due diligence requirements for an initial public offering. In the late 1950s and early 1960s, McDonald's had similar problems raising money from lending markets. In fact, the company resorted to some very innovative accounting techniques such as capitalizing future lease payments in an effort to boost the impression of its balance sheet to attract debt and equity capital.[23]

McDonald's is not an isolated example. In fact, there are only a handful of "public company" franchisors. The vast majority (perhaps more than 95 percent) of all franchising companies are privately held concerns that could not qualify to sell stock in most states. And capital markets are closed to most small companies for a very good reason.

Before franchising, the last great systemic fraud on the American public occurred in the securities industry during the first third of this century. During a time when anyone could sell the stock in their company in the public markets, the sale of "blue sky" was quite popular. The American public gobbled up stock and bonds with a voracious appetite. Margin buying was easy, and paper profits were enormous.

Following the stock market crash of 1929, and leading into the Great Depression, the mechanisms of the great securities scams and frauds of the 1920s became recognized and understood. In response to the unregulated selling of worthless securities to an unsuspecting public, the federal government, and every state, passed investor protection laws to regulate or prevent the selling of "blue sky" to an unwary public. Today, a fabric of securities laws and blue sky laws has developed into a broad range of investor protections.

Under the various state and federal securities laws, a company must produce substantial and expensive economic disclosure before it can sell stock, and most states preclude the sale of stock from startup companies to all but the most sophisticated investors. In fact, speculative securities may only be sold to investors who meet stringent suitability requirements.

It is common for a state to require an investor to have a net worth (exclusive of his or her home) in excess of $250,000 in order to make an investment of as little as $5,000 to $10,000 in a speculative security. Investments of $50,000 or $100,000, or more, truly require a millionaire.

In essence, our securities laws preclude most middle Americans from investing a large portion of their net worth in speculative securities. And even when such investments legally can be made, the specter of speculation hangs heavy over the opportunity so that small investors understand they are taking an inordinate amount of risk.

Since it is safe to opine that the vast majority of franchising companies are relatively young, privately held businesses, it is apparent that most prospective franchisees could not acquire stock in such companies. Indeed, most prospective franchisees could not legally invest even $5,000 or $10,000, in their franchisors. On the other hand, a typical franchise investment can run into hundreds of thousand of dollars when all the aspects of starting a franchise business are considered.

So it is curious, at the very least, that an investor who may be precluded from purchasing a modest amount of stock in a company, can, nevertheless, invest his or her entire life savings in the same company with little government regulation or interference.

But through the "magic" of The Franchise Fraud, not only is the investment of thousands of dollars in young, unproven companies permitted, such investments are promoted by the franchising industry and governmental authorities. Much like the false promise of paper profits in the 1920s, the false image of franchising has created the gold rush of the 1970s, 1980s, and 1990s.

THE FRANCHISEE VICTIMS

The tragedy of franchisee victims is the magnitude of their losses. Typically, franchisees bet the farm when they buy a franchise. Accordingly, when they lose their investment, it is not like dropping a few thousand dollars in the stock market. Usually it means the family home, life savings, and maybe credit rating. Often it means starting over with an albatross of huge debt and bad credit around the former franchisee's neck.

I have seen the following scenario time and again: The franchisee had thought he was investing in an established successful business. He had understood the purchase of a franchise meant the franchisor would train him in the business, would make sure he chose an appropriate business site, and would provide all the necessary backing to ensure the franchise's success. Because, of course, the franchisor could only prosper with a dynamic successful network of franchised businesses. This wistful naïveté of the franchisee going into business, brimming with optimism and high expectations, was dashed by the cold reality that his position was the equivalent to the franchisor's slinging other people's mud at a wall and claiming all of what stuck to the wall as its own.

Ultimately, franchisees come to understand they have provided all the capital for the establishment of the franchise business. Moreover, franchisees are invariably responsible (and accountable) for the selection of the franchise site. Franchisees almost always are responsible for the hiring and the management of the employees of the business. And when the business loses money, *only* the franchisee loses. The employees get paid, *and* the franchisor gets paid, win or lose.

When franchisees fail, the franchisor rarely shares their failure. Rather, the franchise goes back into inventory to be resold again and again.

I recently had a conversation with a lawyer with the Federal Trade Commission. We were talking about franchisee losses, and I was expressing my alarm at the magnitude of the size and the consequences of a typical franchisee failure. The FTC lawyer responded to my comments by noting a fact that had never occurred to me: Virtually every franchisor "prequalifies" prospective franchisee candidates by performing a complete evaluation of their credit and financial circumstances. Effectively, every franchisor is aware of exactly how much money the franchisee has to lose before the franchise is ever sold.

THE FRANCHISOR OWES YOU NOTHING

My frustration with franchising is that the industry claims to have built its reputation on ethical conduct in providing a controlled risk mechanism of entrepreneurial opportunities to a large number of Americans. And yet the franchising industry has consistently denied that franchisors have any legal or ethical duty for the success of their franchisees.

I am particularly frustrated because franchisors realize so many exceptional benefits from a franchise network—the formation of substantial capital, the development of self-committed middle management, protection from ancillary risks, and insulation from the losses of the franchisee. Because these benefits are so compelling, the failure to require franchisors to provide some level of reciprocal commitment to the success of their franchisees is absolutely bewildering to me.

My biggest frustration, however, is that franchisees, many of whom are educated businesspeople and intelligent investors, allow The Franchise Fraud to continue virtually unchecked. In a very real sense, franchisee victims have allowed themselves to be victimized. The problems in franchising are eminently solvable. We don't need more lawsuits, and the job could probably be done without new laws. What is needed is a correction in the franchising marketplace. We need capitalism to work the way it was intended, with a willing buyer and a willing seller negotiating in good faith from equal bargaining positions.

Balanced negotiations will never occur so long as the parties are one franchisee to one franchisor. That is not to say, however, that franchisees lack substantial (collective) market power. As franchisees learn to organize and work together, so will their ability to bargain in good faith improve, and so will they reclaim the American Dream of true business ownership.

Chapter 5

The Franchisee as Indentured Servant

Perhaps the biggest myth of franchising is that a franchisee is an independent businessperson. Most franchisees have fewer rights than common-law employees.

Although most franchise agreements claim the franchisee is an independent contractor, franchisors rarely accord their franchisees any degree of independence. Franchise agreements can run 50 pages or more and are usually subject to many volumes of standard operating procedures manuals. In truth, most franchisees could not meet the legal test to qualify as independent contractors. Rather, most courts would likely rule that many franchisees are really employees under the current Internal Revenue Service definition. However, franchisees rarely have the rights and privileges of employees under the law and therefore invite comparisons to indentured servitude.

Indentured servitude was a master-servant relationship that grew out of feudal times. A peasant or serf was bound into servitude to his master upon some agreement or indebtedness. In feudal times, indentured servitude could last for life—the lord of the manor virtually owned the serf, and the relationship was tantamount to slavery. As recently as the nineteenth century, indentured servitude continued to exist in the United States but arose from agreements whereby the person bound into service received a benefit (often the right to emigrate from a European country to the United States) for which he or she could not pay except by the promise of service.

Indentured servants were legally bound by their contracts to serve their masters for a period of years. Indentured servants did not have the rights or liberties of freemen. They could not own property, vote, or work for hire until their servitude was completely fulfilled. After slavery was abolished, indentured servitude was the closest relationship to bondage existing in the United States. Ultimately, the relationship has been abolished as repugnant to our sense of individual freedom.

Initially it may seem preposterous that I draw a comparison of franchising to indentured servitude. Even though the franchise business model grew out of the feudal economic system, certainly it must be a stretch to suggest that franchisees are lacking in basic human rights and political freedoms. On inspection, however, the franchise relationship as applied under modern law is closer to indentured servitude than to any other commercial relationship.

In signing a franchise agreement franchisees indenture themselves to their franchisors, because an indenture is really no more than undertaking to perform some service or promise in exchange for valid consideration. For franchisees, the indenture undertaken is to promise "service" to the franchisor under the strict rules of the franchise system.

In signing the franchise agreement, franchisees surrender the right to operate their businesses independently and autonomously. More importantly, franchisees cannot terminate their servitude without paying substantial damages to regain their independence. Often, franchisees are restricted from gaining independence at any cost.

When franchisees enter the franchise relationship, they rarely understand or appreciate the expense of trying to exit the system if they are dissatisfied with the relationship. As is covered in Chapter 7, frequently franchisees are simply not permitted to leave.

Like franchising, conceptually indentured servitude was not a "bad" practice. Many people were enabled to emigrate and gain the right of U.S. citizenship by virtue of their servitude, and many masters were kind and protective of their servants. Some indentured servants were treated well and ultimately earned freedom. Similarly, franchisees in many systems are well rewarded for their efforts and benefit substantially for having agreed to be bound to their franchise systems. The fact that there were many benign slaveholders, however, does not change the circumstances of bondage—such is also the case in franchising.

Time and again, we hear of horror stories dealing with the indentured servitude of the franchise relationship. A maid service franchisee of a little-known franchise system would like to leave because he is losing money and gaining no benefit from the franchise, but his phone number and the yellow pages lifeline to his customers are bound to the franchisor. The franchisee of a major engine tune-up system lost $300,000 because the franchisor failed to research the competition in recommending the franchise site. Nevertheless, he was not allowed to quit the system (even to go out of business) without paying damages for the franchisor's loss of royalty income due to the early termination of the franchise agreement.

I have represented numerous franchisees in many different industries who found themselves "indentured" to the service of their franchisors (and paying substantial fees and royalties) while suffering the loss of money and property. These same franchisees, who had paid for their franchise rights, had financed their businesses, and worked 80-hour weeks for little or no pay, frequently existed near the franchisor's company-owned office, which paid a manager a competitive salary and provided paid training, vacations, sick leave, and pension benefits.

There is one glaring difference between a franchisee and an indentured servant. Traditionally, indentured servitude was for a definite term, often seven years. When the relationship ended, the indentured servant was free. Most franchisees never gain their independence. When the franchise ends in the modern franchise, most business rights revert to the franchisor.

THE FALSE PROMISE OF BUSINESS OWNERSHIP

The Franchise Fraud, in part, is the false representation that the franchisee owns a business. The franchise agreement purports to grant rights—to enfranchise—but most franchises in today's marketplace do not impart meaningful ownership.

A company I recently helped to franchise is an excellent case in point. The company was a successful janitorial business that had been around for a number of years. (The building maintenance industry has been a prime market for franchising, and 3 of the top 10 franchisors in *Entrepreneur's* 1992 industrial rankings were from that industry.)

For years, my client had entered into independent contractor agreements granting exclusive janitorial routes to individuals. However, the company had recently been audited by the Internal Revenue Service (IRS) and was assessed substantial penalties because the IRS deemed the independent contractors to be common-law employees and subject to withholding taxes. My client's tax attorney recommended "cleansing" the independent contractor relationship by selling the janitorial routes as franchises, and I was hired to do the job. In fact, the IRS accepted the janitors as independent contractors once they became franchisees. It is important to recognize that the rights and the duties of the janitors never changed, only their title.

Nevertheless, the public identifies a franchisee as an independent businessperson, no matter what his or her rights in operating a business.

From my personal perspective, I cannot imagine a better way to hire a middle manager than by selling a franchise. The typical franchisee makes a substantial investment in the business opportunity and therefore has a vested interest in the operation's success. The franchisee is not paid a salary and is not even entitled to minimum wage. Because the franchisee manager has a vested interest in the enterprise, he or she doesn't use sick leave and doesn't accrue vacations.

Indeed, franchisees even pay for their own training! A typical franchise sale usually allocates $10,000 to $15,000 of the initial franchise fee to training. A typical training program lasts from 2 to 4 weeks. Even with today's high cost of education, $15,000 will still pay for a full year of college at many fine universities.

Perhaps most important, in the typical franchise the franchisor receives a continuing royalty, which is usually a percentage of the gross revenue. This means the franchisor makes money even if the franchisees are unprofitable. In fact, a common criticism leveled at franchisors is that they lack a vested interest in the profitability of their franchise networks.

From the franchisee's perspective, a franchise opportunity only fulfills its promise if the franchisee has the right to operate and exercise the discretion normally associated with business ownership. More often than not, franchising companies pay lip service to the independent status of the franchise operator, but in reality franchisors require strict adherence to the company's marketing system and standard operating procedure manuals.

A good example of an illusory entrepreneur is the 7-Eleven store operator. 7-Eleven has long been regarded the premier franchise opportunity for convenience stores. Southland Corporation claims its franchisees earn substantially higher incomes than the typical convenience store "hired" manager. In fact, many 7-Eleven operators earn between $40,000 and $80,000, and more. Such earnings are more than twice the cost of hiring an in-house store manager.

Although 7-Eleven offers an attractive earning potential, the franchisees' status as business owner is quite suspect.

7-Eleven operators exercise very little discretion in the operation of their businesses. Indeed, all revenues go from the cash register to a floor safe owned by the franchisor, Southland Corporation. Southland collects the revenues daily and deposits are made directly to Southland Corporation accounts. Southland pays for all inventory and purchases, and once a month pays its franchisees their share of the prior month's net profits. In other words, a 7-Eleven franchisees (the so-called business owners) never really touch the store revenues!

And the franchisees have very little discretion in what they sell, or don't sell in the store. I recently represented a 7-Eleven franchisee, who (for reasons best known to her) refused to sell California lottery tickets in her 7-Eleven store. Invoking a provision in the franchise agreement giving Southland the right to require all franchisees to carry products that the general public is ac-customed to finding in a 7-Eleven store, 7-Eleven declared my client in mate-rial default of her franchise agreement for failing to sell lottery tickets. My client was given notice of termination of her franchise unless she immediately began to sell lottery tickets.

Worse, because most 7-Eleven franchisees rent their stores from Southland, Southland is able to invoke a provision in the lease providing that a violation of the franchise agreement is also a violation of the lease agreement, and my client was given a notice of termination of her lease. Needless to say, my client had little discretion over whether or not she could sell the lottery tickets in her store.

THE POWER OF CONTROL OVER THE FRANCHISE LOCATION

The experience of my 7-Eleven client raises an interesting point. The cutting edge of modern business franchising, or more particularly, the cutting edge of franchisor coercion, is the *use of real estate* to control franchise activity and ownership of the franchised business.

In the early days of franchising, the franchisee found a location and signed the lease. In fact, one of the proclaimed benefits of franchising to a franchisor was that the franchisor did not incur lease obligations in all the branch outlets. As a franchisor becomes economically secure, however, it is far and away in the franchisor's best interest to sign the lease and sublet to the franchisee. Later, if the franchisee attempts to terminate, the franchisor gets the premises, and the franchisee must walk away from the business and, usually, his or her share of any business equity.

Once again, the franchisee is out in the cold and has little to show for any so-called equity in the franchise operation.

THE EQUITY ISSUE

The whole subject of what a franchisee really "buys" when acquiring a franchise for many thousands of dollars is increasingly coming under scrutiny in the franchising industry.

The industry extols franchising as a mechanism for an entrepreneur to "own your own business." "In business for yourself, but not by yourself" is the phrase coined by the IFA. Conceptually, a franchisee is buying a business that already has the protection of a strong trademark, a marketing system, and a mentor in the franchisee's corner to help steer the operation on the path to financial success.

More and more, the franchise model of business ownership is being eroded. In most successful franchise systems, the franchisee today is little more than a store manager without a salary, without fringe benefits, and without any significant right to control his or her own destiny. Franchisees usually lack the right or authority to respond to local market demands (by offering new products or services) without the franchisor's specific approval.

Keep in mind that, for the most part, franchisors are not *legally* culpable for this inequitable state of affairs. Most franchisors have not broken any laws or taken any money without fully disclosing all information required to be disclosed by law. Generally speaking, franchising companies spend thousands of dollars a year making sure their disclosure documents and franchise agreements accurately describe in detail a franchisee's rights and obligations.

Notwithstanding the fine print in the franchise disclosure document, most franchise opportunities are marketed as selling an independent business. Claims that franchisees own their businesses are often significant falsehoods. As often as not, the franchise agreement denies the franchisee any ownership equity in the licensed enterprise. For the most part, false claims of ownership are not actionable against individual franchisors because it is the industry, generally, that has spawned the myth, not specific franchisors.

Recently, Philip Zeidman, who is general counsel to the International Franchise Association, spoke before a large gathering of franchise attorneys and addressed the issue of franchisees' lack of any true "equity" in the licensed business. Mr. Zeidman's prescription for solving the problem was to require franchisors to disclose in their franchise documents that a franchisee *acquires no equity* in the franchised business.[1]

Mr. Zeidman's suggestion was typical of the franchising industry's solution to virtually all franchise abuses. Historically, whenever a franchise abuse is identified, the franchising industry has suggested (so far successfully) that more disclosure, rather than industry regulation, will solve the problem. Although I am no fan of increased government regulations, disclosure, without more, does no more than insulate franchisors from liability for franchisee claims of abusive practices.

THE FRANCHISEE IS NOT INDEPENDENT

Most franchise agreements provide that franchisees are independent contractors and *not employees* of the franchisor. Franchisees usually rely on such provisions to bolster their belief that they own an independent business.

However, franchisees should be cautioned to follow the axiom: "Just because the franchise agreement says it, doesn't make it so!" This axiom is of critical importance in representing the interests of franchisees because many unconscionable provisions in a franchise agreement may be unenforceable pursuant to the laws of the franchisee's state. For example, the noncompete covenants found in virtually every franchise agreement are *void* in several states and are restricted in many others. Without knowledgeable legal counsel, however, most franchises would assume these clauses are valid. Franchisees are frequently intimidated by the belief that they will be prevented from working in their chosen profession if the franchise is terminated.

The independent contractor clauses in most franchise agreements also bear close scrutiny. If a franchisor exercises so much control over its franchisees as to create an employee relationship, the franchisor may be in violation (or breach) of its promise to grant independent contractor status as provided in the franchise agreement. The franchisor may even be liable for misrepresenting the franchisee to be independent, when, in fact, he or she is an employee or something different.

Legal scholars have long debated the dividing line between an independent contractor and an employee. No one has been more interested in the subject than the Internal Revenue Service, which seeks to make sure American businesses are not avoiding withholding taxes by disguising their employees as independent contractors.

The IRS has published a series of guidelines to distinguish an independent contractor from an employee, "Twenty Factors to Determine Existence of Employer/Employee Relationship."[2] These guidelines state the general rule that the "relationship of employer and employee exists when the person or persons for whom the services are performed have the right to control and direct the individual who performs the services, not only as to the result to be accomplished by the work but also as to the details and means by which that result is accomplished." The guidelines also state ". . . if the relationship of employer and employee exists, the designation or description of the relationship by the parties as anything other than that of employer and employee is immaterial. Thus, if such a relationship exists, it is of no consequence that the employee is designated as a partner, coadventurer, agent, independent contractor, or the like."

The preceding guidelines were adopted by the IRS in 1987 after many years of debate and evaluation. They were first under discussion in the 1970s but were withdrawn for several years because the IRS had difficulty arriving at a successful distinction between the definition of an employee and independent contractor.

In an ultimate sense, the difference between an employee and an independent contractor is rather obvious. An employee is a "hired" worker under the direct supervision and control of the employer. The employer tells the employee where and how to do the work and is responsible for the employee's workmanship. An employer pays wages to the employee, dictates where and when the employee works, and usually supplies the employee both a work space and tools of the employee's trade.

An independent contractor on the other hand, is also "hired" to perform a job and may be said to be "employed" for the purposes of his or her contract. But an independent contractor does not work under the direct supervision of the employer. Rather, an independent contractor "contracts" to perform an ultimate task under certain specifications for a negotiated price. Beyond the specifications of the contract, the independent contractor usually does *not* work under the employer's direct supervision. Generally speaking, independent contractors provide their own work space and tools, and are fully responsible for the performance of their services.

Ostensibly, every franchised business has an independent contractor relationship with the franchisor. Virtually every franchise agreement specifies the relationship between the franchisor and franchisee is that of an independent contractor and specifically is not that of employer and employee.

Notwithstanding the contract language, however, the terms of many franchise agreements strain the meaning of independent contractor to its logical limits. The janitorial service company discussed at the beginning of this chapter is a perfect example. When my client tried to claim its janitorial technicians were independent contractors, the IRS disagreed and ruled the relationship between the technicians and my client was truly that of an employer and employee.

When my client began to sell franchises to validate the independent contractor relationship, the actual relationship between my client and its janitors did not change substantively. Nevertheless, because my client called the relationship a franchise, the IRS has now accepted the independent contractor status.

The trouble is that most franchise relationships are at least as controlling, if not more controlling, than many employer-employee relationships. Most established franchise systems have extremely precise multivolume operating procedures manuals that all franchisees are *required* to follow precisely. The failure to follow the manual can be grounds for termination. In my experience, franchise operating procedures manuals are at least as pervasive and controlling as equivalent employment manuals in similar industries. The manuals for most well-established franchisors consist of several volumes of specifications that dictate every aspect of the business enterprise. More importantly, franchisors reserve the right to modify their operations manuals at will—such that franchisors are effectively able to substantially amend and alter the franchise system and relationship without any agreement or consent from the franchisees.

Notwithstanding the control exercised by franchisors over their franchise systems, franchisees may be considered to be independent by virtue of their ownership of the franchise location and the tools of the franchise trade. As will be seen, the franchisee's ownership of the assets of the franchise business is frequently more illusory than real.

Although the franchisee provides the financing for most franchise businesses, paying for the business, without the authority to run it, seems an insufficient barometer of whether a master-servant relationship exists. Moreover, modern franchisors increasingly require their franchisees to sell their franchised businesses back to the franchisor on the termination of the franchise system. In such instances, ownership of the franchise enterprise should be carefully scrutinized.

Earlier in this chapter, I described the 7-Eleven operator as an "illusory entrepreneur." Is the relationship between Southland Corporation and its 7-Eleven operators truly that of an independent contractor, or does it more closely resemble the relationship between an employer and employee?

As previously discussed, I am currently representing some franchisees who own temporary employment service businesses. My clients have terminated their franchises claiming the franchisor falsely represented the franchisees were independent contractors. My clients contend they are treated like other employee managers of the franchisor, except that they do not receive salary or benefits and are denied access to training and other support programs offered to managers of company offices. Alternatively, my clients have claimed the franchisor breached the franchise agreements by failing to treat the franchisees as independent contractors.

My temporary employment services clients claim their franchisor completely controlled their business activities. The franchisor provided a thorough operating procedures manual that dictated the operation of their business enterprises. More importantly, the franchisor hired all the temporary employees, directly billed all the clients, collected all the proceeds, paid all the temporary employees and some vendors, and then paid the franchisees their share of the "gross profit."

The franchisees were required to pay all their operating expenses out of their share of the gross profits and frequently had little left for themselves on a monthly basis. My clients did not believe they were in business for themselves as they had intended when they purchased their franchises. When these franchisees attempted to terminate their franchise agreements and go independent, the franchisor sued them claiming it had a right to assume all the assets of the franchised businesses, including ownership of all the customers and employees of the business.

In December, 1993, an administrative judge ruled my clients were employees and not independent contractors as stated in the franchise agreement, and my clients were entitled to unemployment benefits. The would be franchisor will be audited for non-payment of payroll taxes. My client's lawsuit goes to trial in the spring of 1994.

Outside of this case, I am not aware of any lawsuit that has directly challenged a franchisor for failing to deliver a truly independent business enterprise. Unfortunately, my clients simply lack the financial resources to effectively prosecute their claims, especially against the substantial economic muscle of the franchisor. In fact, less than 5 percent of all lawsuits go to trial, and most are settled for economic reasons. Still, in this instance, it would be fascinating to see our appellate court system address the issue of whether my clients are independent contractors or employees.

THE TERMINATION TRAP

Most franchisees do not fully appreciate their entanglement in a dangerous web until they become disenchanted with their franchise and begin paying close attention to the termination provisions in their franchise agreements. This is where franchisees uniformly discover they do not really own the business they thought they "bought."

It is quite easy to generalize about franchise agreement termination provisions. As an experienced franchise attorney, I know what I'll find before reading the contract, and I am hardly ever surprised. Invariably, a terminating franchisee finds a variety of provisions that literally choke his or her ability to remain in business after termination:

- Without exception, every franchise agreement requires the terminating franchisee deidentify from the franchisor. Of course, this is an appropriate provision, because the franchisee should reasonably be expected to take down the franchisor's signs and to cease all benefits of association with the former franchisor. Notwithstanding the reasonableness of deidentification provisions, the expense of deidentification is substantial. It can cost a terminating franchisee many thousands of dollars to gain his or her new identity.

- Virtually every franchise agreement contains a noncompetition clause. These clauses range in severity, but a typical clause provides the franchisee, on termination of the franchise, may not compete directly or indirectly with his or her former franchisor anywhere near an existing outlet or office of the franchisor, for a period of two years or more. Noncompetition clauses usually mandate that a franchisee must literally change occupations. The function of franchising as a job training mechanism is effectively defeated. Franchisors defend noncompetition clauses as necessary to protect the franchisor who invests in training a franchisee and building goodwill of its franchised enterprise at a specific location, and then risks being dumped by the franchisee after sharing all its trade secrets and goodwill.

- Most franchise agreements restrict the franchisee from using or divulging the trade secrets of the franchised business. Franchisors attempt to extend trade secret protection to customer lists and the franchisor's methods of doing business.

- Many franchise agreements provide that ownership of the franchised business reverts to the franchisor on the franchisee's termination. More often, the franchise agreement will give the franchisor the option to purchase the franchise business at a price substantially below market value. Still other franchise agreements severely inhibit the franchisee's ability to sell the franchised business.

- As noted earlier in this chapter, the state of the art of franchise termina-tion provisions involves the franchisor maintaining control over the franchisee's real estate and lease. Again, franchisors employ several methods, all designed to achieve a reversion of the franchise location to the franchisor on termination. The most economically viable fran-chisors simply control or own the real estate, and lease or sublet to the franchisee. When the franchisee terminates, so does the lease, and the franchisee must vacate the premises and go out of business. Franchisors who are unable to afford owning all their franchise locations, or do not want the risk of being the primary lessor at all locations, will have the franchisee and his or her landlord execute a least assignment at the commencement of the franchise relationship. Less effective, but fre-quently used, is a provision in the franchise agreement whereby the franchisee agrees to assign the lease back to the franchisor on termina-tion. This latter device may be effectively attacked if the franchisor has breached the franchise agreement, and the landlord is not a party to the franchise agreement and therefore not required to honor the provision when the franchisee objects. However, faced with termination (and usually in severe financial distress) most franchisees lack the sophistica-tion or resources to attack such contractual provisions proclaiming the franchisor's right to the lease.

The practical effect of the preceding franchise termination provisions is quite simple: When franchisees terminate a franchise, they go out of business and must find a new career.

Admittedly, this text focuses on the franchisees' perspective. Franchisors advance many strong justifications for imposing severe restrictions on fran-chise terminations. Bottom line, franchisors (especially the ethical ones) are intent on expanding their businesses and growing their markets and business networks. More importantly, a franchisor, together with the franchisee, should share a vested interest in the success of the franchise system at each branch and franchise location. After all, the franchisor is interested in some-body operating a business for the benefit of the franchisor at a specific loca-tion, and the franchisor is not anxious to lose the goodwill built up at a location over many years.

In truth, the resolution of the respective rights of franchisors and franchisees on termination is the most difficult issue for the industry to solve. Both sides have legitimate rights and a vested interest in preserving their hard-earned equity.

For most good capitalists, the solution to resolving difficult issues is through negotiated tradeoffs, *quid pro quo*. Given equal bargaining power, franchisors and franchisees can address termination rights through negotiation in a free market.

In theory, parties to a contract can determine their respective rights on termination through balanced, informed negotiation. In a balanced marketplace, negotiation may provide suitable compromises. But the franchising industry is not a balanced market. It is a marketplace in which the franchisor dictates the terms, and the franchisee (usually without the benefit of counsel) has the option to accept the franchisor's terms, or to go look for another business opportunity.

If we stop for a moment, and we review where this chapter has taken us, we find a very revealing scenario. Typical franchisees, believing they have purchased their own business, may have a rude awakening. Generally, they have no more authority than typical managers, but have no guaranteed salary, fringe benefits, or perks. Usually, franchisees are not protected by federal wage and standards laws and have no paid vacations, no 40-hour workweeks, and no big company benefits.

Although a franchisee theoretically "owns" the business, there typically is no equity in the business even though the franchisee may have an investment of many thousands, or even hundreds of thousands of dollars.

If franchisees breach the franchise agreement, they may face termination and immediate loss of their total investment. Finally, if franchisees seek termination, forfeiture of the franchise investment is virtually assured.

I recently had an experience that ironically, almost comically, demonstrated the myth of a franchisee's ownership of the franchised business. I was retained by a company that was interested in franchising a unique carpet treatment service. My client had been in business for about a year and had developed a unique and profitable carpet treatment business, such that he had several people interested in acquiring franchises for his carpet treatment system in other cities.

When advised it could take four to six months to complete a franchise registration in the state of California, my client complained he needed to move ahead immediately. He asked if we could develop a business arrangement to emulate a franchise without such a substantial time delay.

Attempting to satisfy my client, I suggested the creation of a partnership with prospective investors, providing an option to convert the businesses to franchises at some future time. I suggested the partnerships be designed to emulate franchises without meeting the legal test of a franchise. I further advised the partnership arrangement should be less enticing to the prospective operators than an actual franchise so that when my client was able to sell franchises, each of his prospective venturers would immediately opt to convert to the franchised enterprise.

My client agreed to my plan and sent me to work in preparing a partnership agreement along my suggested guidelines. I prepared a partnership agreement whereby my client had complete control of the operation of the business and the prospective investors were responsible for the day-to-day operations. My client had no liability for any of the debts of the partnership, and the prospective investors would agree to indemnify and hold my client harmless for any such liabilities. The prospective franchisee/partners were required to put up all the capital and assume all the risk. On termination of the partnership, my client was entitled to buy the partnership assets on favorable terms.

The prospective franchisee/partners immediately balked at the onerous terms of the proposed partnership. Why—they and their attorneys asked—should they agree to a partnership that provided the prospective franchisee/partners put up all the capital, all the risk, but submit to the business control of my client as the managing partner? Why—when my client was not going to be involved in the day-to-day operations of the business—should he be preferred in the payment of fees over the prospective franchisee/partners?

I asked each of the prospective franchisee/partners if they were prepared to immediately purchase franchises from my client. Each of the parties, and their counsel, were immediately prepared to move ahead with the franchised enterprise. I then calmly explained that if we proceeded with a franchise, each of the prospective franchisee/partners would put up all the capital of the business and would bear all the risk, that my client would be insulated from liability, that my client would control the conduct of the business through its standard operating procedures manuals, and that my client's franchise fees would be preferred over the new franchisee's right to remuneration through the franchise business.

I could have also explained to the prospective franchisee/partners that under the partnership agreement, my client's fees were deferred until after all the partners had received compensation for their services. This factor made the partnership agreement immanently more favorable to the prospective franchisee/partners than did the ultimate franchise design. Nevertheless, the aura of business ownership characterized by the myth of franchising rendered the purchase of a franchise acceptable, while my proposed partnership agreement was not.

DEBTOR FRANCHISEES

When I testified before the House Committee on Small Business in the summer of 1991, Congressman John LaFalce asked me if I thought the typical franchise relationship was not more like the relationship between an employer and employee. My immediate response was that the franchisor-franchisee relationship was even closer to the relationship between a master and an indentured servant, or a lord and his serf.

I have witnessed and represented scores of franchisees who have become heavily indebted to their franchisors because of their inability to pay franchise fees and royalties. It is most common to find debtor franchisees encumbering their homes, liquidating pension benefits, and exhausting a lifetime of savings to ward off the burden of indebtedness to their franchised businesses.

Once a franchisee's investment is complete, he or she is a trapped person. Unless franchisees can sell their business with the franchisor's approval, they usually find themselves in a very vulnerable place—rather than achieving business independence, they find themselves imprisoned for life. Franchisees are thus indentured to their franchisors.

Chapter 6

Promises Unfulfilled

Although the franchising industry crows about substantial support and guidance provided by the franchisor to its franchisees, most franchise agreements promise nothing beyond a license to use a trademark and operational system. Conversely, franchise systems that provide substantial support and are dedicated to their franchisees as their primary method of product and service distribution can deliver all the substantial promise of franchising. Examples of successful and unsuccessful franchise systems are analyzed.

In my experience, the number one complaint of dissatisfied franchisees is their franchisor's lack of guidance and support. Franchising is touted as providing a would-be entrepreneur with training and operational support to ensure success. The following excerpt from a brochure touting franchising is representative:

> Why a franchise? Because with a franchise you buy an entire way of doing business—it starts with initial training in all aspects of running the business and continues with ongoing managerial support for as long as you own your franchise. You learn how to run your business from a mentor who has a vested interest in seeing you become profitable.[1]

Similar themes are echoed in a multitude of articles about franchising, such as a recent article highlighting the *Entrepreneur* Annual Franchise 500®. The article was entitled "R-E-S-P-E-C-T: Franchising Puts Small Business in Fast Lane":[2]

> What is franchising's secret for building almost instant credibility? "There's the name recognition factor" says (franchising expert) Edward Kushell,

"franchises also provide proven systems and methods of doing business. With the initial training and ongoing support of a franchisor who knows the business, almost any type of company can be very successful."

In fact, the explosive growth of franchising is almost entirely based on the promises of franchisors to train and support franchisees in the ownership of a proven marketing system. These promises of franchising are touted by the industry, by government publications, and by a steady diet of articles in the press. Even this book begins with a chapter dedicated to the substantial promise of franchising.

Every franchisor produces marketing materials enticing prospective owner/operators with promises of complete training, ongoing support, the establishment of a viable network, an impressive management team, and the ever-knowing presence of a dedicated franchisor standing in the background, parentlike, trying to make sure every franchisee succeeds.

The examples of A&W Root Beer and Chick's Natural (see Chapters 1 and 4) are typical.[3] Each in its own way—franchisors and the franchising industry—extols the virtues of the partnership attributes of franchising. Franchisors advertise teamwork, support, uniformity of system, combined advertising muscle, and similar concepts of mutual benefit as the foundation of their franchise systems.

But a comparison of franchise agreements reveals a far different reality from the rosy representations of most franchising advertisements. Very few franchisors are *contractually obligated* to provide *any* services beyond initial training and trademark protection to their franchisees. More importantly, a substantial number of franchisors (I would contend a large majority) fail to deliver even what little has been promised in the franchise agreement.

THE "SHALL VERSUS MAY" EFFECT

A typical franchise agreement is laden with the franchisees' obligations to adhere to the franchisor's system, to file reports, pay royalties, comply with the standard operating procedures manual, attend ongoing training sessions, pay advertising fees, honor the franchisor's warranty program, and more.

But rarely does the franchise agreement require similar compliance of the franchisor.

I call the exchange of promises in the typical franchise agreement the *shall versus may* effect. Universally, the franchise *"shall"* perform its duties and promises, while the franchisor only agrees that it *"may"* provide those services which the franchisor "in its sole discretion" decides to provide. Typically, the franchisee must agree to adhere to the provisions of the standard operating procedures manual "as it may exist from time to time." In other words, the franchisor is not required to provide a manual, but if it does, the franchisee must follow it religiously.

The case of a transmission repair franchisee I represented several years ago is most illustrative. My client (we'll call him Stan) was a former Air Force colonel who retired from active duty after 20 years in the service. Having a strong mechanical background, Stan was attracted to the transmission repair business because of his favorable impression of AAMCO, the recognized industry leader. Unfortunately, AAMCO had no nearby franchise opportunities, and Stan was enticed by a competing franchisor ("Franchise A"). Franchise A required no prior experience and promised complete training and the strongest customer warranty in the industry.

After paying his franchise fee, Stan received a two-week training course at Franchise A's training center in Alabama. He never saw a transmission. The training consisted solely of teaching franchisees how to *sell* transmission services, and how to fill out weekly reports required by the franchisor to make sure royalties were paid timely. The customer warranty was indeed a strong one—a defective transmission would be repaired or replaced free of charge at any Franchise A Center in the United States. *However, it was the franchisees who were bound to honor the warranty, not the franchisor.*

What did my client learn about repairing transmissions? He was told to hire experienced transmission rebuilders. Knowing how to choose a good rebuilder, or to supervise him, was not part of the training. Stan proved very good at developing business, but not good at hiring qualified transmission rebuilders. Moreover, he had no personal ability to do the work himself, or to train his employees in transmission repair. My client experienced a large amount of poor repair jobs, which meant a lot of warranty work, substantial expense, and business losses.

Stan appealed to Franchise A to provide his transmission rebuilder with additional training. He was told to fire the rebuilder, but he couldn't find an adequate replacement. Moreover, he recognized his rebuilder was a hard-working employee who merely lacked experience and training. Stan again appealed to Franchise A for assistance. But the only Franchise A representatives to visit Stan's shop were auditors who wanted to make sure Stan was reporting his sales and paying his royalties.

Ultimately, Stan terminated his Franchise A franchise. It took a lawsuit to gain independence, because Franchise A claimed ownership of Stan's transmission shop. Once independent, Stan learned his trade, and his young mechanic became a master transmission rebuilder. For the past five years, Stan has established himself with a viable independent business and is respected for the quality of his service. He has never regretted his decision to stop paying a 6 percent royalty to Franchise A. In fact, within a few years of the termination of his franchise, Franchise A filed bankruptcy, and has quietly gone out of existence. Stan was most lucky to have successfully escaped his franchisor. I had other Franchise A clients who were not so fortunate.

Franchise A was one of the early franchisors to require its franchisees to sign a lease assignment, and have it accepted by the landlord, *before the commencement* of the franchised business. I represented two Franchise A franchisees who had given lease assignments and later attempted to terminate their franchise agreements. Both of these clients claimed Franchise A had materially breached their franchise agreements and attempted to invalidate the lease assignments by legal action. Neither client could afford the legal expense. One went out of business before the action could ever come to a hearing. The second client actually won a preliminary motion and then reached a settlement agreement with Franchise A whereby my client was entitled to deidentify and retain his business location. But the process had taken its toll, and my client closed his doors within a couple of weeks of winning his legal victory.

All of my Franchise A clients echoed the same complaint. They received no benefits from their franchise relationship, and they only heard from the franchisor when they were late in paying their royalties.

As I write this, I am constantly troubled that I am painting too one-sided a picture. Certainly, many franchisors have developed valuable franchise systems and provide substantial benefits to their franchisees. However, even the franchisors who deliver the promise of franchising do so without being obligated by their franchise agreements.

Chapter 9 is dedicated to identifying quality franchise opportunities. In truth, however, there is *very little to recommend* in today's franchise marketplace! Franchisors have discovered that the buying public is not demanding or discerning—buyers are lured, in Pied Piper fashion, by the image of success and fast-growing systems. If there are lots of units in business, most buyers presume someone must be doing something right. *Somehow, some way, the public must wake up and demand quality, equity, and fairness—only when the marketplace demands value will the franchising industry deliver value.*

Without exception, the franchisors who provide substantial backing and support to their franchise networks exemplify what I believe is the cardinal rule in franchise selection. The most successful franchise systems, and the only franchise systems that I can recommend to a prospective franchisee, are in business to distribute products and services to ultimate consumers, and are dedicated to a franchise system of distribution as their primary (if not only) method of product and service distribution. It is a two-part rule and both elements are absolutely critical to the recommendation.

There are many examples of companies that are in business for the purpose of distributing products and services, but are not dedicated to franchising. Invariably, such systems have a long history of franchisee turbulence. Thus proud names such as Häagen Daz, Marie Callender, Texaco, Carvel, and Western Temporary Services, to name just a few, have all encountered substantial disputes with their franchisees due to the establishment of multiple channels of distribution in competition with their franchise networks.

Even more ominous are franchise systems that depend on the sale of franchises (as opposed to products and services) as their primary source of revenue and profits. Such companies feed off the popularity of franchising and the established reputations of proven competitors for whom franchises are already sold or are otherwise unavailable.

Franchise A, for example, was a franchising company pure and simple. It was not a company with superior expertise in selling or rebuilding transmissions, or even in running successful transmission shops. However, Franchise A developed a transmission business format in competition to the very successful AAMCO Transmissions.

Franchise A appeared to offer a very competitive franchise to AAMCO and was a particularly attractive opportunity for prospective franchisees who could not qualify with AAMCO or could not obtain an AAMCO Transmission Center in a desirable area.

AAMCO had built a solid reputation for quality and service that established it as the industry leader in transmission repairs. AAMCO's corporate purpose was to perform quality transmission repairs through a nationwide network of exclusively franchised offices. AAMCO operates no company-owned service centers.

Franchise A, on the other hand, was dedicated to franchising but not to delivering quality transmission services to its customers. That is not to say that all Franchise A franchisees were bad operators because some capable transmission mechanics happened to buy Franchise A franchises, hoping to gain the benefits of a franchised network. Such operators turned out a quality product. Nevertheless, the inexperienced purchasers of a Franchise A Transmission Center stood an excellent chance of losing their entire investment because they did not receive promised training and support services necessary to operate a successful business.

An interesting (and happier) example of the importance of making sure your franchisor truly has a product and service to distribute to the general public involved a travel agency franchise system specializing in sea cruises.

The company's business plan recognized cruises constitute big ticket travel packages that give a travel agent a substantially higher revenue per client than a general travel agency, which earns relatively small per transaction fees for booking airline tickets. The business plan also contemplated developing an enormous volume of cruise bookings, which created the opportunity to negotiate substantial volume discounts, creating greater margins for the company and the franchisees, as well as good value for ultimate consumers.

While the business plan seemed well conceived, the company's financial projections had some serious flaws. Notwithstanding its good intentions, the company found itself desperately needing to sell more franchises to cover operating expenses. The company's revenues from cruise sales were insignificant compared with revenues from franchise sales, and the company's survival depended on an ever-growing volume of franchise sales with little attention given to expanding the ultimate consumer product line. Because the company was unable to provide superior high value cruise packages, the franchisees struggled, and there was substantial systemwide discontent.

Fortuitously the cruise franchisor was bought out by a group headed by a former franchisee who appreciated the intelligence of the original business plan. New management understood that providing superior cruise products to ultimate consumers through the franchise system was the future of the company. The company went hard to work producing special cruise packages, specialty cruises, and exceptional value options. The company used its buying power to get substantial discounts from cruise lines, and the company had the good sense to pass these economies onto ultimate consumers while maintaining decent profit margins. Franchisees, armed with new and powerful products, could finally become competitive, and do their jobs. Predictably, the company's fortunes have turned, and franchisee dissatisfaction has turned to praise for new management.

It is good and important to tell some successful stories about franchising that show the enormous promise of franchising can be very real. When the promise is delivered, the results can be beneficial for both the franchisor and the franchisee, and franchising can be the very win/win/win opportunity it is promised to be. Unfortunately, more often than not, the promises are empty. Neither the industry nor the government regulators have provided any mechanism to ensure the promises are delivered.

The story of the cruise travel agency underscores the importance of having a franchisor whose business purpose is to deliver goods and services to the general public. The story also exemplifies how well franchising can work when franchisor and franchisee are in sync with the common goal of consumer sales. The story also demonstrates other important principles of business success. Deliver your customer (and by this I mean both the franchisee and the ultimate consumer) more than is expected and more than you are required to give, and your customer will return and be loyal.

From my perspective, the most important lesson from the travel agency story is one that I hope is behind every page of this book. Buying a franchise is no guarantee of success. Buying into a successful, proven franchise system that has established a reputation of quality and value for its goods and services, and has demonstrated a business purpose of delivering its goods and services to the general public through franchising, is frequently a formula for a very successful franchised business.

Unfortunately, too many franchising companies are in business to sell franchises and, at the very least, have lost sight of the underlying goal of product and service distribution. The franchisor's "be-all and end-all" is the collection of franchise fees, royalties, and advertising fees. I have encountered franchising companies with only two divisions, franchise sales and contract administration (i.e., collections).

The reader should not assume that only unproven franchisors are guilty of poor support of their franchise systems. In many respects the more powerful the franchisor, the less responsive it needs to be to its franchisees. For example, some recent clients of mine lost big time with a major fast-food franchise. Their story is particularly telling because they literally did everything right from the viewpoint of most prospective franchisees.

My clients, a father and son, were naturalized U.S. citizens. The father, Vinnie, had owned a small trucking company before immigrating to the United States. After arriving in this country, Vinnie had worked as a bakery truck driver and advanced his career to a point where he acquired his own route in San Diego. In 1978, Vinnie sold his bakery route to acquire a business with more potential.

The son, Chris, was 19 years old when he immigrated to the United States with his parents. Chris was educated, with a college degree in computer sciences, and had earned his living working as a computer programmer. Desiring career stability and the opportunity to own a business with his father, Chris began investigating franchises in late 1986 and early 1987.

Like most prospective franchisees, my clients were attracted to franchising because of the industry promise that entrepreneurs could acquire an independent business while benefiting from the experience and expertise of the franchisor and obtaining complete training in the franchisor's field.

Chris carefully researched several different industries and companies. He attempted to identify the best possible restaurant opportunities for which he and his father could qualify given their financial circumstances and net worth.

Although he looked at several frozen yogurt franchises, Chris worried that yogurt shops were a fad, and perhaps over saturated. Chris and Vinnie rejected certain hamburger franchises as being also-rans to McDonald's, Burger King, and Wendy's (which were all beyond their means).

In the summer of 1987, my clients were attracted to an advertisement in *The Wall Street Journal* placed by a major fast-food company, "Franchise B," who represented itself to be a strong system that gave substantial support to its franchisees. My clients were well aware of Franchise B, and believed it controlled a distinct market segment, and they felt they could meet Franchise B's net worth requirements.

Chris responded to *The Wall Street Journal* ad by contacting Franchise B about acquiring a franchise in California. Franchise B sent Vinnie and Chris separate packages of marketing materials and two financial prequalification applications.

My clients were completely inexperienced in the restaurant business, and they were attracted to Franchise B, in substantial part, because it claimed to provide complete training in all aspects of the restaurant business, including site selection, restaurant design, and operation. The marketing materials provided by Franchise B promised written guidelines and counseling regarding site selection, and also represented that all sites must be approved by Franchise B prior to the start of construction.

After receiving Vinnie's and Chris's separate applications, Franchise B provided my clients with a uniform franchise offering circular (UFOC) as required by Federal and California law. After reviewing the marketing materials and the offering circular, Vinnie and Chris continued to pursue their interest in a Franchise B's franchise. They were referred to the company's regional franchise manager in San Diego County.

The regional franchise manager reviewed the clients' combined financial statements. Together, Vinnie and Chris met Franchise B's minimum requirements, but they were advised they could not afford to construct a new freestanding restaurant. The regional manager recommended Vinnie and Chris look into purchasing an existing franchise.

Some time later, Franchise B's regional manager alerted Chris to a Franchise B location that was up for sale. The regional manager told Chris the store was not doing well but blamed the store's poor performance on an absentee owner who wasn't minding the store. Chris was told the restaurant had great potential and a great site, and could be successful if it were properly managed. Franchise B's regional manager referred Chris and Vinnie to the business broker who was representing the existing franchisee.

When Chris and Vinnie met with the business broker, they were told the restaurant was on the market for $275,000 but could be purchased for closer to $250,000.

Franchise B's offering circular had represented the high-low range for the acquisition and development costs of a typical Franchise B's franchise to be between $485,000 and $800,000. Consequently, the restaurant seemed like a bargain. Nevertheless, Chris contacted the Franchise B's regional manager for his opinion and advice.

The regional manager again confirmed the quality of the location, but advised Chris to offer only $225,000 so he and his father would retain $25,000 in operating capital. Chris and Vinnie made an offer subject to Franchise B's approval of the transaction, and the offer was accepted.

Several weeks passed. Chris had not heard from Franchise B. Anxious to start their new business, Chris contacted Franchise B's headquarters in Atlanta to find out what was delaying approval. Chris was told by a transfer approval manager that Franchise B was taking a hard look at the numbers, because Franchise B wanted to make sure Chris and his father would be successful. Franchise B's representative further told Chris that Franchise B would attempt to negotiate better terms.

Unbeknownst to Chris, the transfer approval manager had written a letter to the selling franchisee advising that the restaurant was substantially overpriced. The letter claimed that if the transaction was approved as negotiated, my clients would lose $5,200 per month, and could not survive even a full year in business. Franchise B's letter suggested the restaurant was worth no more than $75,000 and indicated Franchise B would not approve the sale for a greater amount.

Internal company memorandum suggested that the transfer approval manager's recommendation was ignored or over-ruled. My clients were never advised of the transfer approval manager's letter, nor did they ever see a copy of Franchise B's letter of disapproval. Two weeks after Franchise B threatened to reject the proposed sale, the offer was approved at full price. The terms of payment were slightly modified to reduce the monthly payments during the first two years.

Because they were not advised of Franchise B's letter and also because the terms were negotiated to the clients' apparent benefit, Chris and Vinnie were confident Franchise B had negotiated in their behalf and had even obtained an improvement in terms as promised.

What Vinnie and Chris did not know was that the selling franchisee owed Franchise B more than $38,000 in past-due royalties. Together with the $13,500 franchisee fees my clients would pay, Franchise B stood to gain $50,000 from the transaction. Vinnie and Chris were also unaware the restaurant failed to meet Franchise B's requirements for signage and could not support a drive-thru as recommended by the franchisor. In fact, it turned out Franchise B had originally approved the location five years earlier on the understanding the restaurant would have both a drive-thru and street signage.

As predicted by Franchise B, my clients were out of business within seven months and had lost their life savings. Chris was able to fall back on his talents as a computer programmer, but he now must support his father who is in ill health and in his 60s.

My clients sued Franchise B for misrepresenting the potential of the restaurant and for failing to abide by their promises to provide honest site evaluation services.

But my clients could not match Franchise B's firepower in court. The resources of most franchisees are wholly inadequate to match well-heeled franchisors. As part of its defense, Franchise B charged that my clients failed to hire an attorney or an accountant to make an independent evaluation of the franchise opportunity. In fact, the franchise offering circular did advise that all prospective franchisees should seek legal counsel before acquiring a Franchise B franchise.

My clients' response was typical of the vast majority of prospective franchisees. *They thought they had hired a franchise expert to guide them into business ownership.* In fact, they had researched the industry to try to find the best expert they could afford, and they paid $13,500 for the expert's wisdom. In my clients' eyes, they had hired Franchise B as their expert. After all, this was the promise of franchising.

Truly, Vinnie and Chris were victims of The Franchise Fraud. They believed the industry line about the safety of acquiring a franchised enterprise. They had been careful to isolate a blue chip, proven franchisor, that "promised" substantial guidance, training, and support. Their franchisor sold them a franchise which was a certain failure. Franchise B's only interest was in collecting its past-due debt from the franchisee who had already failed—there was no concern for the welfare of the next franchisee *victim* in line.

ILLUSORY PROMISES

Although it is easy to say a disenchanted franchisee's most common complaint is lack of franchisor support, it is equally true most franchisees cannot tell you what promises their franchisors have failed to keep. Commonly, the franchisee is losing money and is facing some major obstacle to the operation's success. The franchisee expects to turn to the franchisor for assistance, and even financial help. Far from helping matters, the franchisor is usually standing on the doorstep, in line with the other creditors, demanding payment of past-due royalties and advertising fees, and threatening franchise termination.

And the troubled franchisee always asks, in effect, "What happened to my mentor, to my kindly franchisor who would be there to show me the way and help me out of troubled waters?"

In example after example, I have found that a franchisor whose purpose is to distribute products and services to the ultimate public, will bend over backward to preserve a franchisee with potential. That is not to say a franchisor won't be quick to terminate a franchisee who is a discredit to the franchise system. The "enlightened" franchisor, however, understands the need to keep good franchisees in place, and to help them through difficult times.

An enlightened franchisor recognizes the tremendous savings in developing a franchise system of distribution. It understands what it would cost to maintain a distribution system of company-owned operations. Enlightened franchisors understand the cost of training employees as compared with having franchisees pay for their own training.

Enlightened franchisors understand a branch office losing money means corporate headquarters is losing money. With franchising, the franchisor is insulated from branch office losses. Indeed, in the usual case, the franchisee incurs obligations to pay royalties even while losing money. Enlightened franchisors also recognize they would pay salaries to branch management, whereas in a franchise system, the franchisee may work for nothing to preserve perceived equity and investment.

When seen in the light of the advantages of a franchise system of distribution, it becomes difficult to understand why a franchisor would not forgo royalties, and even provide financial assistance through loans and advances, to help a franchisee get through troubled times. From the franchisees' perspective, the reason to expect assistance from the franchisor is even simpler. It was what they were told they should expect when they purchased their franchise.

It is no wonder franchisees are angered when their cries for help are drowned out by a bill collector's demand for royalty payments, and franchise termination notices arrive in the mail. What happened to the promise of franchising?

Perhaps it is useful to analyze exactly what franchising promises to provide. To the prospective franchisee, the promise is to be set up in business, fully trained, well stocked, in a professionally selected location and a viable business enterprise. It is further the promise of an advisor, mentor, and support team standing at the ready to help the franchisee over difficult times and provide guidance on the path to success. The promise of franchising certainly includes a recognized trade name and a powerful marketing system bombarding consumers with a steady message of the quality and value of your services and products.

In reality, the contractual promises made by franchisors fall well short of the conventional perception of what franchisees get when they buy a franchise. Franchise agreements commonly promise the following:

1. The franchisee is granted a license to operate under the franchisor's trademark and trade name, and to use the franchisor's marketing system to the extent it exists. Usually there is no promise to produce a marketing system, and sometimes (hopefully not the norm) the franchisor does not even own the trademarks. The grant of a license to operate under the franchisor's trademark and to use the franchisor's business format must, by definition, exist in every franchise opportunity.

2. Almost without exception (but there are exceptions), the franchisee receives training on how to operate the franchised business. It is important to recognize the franchisee's training is included in the franchise fee, which means the franchisee pays for instruction. Franchisor

training courses vary widely in length of time and quality of training. Training may last a few days or several weeks, and may vary in completeness from observing the franchisor's operations to completing a prescribed course of study and receiving a diploma at McDonald's Hamburger University.

Franchising training courses typically cost $10,000, plus living and travel expenses, and training courses rarely exceed a month in duration. Compare the cost of training with the costs at most state universities, and you may discover that in many instances, you could pay three years of college tuition for the cost of three weeks of franchise training.

Most franchise training courses involve learning how to run the franchised business, including filling out forms and performing required accountings. Many franchisors advertise no experience is necessary for prospective franchisees; the franchisor will provide complete training, not only in the conduct of the franchise, but in the business and service the franchise offers the general public.

3. In fact, in many instances, there is no number 3. Beyond the grant of a license and the offer of some form of training, many franchisors make no additional promises. On the other hand, there are additional requirements in all franchise systems, such as the requirement of adherence to the business marketing system, and the requirement to purchase goods and services from franchisor-approved sources. These requirements may, in essence, constitute additional promises as well. For example, the requirement of adherence to the franchisor's marketing system may amount to a promise to provide a uniform franchise system that benefits all franchisees. The relevant point here is that the failure of a franchisee to adhere to the program may be a breach of the franchise agreement, but the franchisor's failure to require performance may also be a breach of contract that is actionable by other franchisees.

4. Many competent franchisors do make additional material promises to their franchisees. The following are examples of the kinds of promises a prospective franchisee should look for:

   • A franchisor-backed consumer warranty providing a network to protect all consumers who buy from the franchisee.

- Franchise network marketing assistance and contributions by the franchisor to marketing for the benefit of the entire system. Usually, the marketing fund comes from the franchisees' contributions, which may be spent by the franchisor. Often, the franchisor can use marketing funds for any kind of marketing, including the sale of franchises. Frequently, franchisors receive income from advertising fees.

- Valuable customer services, consumer hotlines, relocation networks, inventory control systems, vendor discounts, insurance breaks, and other franchising perks that take advantage of franchising's ability to benefit from volume purchasing. In most instances, all these franchising perks are probably not required by the franchise agreements. Consequently, the failure of a franchisor to provide many valuable services may not be a breach of the franchise agreement even though it is a breach of the franchisor's customary support of its franchisees.

My temporary employment service clients offer an excellent case in point. One of my clients' complaints is that over the years the franchisor always provided business forms and marketing materials to franchisees without charge. A few years ago, and without any prior notice, the franchisor began to charge franchisees for all these materials. The franchise agreement promised only that the franchisor would provide the materials; however, the agreement is silent as to who pays for the materials. Nevertheless, for many of these franchisees, the knowledge that the franchisor had provided the materials without charge was a material inducing factor in the decision to acquire the franchise.

In essence, most franchisors promise little but to train you for a fee and allow you to use their trademark and marketing system in exchange for the payment of a royalty. This is the essence of franchising. That is not to say prospective franchisees cannot insist on franchisors committing additional promises to writing in the negotiation of franchise agreements. In a buyer's market, sellers of businesses will make numerous promises to accomplish a sale in a competitive situation. Franchisors are no different. Indeed, I have witnessed many hungry franchisors make substantial concessions in franchise agreements, notwithstanding claims that state law forbids negotiated changes.

The lesson of this chapter is quite simple. The pervasive conventional wisdom that franchising automatically signifies a powerful marketing system with the substantial resources of the franchisor solidly supporting all the franchisees of the network is a myth. For the most part, ongoing and meaningful support by franchisors is more the result of forward-thinking company policy than it is a matter of contract between franchisor and franchisee.

Although franchisees can protect themselves somewhat by attempting to select "forward-thinking" franchisor systems, unless the franchisors' support obligations are bound by the terms of the franchise agreement, the franchisee is vulnerable to policy changes, changes in management, and the possibility that the franchise system will be sold to a new, less caring, and less forward-thinking franchisor.

Many such examples abound. I have represented and interviewed numerous franchisees of the Dunhill Personnel Systems who wanted to retain policies and support efforts of the founder of the company that my clients claim were changed and abandoned when the company was sold to a large public corporation some years ago. Similarly, franchisees of Western Temporary Services have complained that their franchisor seemed to change its corporate policy some years ago from an emphasis on franchise-based offices to an emphasis on company-owned offices. In each instance the franchisor denied the charges.

I have had many similar complaints from such franchising companies as Marie Callender's, which now has more company-owned restaurants than franchised restaurants. Franchisees commonly complain that training programs for company managers are not available to franchisees, and that the company sells its products in supermarkets in competition with franchised restaurants.

Recently, Encyclopaedia Britannica decided to get out of one of its subsidiary businesses, the operation of company-owned and franchised Britannica Learning Centers across the United States. Britannica developed and owned various learning programs that were marketed exclusively through Britannica Learning Centers. The company sold its learning center network in a transaction that was expected to convert most of the Britannica Centers into Sylvan Learning Centers.

Most Britannica Learning Centers were company owned and could be merged with existing Sylvan centers, or converted to Sylvan where there was no competition. Britannica franchisees were given the option to convert to

Sylvan (if there was no existing Sylvan competitor) or to terminate their franchise. But many existing Britannica franchisees could not convert, or did not want to buy their franchise all over again, and were effectively left out in the cold because they needed access to learning programs to stay in business.

Other times, franchisors fall on bad times, and the franchisees whose businesses are integrally tied to the fortunes of the franchisor find themselves dragged down by the franchisor's financial distress. Such problems have befallen such systems as Jack-in-the-Box, which suffered enormous problems when *E. Coli* bacteria caused illness in hundreds of customers. Recently The Diet Center and Nutri-System franchisees were buffeted by the financial crises that befell their respective franchisors.

Although it is important for prospective franchisees to judge the quality and level of services provided by the franchisor, and the franchisor's attitude of compassion and equity toward its franchisees, franchisees must nevertheless protect themselves by ensuring that promised behavior is contracted behavior. In a time when the negotiation of franchise agreements appears to be difficult, at best, *it is incumbent upon franchisees to ferret out or demand equitable franchise agreements.*

Until franchisees learn to say "no" to inferior franchise arrangements, and to say "no more" to imbalanced relationships, the franchising industry will continue to deliver a very subservient relationship. It is an obvious and unfortunate truth that the only way to assure fulfillment of the promise of franchising is to embody the commitment to the promise in the language of the franchise agreement. The only way to accomplish this task is to change the franchising marketplace.

Chapter 7

You Can Never Leave

This chapter examines various provisions in franchise agreements that prevent a franchisee from terminating a franchise, or from continuing in the same occupation on termination. Franchising is touted as a mechanism of job training, but on franchise termination, most franchisees are unable to compete with their franchisors or even stay in the business for which they have been trained. The chapter also examines several devices used by franchisors to control the franchise relationship and to prevent the franchisee from ever leaving the system.

This chapter and Chapter 8 may, at first, seem inconsistent and contradictory. In this chapter, we examine what happens when franchisees want to leave the franchise network for a variety of reasons, and find they are contractually and legally prevented from doing so.

The next chapter deals with various practices employed by franchisors that effectively sacrifice franchisees through planned attrition to achieve rapid and profitable system growth. Many franchisors are guilty of exploiting their franchise systems by using franchisees to absorb all the risks of business expansion. Through various mechanisms, many franchisors purposely plan to turn the most profitable operations into company-owned branch offices. Franchisees may be terminated or forced out of business for a variety of reasons with little or nothing to show for their investment.

Although at first it seems paradoxical to claim franchisees are not allowed to escape their franchise systems on the one hand, but are expendable on the other, both phenomena are characteristic of the franchisor's efforts to exercise ownership and control over the franchised location.

WHY FRANCHISE TERMINATIONS OCCUR

Franchise terminations happen for many diverse reasons. Usually the desire to end the relationship (for both parties) is economic—the relationship is not profitable (or sufficiently so) for either or both parties. When the franchisor terminates the agreement, it usually claims the franchisee has violated a "material" provision of the franchisee agreement giving cause for the termination. More often than not, the franchisee is behind in royalty payments, but as will be seen hereafter (and in Chapter 8), the franchisor has many options to choose from when termination is desired.

When franchisees decide they no longer want to be affiliated with their franchisor, or any franchisor, they tend to claim the franchise is not providing any benefits, or that the expense of the franchise (in terms of royalties and franchise fees) cannot be justified. Frequently, the franchisee is not making adequate income, and sees the 5 percent to 8 percent of gross revenue going to the franchisor each month as the difference between the success and failure of the locally owned business.

Sometimes the franchisee loses confidence in the franchisor's product. Frequently, and this is the most common complaint, franchisees claim that their franchisors are not providing any kinds of significant services to justify the expense of the franchise.

Sometimes the franchisees are right, and sometimes they are wrong. It really doesn't make much difference, because either way the issue is whether the franchisee has a right to terminate the franchise relationship and continue in business as an independent operator.

In the hypothetical perfect franchise, the respective rights of franchisor and franchisee are all sorted out when the parties *enter into* their franchise agreement. Ideally, the parties carefully discuss their relative concerns as to what happens when one or the other party wishes to terminate the relationship. Each party retains competent legal counsel, and there is a thorough and complete negotiation of each party's respective rights when the franchise ends.

In the real world, franchise agreements are rarely negotiated. Rather, franchise agreements are routinely preprinted form contracts that are offered to franchisees on a take-it-or-leave-it basis. In fact, many states that regulate the sale of franchises will not allow franchisors to deviate from the contractual terms

lodged with the states on registration. I might add that I have never understood the regulator's refusal to allow negotiation between franchisors and
franchisees, but we will leave that discussion for Chapter 11.

THE FRANCHISEE HAS NO RIGHT TO LEAVE

Along with the shall versus may effect discussed in the previous chapter, the
termination provisions of most franchise agreements are the most blatant examples of inequality of bargaining leverage between franchisor and franchisee.
Typically, the franchisee is accorded no right to terminate the franchise, for
cause or otherwise.[1] Conversely, franchise agreements invariably state many
grounds on which the franchisor may terminate, with or without cause, and
with or without advance notice to the franchisee. While most franchise agreements have no provision for termination by the franchisee, it is not uncommon
to see as many as 30 separate grounds on which the franchisor can end the
franchise relationship.

In terms of the written document, the franchisee is not even given the
right to terminate the agreement *for cause*. In fact, most franchise agreements
spell out the consequences of the franchisee's breach or default of the contract
in detail, explaining every penalty, fee, punishment, right, and privilege the
franchisor may invoke if the franchisee fails to abide by the strict terms of the
agreement. Contrariwise, rarely does the franchise agreement even mention
the possibility that the franchisor may breach, let alone accord the franchisee
any powers of punishment or enforcement.

If the disparity in termination rights is glaring, the consequences befalling
the terminated franchisee are devastating. For the reasons detailed in this
chapter, in most instances terminating a franchise means going out of business
altogether. Thus the title of this chapter—if you, as a franchisee want to stay in
business in your chosen profession, "You Can Never Leave" your franchise
system.

In most franchise agreements, the franchisee is required to completely
cease the use of the franchisor's trade name and trademarks, must surrender its
telephone numbers and yellow pages listings, must immediately pay all sums
due the franchisor, and must abide by the noncompetition provisions of the

franchise agreement to the extent allowed by applicable law. The typical agreement also provides the franchisor the option to purchase the franchisee's business for the depreciated book value of the business. It is also common for the franchisor to take over the franchisee's lease, to demand the franchisee's customer list, and even to claim the franchisee's accounts receivable.

Increasingly, franchisors also claim to own the look and feel of the business format—something called the franchisor's "trade dress." Franchisors claim that the distinctive look of their business motif is just like a trademark, and demand that the franchise completely redecorate so the franchisee cannot benefit from any of the franchisor's goodwill after termination.

MUTUALITY OF OWNERSHIP RIGHTS

In many ways, this chapter has been most difficult to write, because we are dealing with the grayest of areas: Both the franchisor and the franchisee claim important and valid equity interests in the franchised business. At issue are the relative ownership rights of the franchisor and the franchisee to the enterprise (the franchise) conducted jointly by both.

In its purest form, the notion of granting a franchise contemplates a *mutual* enterprise between the owner of a trademark describing a particular product or service and a local independent operator who wants to establish a self-owned business. The local operator and the owner of the service mark each see natural advantages for entering into a joint enterprise. The local owner expects a substantial benefit from using the well-recognized service marks, from benefiting from an established uniform operating system, and from receiving substantial training provided by the franchisor.

On the other hand, the franchisor expects a dedicated manager at the local level who has a pride of ownership in a self-owned business. Equally important, the franchisor expects the local owner/operator will invest financial resources to create a long-lasting presence for the franchisor's brands (of products and/or services) in the owner/operator's specific locality.

Perhaps the most important consideration is that both the franchisor and franchisee invest a substantial amount of time, effort, and money in building the business connected with the franchisor's trademark and trade name at the owner/operator's place of business. I cannot over emphasize the importance of the mutual contribution of the franchisor and the franchisee, because it is their intertwined interest in the franchised enterprise that is so difficult to unravel when either party decides to terminate the relationship.

Nevertheless, on termination, both the franchisor and the franchisee usually claim the right to "hold the turf" of the franchised location. Each believes it "owns" the location and has the right to continue in business there. The franchisor's customers have come to expect its products and services to be delivered at the existing location. Similarly, the franchisee has developed local and personal goodwill with his or her customers. Especially when the decision to terminate is due to a perceived lack of support from the franchisor, franchisees are adamant that they should not be forced to abandon their locations.

In trying to explain to my clients (and frequently to courts) that both sides have legitimate claims to the business conducted at the franchise location, I have come to liken franchise terminations to child custody disputes and other issues relating to the termination of a marriage. These are issues to which many people can relate. When each parent claims a right to shared custody over the children of a marriage, the courts must painstakingly resolve those rights on a case-by-case basis.

Similar debates occur with respect to prized possessions acquired by a couple during their marriage. Frequently, the process for parceling out the important jointly owned assets piece by piece is more expensive than the total value of all the property divided.

So it is with the termination of a franchise. Both franchisor and franchisee rightly claim a vested interest in the business. Both have a long-term investment in the development of substantial goodwill at the existing location. Just as with many child custody suits, courts must painstakingly weigh conflicting interests to evaluate who gets "custody" of the formerly joint enterprise.

ANALYSIS OF TERMINATION ENFORCEMENT PROVISIONS

Suffice it to say, franchise agreements are only infrequently negotiated instruments, and most franchise agreements provide broad restrictions on a franchisee's right to stay in business following the termination of the relationship.

A typical franchise agreement will include several kinds of restrictions such as the following:

1. The covenant not to compete typically provides the franchisee must not compete, directly or indirectly, with the franchisor for a period of two years or more following termination of the franchise.

2. Frequently, franchise agreements provide the franchisor has exclusive ownership of all the trade secrets of the business, and the franchisee agrees to not use or divulge any of those trade secrets.

3. Franchise agreements also frequently give the franchisor the option to purchase the franchise business on termination for a price substantially below the fair market value of the business enterprise.

4. The franchisor's single most powerful weapon for controlling owner-ship of the franchised business is through ownership or legal possession of the franchise premises. In most situations, the franchisee's rights to continue in business are meaningless if the franchisee cannot keep the location. As a practical matter, whoever owns or controls the physical office, store, or restaurant site usually is entitled to retain the business.

The Enforcement of Noncompete Covenants

Historically, and uniformly, franchise agreements contain provisions whereby the franchisee agrees not to compete with the franchisor on termination of the franchise agreement. Nearly all noncompetition clauses prohibit the fran-chisee from competitive activities at or near the franchisee's former location. Frequently, franchisees are also prohibited from competing near any other franchised or company owned location as well. Imagine terminating your Coca-Cola® distributorship and discovering that you could not be a compet-ing distributor of somebody else's soft drinks products anywhere in the world where Coca-Cola® was doing business.[2] Needless to say, it would be time to find a new profession. Or move to Venus!

In fact, most noncompetition clauses restrain the former franchisee from competing directly or indirectly with the former franchisor. Frequently, this means that a former franchisee cannot even return to work as an employee of a competitor.

Noncompetition clauses, if valid, are terrific deterrents to a franchisee ever terminating the franchise agreement, because the noncompete covenant effectively restrains a franchisee from future employment unless the franchisee is prepared to change careers.

At the time of purchase, few franchisees consider what will happen should they ever want to leave their franchise system. When they seek to terminate, most franchisees are caught by surprise when they come face to face with the termination clauses in their agreements prohibiting competition with the franchisor for two years or more. Frequently, termination provisions restrict the franchisee from competing within 25 to 50 miles of any other franchise location.

While most states prohibit or restrict enforcement of noncompetition clauses against former employees, the clauses are frequently enforceable in franchise agreements. Consequently, if a franchisee wants to continue in business, the practical effect of a noncompetition clause is to deter a franchisee from terminating the franchise.

The justification for noncompete covenants has its roots in basic contract law. As a society, American jurisprudence honors the sanctity of contracts. If two people agree that one will not compete with the other on termination of a business relationship, the courts (in the absence of some important public policy) will honor the agreement. In fact, many states restrict the enforcement of noncompetition clauses because a citizen's right to work is a compelling public policy.

In a truly negotiated contract, sanctity of contract makes sense. The premise of a willing buyer and a willing seller coming to terms with respect to some legal purpose is a time-tested and honored principle. Public policy aside, courts seek to enforce the agreed performance set forth in legally formed contracts.

Moreover, it is logical that a franchisor desiring to expand its business into a new territory would require a condition that the right to operate within the territory be retained on termination. After all, the franchisor trains the franchisee in all operational details and literally makes it possible for the franchisee to go into business and represent the franchisor's product or service.

111

But what about the franchisee's investment? In the typical scenario, the franchisee acquires a franchise and right to initiate an independent business. The franchisee provides all the operating capital and further invests the blood, sweat, and tears in building the franchise business as an independent contractor. Frequently, the franchisee has already been in business as an independent but takes on the franchisor's line or trademark to enhance market recognition or product quality. More often, a prospective franchisee has invested in a franchise to gain job training—to secure productive vocational training.

In Chapter 2, I made note of a client who owned a motel that converted to a major motel franchise. Unsatisfied with the franchise relationship, my client decided to go independent and found that the terms of the franchise agreement and its noncompete clause, provided he couldn't get out of the franchise without getting out of business, and perhaps selling his motel to the franchisor for book value. Ultimately, the franchise agreement was not enforced, but the process of winning his independence cost my client many thousands of dollars.

The pros and cons of noncompete covenants in franchise agreements are the grayest of issues. In fact, there is a real split concerning the enforcement of noncompete covenants throughout the United States. Every state allows noncompetition agreements in certain circumstances, but for public policy reasons, very few jurisdictions will honor a noncompetition clause that prevents an individual from earning a living.

Nevertheless, with the exception of California, virtually every state will enforce a noncompetition provision in a franchise agreement, provided the noncompetition clause is reasonable as to time and distance. This means a terminating franchisee may be restrained from competition with the former franchisor within a reasonable radius of the franchise location and for a finite period of time (usually no more than two years).

Where noncompetition clauses are enforceable, the practical effect is to close down the formerly franchised business. If the franchisee is required to move ten miles away for a period of two years, the franchisee is faced with starting all over and completely abandoning the established business.

My home state of California has a unique approach to noncompetition clauses. Generally, noncompetition clauses in California are *void,* as violating the state's strong public policy in favor of an individual's right to work.

Even in California, however, there are some notable exceptions to the general rule prohibiting noncompetition clauses. For example, an employer can restrain an existing employee from moonlighting. More importantly, if a business owner sells a business, including the goodwill of the business, a non-compete clause, reasonable as to time and distance, will be enforced by the courts. By statute, California courts also enforce provisions in partnership agreements that restrict competition between the partners on termination of a partnership.

It is most interesting that franchisors in California have attempted to rely on all three California "exceptions" to enforce noncompete clauses against franchisees. Most often, franchisors claim that a franchise termination amounts to the sale of the franchisee's goodwill back to the franchisor, thus permitting the enforcement of a noncompete covenant. Franchisors have also attempted to show that a franchise is analogous to either an employee or a partner.

The analogy of a franchise relationship to a partnership is most ironic. Indeed, franchisees uniformly believe they are gaining a partner when they sign their franchise agreements. Franchising companies liberally describe the relationship in partnership terms.

But partnerships create fiduciary relationships between partners. Partners owe one another the highest duty of good faith and loyalty that the law imposes. Partners have a legal duty to look out for one another's interests. To the contrary, the courts in the United States have uniformly rejected the premise that a franchisor owes a fiduciary duty to its franchisees. Rather, courts have consistently held that franchise relationships are *negotiated commercial relationships* with each side of the transaction expected to protect its own interests.

In essence, the franchising industry holds itself out to be a protective relationship. On the other hand, the law says that franchising represents one of the last vestiges of the doctrine of *caveat emptor* (let the buyer beware).

Sadly, franchisees rarely "beware" of the catastrophic consequences of the termination provisions in their franchise agreements. Only a small percentage of prospective franchisees even bother to seek legal advice when entering a franchise relationship. Recognizing that franchise agreements are not negotiable, franchisees do not perceive any benefit in hiring an attorney to attempt negotiation. When franchisees do seek legal advice, they are told that the restrictive clauses in franchise agreements are typical, and franchisees recognize such advice to mean that take-or-leave franchise agreements are acceptable.

Franchisors, on the other hand, vigilantly attempt to enforce noncompetition covenants in their franchise agreements. Franchisors are quick to point out that if they fail to enforce these important clauses, franchisees will feel free to break away from their franchise enterprise on any excuse. It is the franchisor's purpose to gain market recognition at a specific location. Consequently, both the franchisor and franchisee have a vested interest in retaining the rights to the business enterprise.

When the promise of franchising is being delivered, both the franchisor and the franchisee are working hard to make a success of the trademarked enterprise. Both the franchisor and the franchisee recognize their mutual interdependence—each must succeed and prosper to achieve success for their common enterprise. It is appropriate that the law and commercial principles focus on benefiting the common enterprise. When the enterprise fails, it is essential the termination of the enterprise provides an equitable balance to the interests of both the franchisor and the franchisee.

Who gets to keep the business will depend on the facts of each individual circumstance. Utilizing my earlier analogy, who gets to keep the franchised "child" should depend on who is the most deserving, capable parent. The terms of the franchise agreement (franchising's equivalent to a prenuptial agreement) should be considered; however, prenuptial agreements are only enforced if both spouses are represented by legal counsel and there has been opportunity to negotiate the terms of the agreement.

The restrictive covenants in franchise agreements should only be enforceable to the extent there has been balanced negotiation, and the interests of both parties to the agreement have been dealt with fairly. In other words, if a non-compete covenant is honored, the franchisee should be compensated for the goodwill in the business that is relinquished. On the other hand, if the franchise is terminated because of a failure of the franchisor to provide a promised service, the franchisee, and not the franchisor, should have the right to continue the operation of the business at the franchise location.

Dividing the Trade Secrets of the Terminated Business

My analogy to child custody lawsuits is an apt one. Frequently, franchise terminations evolve into trade secret "custody" disputes. Most franchise agreements claim trade secret status for many aspects of the franchised business. On termination, franchisees are restrained from using and divulging the trade secrets of the business.

If the trade secrets in question are trademark specific, such as a secret marinade, a soft drink formula, or a unique formulation of a product or service, there can be really little debate over the franchisor's right of ownership in the secret as well as the right to deny the continued use of the trade secret after the franchise terminates.

In practice, however, pulling the use of a trade secret out from under a franchise operator can be devastating. But for all of the justification a franchisee may have for going independent, he or she may be prevented from doing so if dependent on the use of the trade secret product or service. The Britannica Learning Center franchisees discussed in Chapter 6 were dependent on Encyclopaedia Britannica to provide their learning programs, and could not continue in business without a satisfactory replacement.

In other instances, confidential aspects of the franchise business are not trademark specific and provide issues of major debate as to whether they are owned by the franchisor even if trade secret protection is claimed in the franchise agreement. The customer lists of the business, for example, frequently are developed through the exclusive effort and expense of the franchisee. When the franchisee seeks to terminate the franchise relationship, the franchisee understandably regards customer lists as trade secrets belonging to the franchisee. Predictably, however, most franchise agreements claim the customers to be the franchisor's exclusive property and confidential trade secrets. The franchisor claims the customers have been developed as a result of the goodwill developed by the trademark or service mark of the business. In any event, the franchisee cannot leave the franchise system without resolving (and usually litigating) the issue.

Often franchisors will claim trade secret status of products, processes, or services that are not truly confidential. A few years ago, I represented a group of franchisees of a company called Contacts Influential. The company sold marketing data and mailing lists to businesses throughout the United States. Each franchisee was responsible for developing a database of the city that represented its exclusive territory. For example, one of my clients had an exclusive territory of Denver, Colorado. The client developed a database through his personal efforts and expense and sold the data to businesses within its territory.

Other franchisees could also sell Denver's data, and the revenue was split according to the franchise agreement.

Notwithstanding that each franchisee developed a database from scratch, the franchise agreement provided that all the databases belonged to the franchisor and were the exclusive property and trade secrets of the franchisor. Indeed, this most incredible agreement required that the franchisees agree in advance to whatever the franchisor claimed as trade secrets, even if (after disclosure) the information was obvious and of public knowledge. The actual "secret" was "use the phone book," something millions of us nonrocket scientists have been doing daily for years.

On termination of the franchise agreement, the franchisor claimed it had exclusive rights to the database because it was developed from a "trade secret" technology, even though each of the franchisees had gone to the expense and effort of developing and maintaining the database. My clients ultimately were able to preserve the ownership of their valuable assets but invested several hundred thousand dollars in legal fees in the process.

Similarly, I have represented numerous franchisees in the temporary employment services industry. This is a heavily franchised industry, with such notable franchisors as Snelling & Snelling, Dunhill, Western Temporary Services, Norrell Temporary Services, Manpower Employment Services, and many others. Temporary employment service franchisors develop a national reputation as resources for the hiring and placement of temporary employees. However, the local franchisees have the responsibility of recruiting temporary employees, marketing the services of the business, and placing temporary employees with client customers within their franchised territories.

As you might guess, on termination of a temporary employment services franchise, the inevitable dispute is over who owns the customers and who owns the employees. The franchisor, who often is responsible for paying the temporary employees, billing the customers, and collecting all receipts, claims the exclusive ownership of the customers and the employees. On the other hand, franchisees make a persuasive argument that they own the customer and employee contacts that they have developed with much expense and personal effort.

For example, one of my temporary employment agency clients (I'll call him Dave) had owned and operated a permanent employment agency business since 1972. After eight years in business, Dave began to investigate adding a temporary employment services division to its existing business for purposes of expansion.

Unlike a permanent employment agency that really performs the service of recruiting job candidates for employers and earning commissions for successful placements, temporary employment agencies actually hire or "employ" temporary laborers for placement with customers who have temporary needs. Consequently, there is a substantial payrolling expense in the operation of a temporary employment services business.

The business owner's need for capital to finance the temporary employee workforce has made an attractive opportunity for several franchising companies. The franchisor typically provides the service of payrolling the temporary employees, billing the customers, collecting the receipts, and dividing the gross profits from the business between the franchisor and the franchisee.

When Dave decided to incorporate a temporary employment services franchise as part of his overall business, his franchise agreement had a specific provision in it allowing him to continue to operate his permanent employment agency as a separate business. However, the contract also provided the customer lists of the temporary employment services business were a trade secret and could not be divulged on the termination of the franchise.

After several years, Dave became disenchanted with the franchise relationship for a variety of reasons. Predominantly, Dave claimed that the franchisor's policies toward its franchisees had changed in a fashion in which the franchisor strongly favored company-owned stores over franchise relations. Additionally, the franchisor had literally forced several franchisees out of business so it could take over the formerly franchised office as a company-owned operation.

Deciding to retire rather than fight the franchisor for ownership rights, Dave notified the franchisor of his intent to terminate the franchise, and he sold the permanent employment agency to his daughter, including the sale of the customer list of the permanent employment agency. Obviously, both the permanent agency and the temporary agency utilized a substantially similar customer list. The daughter went into business for herself providing both permanent and temporary employment services under a new name.

Predictably, the franchisor sued both my client and his daughter for violation of a noncompete covenant, and for unfair competition for the improper use and sale of the franchisor's trade secrets.

This action is still pending, and it has been a bitter and expensive contest for both sides. Even if my clients ultimately win the right to the continued use of the customer lists, it will only come at a substantial cost.

In fact, most of my franchisee clients who have had the economic ability to assert their ownership claims have ultimately prevailed in retaining use of the claimed business assets. Usually, a franchisee "settles" by paying the former franchisor for the right to use the contested "secret" or process in order to stay in business and avoid the substantial legal fees involved in testing the issue in court. As a practical matter, however, the expense of retaining important rights necessary to stay in business has made for very hollow victories. In reality, most franchisees do not have the economic wherewithal to confront their franchisors. More often than not, franchise termination means cessation of business.

Retained Purchase Options

Another mechanism frequently used by franchisors to retain a franchise location is to provide an option to purchase the franchised business on termination of the franchise. Conceptually, a franchisor's purchase option is an equitable solution, provided the franchisor pays a reasonable price for the franchise business. Proponents of franchisee protection legislation have long promoted laws requiring a franchisor to purchase the franchised business on termination for the fair market value of the enterprise.

The problem with most franchisor purchase options is that they provide for bargain basement purchases, rather than fair market value. Frequently, the franchisor can pick up the franchised business at book value, or for an arbitrary amount that bears no relationship to the true value of the business. In my own practice, I have seen purchase options for a price as little as two weeks of gross revenue, or $1,000, whichever was the greater sum.

If a franchisor can enforce a modest purchase option, the franchisor can also protect the noncompete covenant because it has "purchased the goodwill of the business." However, the purchase option device is no more than a boondoggle when the franchisee is not paid a fair value for the business. As always, the provision in the franchise agreement is rarely negotiated, and frequently the franchisee is not even aware that the retained option is present in the contract.

Notwithstanding the complaint that purchase options give franchisors the ability to buy the franchised business at a bargain price, the options are rarely exercised. Franchisors are usually able to take advantage of their other powerful options to retain control of the franchised businesses without paying anything at all.

The Franchisor's Control of a Franchisee's Real Estate

Maintaining control of a franchisee's real estate has become the cutting edge of sophisticated efforts of franchisors to retain control of a franchised enterprise on termination. McDonald's is generally credited as the pioneer of fast-food franchising and modern-day franchising generally. McDonald's is also the pioneer of controlling the franchisee's real estate. It has been said that McDonald's substantial wealth emanates more from the real estate it controls than from the hamburgers it sells.[3]

In a typical McDonald's transaction, McDonald's either purchases the real estate of the proposed location or negotiates the master lease. McDonald's then leases or subleases, as the case may be, the specific location to its franchisee. Either way, McDonald's controls the real estate, and the franchisee cannot stay in business without its lease.

Southland Corporation has long controlled the real estate of most 7-Eleven franchisees. The lease between Southland and its franchisees provides that a breach of the franchise agreement is also a material breach of the lease.

The 7-Eleven franchisee who refused to sell California Lottery tickets (discussed in Chapter 5), received a Notice of Breach of the franchise agreement, Notice of Termination of the Franchise, and Notice of Termination of the licensee's real estate lease.

If the franchisee defaults, control of the licensee's premises through a mortgage or long-term lease is the most powerful tool in the franchisor's arsenal. When the franchisor has the economic wherewithal to purchase the real estate or own the master lease, the franchisor can effectively put the franchisee out of business on termination of the franchise.

Fortunately for franchisees, the mechanisms for controlling the franchised premises have substantial drawbacks. First, the franchisor must have significant financial resources to purchase the property. More importantly, most franchisors utilize franchising to reduce their economic liability, not to increase it. Consequently, most franchisors do not want to be on the hook to pay a mortgage or a long-term lease if the franchisee defaults. Also franchisors who do not have substantial financial statements are unable to purchase the real estate or control the leases in the first instance.

By the same token, if the franchisor is able to own and control its real estate, the franchisee may achieve some positive benefits. By owning the real estate and building the franchise unit, the franchisor is effectively providing financing to the licensee. In such circumstances, the franchisee who has leased premises directly from the franchisor has very little to complain about. Nevertheless, to the extent a franchisee fancies being an independent businessperson, there is little independence when your franchisor is also the landlord.

Although it is easy to defend a franchisor's control of the business real estate when the franchisor has put hard dollars into the location, the franchisor frequently attempts to control the rest estate without any investment whatsoever. Many modern-day franchisors require a franchisee to agree to an assignment of lease on termination. The more careful franchisors actually have the lease assignment signed by the landlord and the franchisee at the outset of the franchised enterprise. Using this tactic, the franchisee leases the property directly from the landlord. Simultaneously, the landlord, franchisor, and franchisee all sign a lease assignment that is held by the franchisor. On termination of the franchise, a franchisor merely delivers the previously drawn and executed lease assignment to the landlord and the franchisee is evicted from the premises.

The lease assignment tactic, and various similar alternatives, give franchisors substantial leverage in termination transactions. In order to preserve an equity interest in the business location, a franchisee must go to court and obtain a restraining order preventing the landlord from delivering the premises to the franchisor. The franchisee always has an uphill battle, because most courts attempt to honor contractual commitments.

In Protecting Your Rights to Be in Business, the Best Defense Is a Good Offense

All the techniques utilized by franchisors to retain a franchise location after the franchise relationship is terminated have a uniform goal and similarity: to ensure the franchisor's name and goodwill continue to exist at a franchise location on termination of the franchise. For the franchisee, the ability of the franchisor to keep the location is the denial of the franchisee's ownership of his or her own business.

Most franchisees fail to pay attention to the devastating provisions concerning termination that are set forth in their franchise agreements and offering circulars, until they are ready to break away. Then it is too late. In this instance, as with all aspects of buying a franchised business, a good offense is the best defense. Do not buy into adhesive and unjust franchise relationships; and at the very least, negotiate equitable terms.

It is fairly clear that the relative rights of the terminating franchisee or franchisor depend on the negotiating power and leverage that one has *vis-à-vis* the other. But the common theme of this book is that negotiation works when there is a balance of power. Meaningful negotiating balance has been sadly missing in the franchising industry, and the lack of balance is perhaps most evident in the existence of restrictive and abusive termination provisions and franchise contracts.

Surprisingly, very few prospective franchisees even try to negotiate the terms of the agreements, and rarely do they pay attention to those unsavory provisions that talk about getting out. Just as couples "in love" disdain talking about prenuptial agreements because they do not want to spoil the romance of their marriage, franchisees seldom want to deal with the negative aspects of their franchise agreements. Often, however, franchisors will negotiate (even when state law restricts their ability to do so). Especially with new franchisors, or particularly attractive franchisees, the opportunity is present to adjust the inequitable provisions at the outset of the relationship.

The franchising marketplace will only make adjustments as buyers become more demanding and more savvy. Only when franchisees *say No!* to inequitable franchise agreements will franchisors *meet the market* by providing a salable product. Keep in mind that just 30 years ago, *the typical franchise agreement provided a protected territory and was terminable by the franchisee at will.*

As a practical matter, most franchisees can only enjoy the benefits of their enterprise if they stay with the franchise. If ever a franchisee tries to go independent and abandon the franchise, the value and the equity in the enterprise disappear as if by magic.

Stated simply, the franchisee can never leave.

Chapter 8

Expendable Franchisees

One of the most common manifestations of The Franchise Fraud is the franchisors' efforts to oversaturate their franchise systems. As franchisees suffer more and more intrabrand competition, the value of their franchises and earning capacities is seriously impacted. Conversely, many franchisors utilize franchise systems to pave the way for company-owned stores. Some franchisors set their franchisees up for failure so that the franchisor can open a company-owned store in successful markets or avoid unsuccessful markets. It is also common for major chains to retain their best locations for company-owned stores and franchise only those locations that do not meet the companies' rigid quality standards.

While the preceding chapter examined various mechanisms used by franchisors to prevent franchise terminations, this chapter examines the seemingly paradoxical methods franchisors use to squeeze franchisees and force them out of business. It may seem ironic to discuss the methods used by franchisors to prevent franchisees from leaving a franchise system in one chapter, and then to talk about franchisees being expendable in the next. Both phenomena, however, represent widespread practices within the franchising industry. For many franchising companies, including many major franchisors considered to be blue chip, the expendability of individual franchisees is a harsh reality.

SUCCESS BY ATTRITION

Keep in mind that one of the major advantages of expansion through franchising is achieving risk-free venture capital from franchisees. In a very real sense, franchisees represent the pioneers going out and staking new territories. I once heard a definition of a pioneer: *Someone staggering out of the forest with an axe in his back!*

The truth be known, most franchisors depend on their population of franchisees to take the risks and to provide the capital, site selection, and sweat equity necessary to grow the system. Like a person flinging mud at a wall and hoping some will stick, franchisors have little to lose, and much to gain, by opening as many franchise outlets as possible.

Certainly, franchisors would like all their franchisees to succeed, but frequently (and against the popular notion) franchisors have no vested interest in the success of their franchisees. It is imminently preferable for a franchisee to fail than a company-owned outlet. The losses of a company-owned unit hit the franchisor in its pocketbook. Franchise failures do not.

In many franchise systems, the franchisor makes money on every service provided to the franchisees. Franchisees pay substantial initial fees and training fees. Frequently, fees are charged for design and location services. Royalties, marketing fees, and other service fees represent substantial cash flow for franchisors. In fact, most start-up franchisors depend on the cash flow from franchise sales to stay afloat and could not survive solely from royalty income.

To establish a beachhead in a given market area, a franchisor typically must open numerous units hoping enough will succeed to establish a presence. The analogy to establishing a beachhead is accurate. Franchisees are like the marines or the infantry and are the first on the beach in the primary assault of a company to establish its market. And like most efforts to establish a beachhead, there are normally heavy casualties in franchising when a franchisor begins to establish its network.

Notwithstanding the industry claims of impressive success rates, many new franchise systems have massive unit failures in their initial years. Most franchisors never live long enough even to be a part of industry statistics.

Examples of mass failures of franchise systems are too numerous to name. A person need only compare annual franchise compilations from year to year to realize that a substantial number of "fly-by-nights" disappear every year.

It is far more revealing to note some of the ultimately successful companies who experienced initial failures on their way to substantial success. For example, it has been chronicled that Ray Kroc alienated a gang of golfing buddies from Rolling Green Country Club because of their difficulties as the initial

McDonald's franchisees.[1] Popeye's Fried Chicken, a major chain that has achieved significant growth, almost went bankrupt in its first year in business. The company later had a dismal record in trying to establish a Southern California foothold. In 1972, Carvel Corporation, which already had an established network with 600 ice cream shops on the East Coast, ventured into California. Of its 34 initial franchise units, 33 shops failed.

It is important to note that each franchise failure represents income and cash flow to the franchisor, even while the franchisee is losing his or her entire investment. Moreover, each unit failure means a franchise returns to the franchisor's available "inventory" of franchises, another investment "opportunity" for the next person in line to try to salvage. Good locations will ultimately succeed. And once a beachhead is established, a franchisor can go on to become a successful chain.

In Chapter 4, we identified a new franchisor, Chick's Natural, which featured a delicious and healthy fast food (rotisserie chicken). The founders decided to base a franchise system on their profitable first restaurant. The initial nine units all lost substantial sums, and eight of the nine ultimately went out of business. The remaining original franchisee had sufficient capital to withstand early losses and ultimately bought out the original franchisor. Twelve new franchisees have taken the place of the original eight, and the chain now claims to be doing better.

The point is that franchisees, like foot soldiers in a war of attrition, are expendable in most franchise systems.

The franchising industry would like us to look at franchising as a mechanism of reducing the odds of business failure. And given a balanced industry, I am confident this image can be true. In practice, however, franchising improves the franchisor's odds of success because the franchisor is able to entice others to pay a fee to serve as advance scouts.

SELLING FRANCHISES CAN BE A PROFITABLE BUSINESS

Just as franchisors have found more and more sophisticated methods for controlling the franchised enterprise following termination, so have franchisors developed intricate schemes and devices to exploit the expendability of franchisees. On the other hand, when a franchisor is dedicated to a franchised system of product and service distribution, the franchise relationship can grow and prosper for both the franchisor and the franchisee. In an economically balanced franchise system that respects the interests of both franchisor and the franchisee, franchising remains a magnificent vehicle for business and capital expansion.

The abuses discussed here, and in other chapters of this book, are the result of a franchising industry that lacks economic balance. When franchisors are able to get away with substantive abuses, they will. This is not to blame the individual franchisors so much as to blame our economic system for the lack of a stabilizing influence to prevent abuses.

Franchisors are increasingly discovering they can take advantage of the expendability of their franchisees to generate substantial revenues from the sale of franchises and to engineer a franchise network into a company-owned network. Notwithstanding the intent of franchising to be a mechanism of product and service distribution, more often than not it is the sale of franchises that drives the revenues and profits of franchisors. Make no mistake, a successful restaurant operator who begins to sell franchises has gone into a new line of business. He or she may still be in the restaurant business, but the individual now is also a member of the franchising industry.

Many franchising commentators deny there is a franchise industry. Franchising is claimed to be merely a system of product and service distribution, and not an industry in and of itself. I simply do not agree. Indeed, several major companies, such as Pepsico and Grand Met, have developed several chains of franchise systems. These companies are primarily in business for the purpose of selling franchises. *Remember the Cardinal Rule: Always choose a franchisor whose purpose in business is to sell products and services to ultimate consumers. Franchisors whose prime directive is selling franchises, rather than products and services, present a major danger signal.*

MARKET PENETRATION VERSUS ENCROACHMENT

Encroachment (selling a new franchise in close proximity to an existing one) and oversaturation of franchises within a geographic territory have become major issues among franchisees. The mutual issues of encroachment and over-saturation have become the number one concern of McDonald's franchisees, long considered the cream of franchise opportunities. "Impaction" (the word utilized by McDonald's franchisees to describe oversaturation and encroach-ment) is crimping the profitability of many McDonald's operators. The truth is McDonald's is a company with a saturated market, but whose continued growth depends on an ever-growing population of franchises throughout the United States and around the world.

The McDonald's corporation defends its practice of purposefully saturat-ing markets as being in the best interest of the entire system as well as existing franchisees. McDonald's points out that market penetration provides the capi-tal to support an enormous marketing effort which, in turn, boosts sales while reducing the per franchise cost of advertising. More franchisees are available to share the marketing burden jointly. Franchisees readily acknowledge the im-portance of market penetration, but when per unit sales and profits begin to decline, franchisees experience diminishing returns. A sales and profit increase for McDonald's is seen to be at the franchisees' expense.

I currently represent a group of franchisees with the opposite problem. My clients own franchises of a prominent haircutting system in the Midwest that sought to penetrate the California market a few years ago. Franchisees were recruited on the success the company had achieved in other areas of the country and, my clients claim, on promises that the franchisor would establish enough units in California for the system to be a serious competitor to Super Cuts and Fantastic Sam's (the two largest haircutting franchises).

Four years later, the franchisor has only established a handful of California units, a wholly insufficient number to advertise aggressively. Most of my clients are losing money. Many are close to failing. Indeed, the franchisor has offered to allow my clients out of the franchises *without penalty,* seemingly willing to accept its failure to gain a foothold in California. My clients con-tend there was a promise to support the system by opening enough units for the system to compete effectively. Allowing these franchisees to withdraw their franchises will not save them; more likely, it will seal their doom.

Failure to achieve market penetration and the achievement of market saturation are both manifestations of franchisee expendability. But these po-lar mechanisms also represent a true paradox for well-meaning franchisors who must strike a delicate balance to achieve market penetration without encroaching the franchisees' existing markets. Nevertheless, franchisees are squeezed by the existence of both devices—sometimes even in the same system. It is common to hear franchisees complain, "You didn't sell enough!" while others are protesting, "You sold too many!" Usually, both complaints are accurate charges of franchisee expendability.

MANIFESTATIONS OF FRANCHISEE EXPENDABILITY

Franchisors employ many tactics and devices that establish and strengthen the franchise system through the sacrifice and expense of existing franchisees. Whether franchisors explicitly intend to develop strong systems through the attrition of franchisees, many franchise systems have a Darwinian "survival of the fittest" evolution. Perhaps it is merely logical and unavoidable—the better operators in the best locations will survive, and the poor operators with poor locations will fail or be replaced by better operators.

The principal problem is that franchising is not sold on the basis of survival of the fittest; rather, franchising boasts it is a *fit* method of business that assures *survival* of the many. On the contrary, not only is there enormous risk in opening a franchise business, often the franchisor intentionally employs tactics designed to sacrifice its franchisees, or at least to use them for the franchisor's purposes without due regard for the franchisees' welfare.

Most prospective franchisees are completely unaware of the propensity of franchisors to cannibalize (this is the industry's term—not mine—but it fits) their franchisees for the purposes of system and profit growth. Lacking education and market power, franchisees continuously are led to franchising, and too often to slaughter. Perhaps the following descriptions of common cannibalizing tactics will open the eyes of would-be and existing franchisees.

Growth by Attrition

Having already discussed this practice, it is sufficient to comment that most franchisors grow by attrition, at least in their early phases. Ideally, franchisors carefully select only the best candidates to be franchise owners, and as a franchisor gains stability and popularity, careful franchisee selection often becomes a reality. Unfortunately, start-up franchisors are hungry for sales—a warm body with a franchise fee and sufficient funds in hand to build, stock, and operate the business are the only requirements. On second thought, forget the warm body, and operating capital is a nice (but not necessary) plus.

The franchisor's goal, indeed its only goal, is to survive and prosper. The franchisor *must* establish its markets; it must have capital and retail outlets. Franchisors know they will have failures—one of the very advantages of franchising is the ability to fail with "other people's money." Growth by attrition is neither illegal nor immoral; *representing that franchising is a protective order is the fraud.* Perhaps if franchisees would finally recognize how much franchisors need for them to be the risk takers, they would demand more rights and privileges—and actually begin to negotiate their contracts.

Encroachment

To most franchisee victims of established franchise systems, encroachment represents a major manifestation of The Franchise Fraud. Opening a competing unit of the same system within an existing franchisee's perceived market is the ultimate insult to franchisees who have worked hard to develop their markets. For most franchisees, encroachment exemplifies franchisor cannibalization; it represents the franchisor eating its young, its loyal warriors who have worked hard to establish the franchisor's beachhead and are now denied the fruits of their labors.

Twenty years ago, most franchisors guaranteed an exclusive operating territory to each franchise granted. As franchising became more and more popular, franchisors discovered exclusive territories were not necessary to entice potential franchise purchasers. Today, the norm is the "location only" franchise. More often than not, there is no limitation on the franchisor from opening multiple units across the street from one another. Franchises are granted only for the specific address, with no territorial protection.

As noted in the previous chapter, franchise agreements today rarely grant any market protection. If a franchisee successfully builds a territory, the franchisor is contractually empowered to sell more franchises. Given the importance of market penetration, franchisors often claim they are duty bound to grow their systems. Often, franchisees are given "first refusal rights"—the right to protect their markets by purchasing each new adjoining franchise the franchisor offers for sale. If at first this seems like a suitable compromise, franchisees invariably perceive exercising a first refusal right as being forced to buy the same franchise over and over again.

Like so many issues in franchising, territorial encroachment is as good for the franchisor's bottom line as it is bad for the franchisee's. You cannot blame the franchisor for wanting to sell as many franchises as possible, any more than you can fault a franchisee for wanting territorial protection. But The Franchise Fraud denies the problem exists; it boasts instead that the franchisor is there to support and nourish the franchisee.

Multiple Chains of Distribution

Once a franchisor's trade name and trademarks, God willing, become established and in demand, franchisors often find they can reach their markets in many ways in addition to their franchise network. Perhaps the franchisor will begin selling trademarked products in supermarkets, through distributors, and mail order. Worst of all from the franchisee's perspective, the franchisor may distribute through discount houses and the popular "club" stores, where the franchisor's price to the public may actually be less than its price to the franchisees!

When a franchisor begins to exploit alternative chains of distribution, the franchisees' markets are again cannibalized. Sometimes, the franchisees' products are more accessible through supermarkets (this has been a particular problem with ice cream and soft drink franchisees) and less expensive to boot.

Franchisors argue that multiple chains of distribution boost the image of the franchisor's trade name and marks. Franchisors claim the result will be greater sales and even more traffic for franchisees. Franchisees fear the reverse is true: The oversupply of franchisor product can reduce demand and have a declining impact on prices and revenues. Mostly, franchisees simply fear that supermarket and mail-order sales will diminish their local markets and detract from the marketing priority of the franchise system.

Reservation of Franchisees to
Less Desirable Territories

Another unfortunate but frequent franchisor tactic employed to the detriment of franchisees is the development of company-owned, high-profit stores in the best locations and the reservation of inferior locations for franchising. A few years ago, the president of Foodmaker, Inc., the California franchisor of Jack-in-the-Box franchises, appeared at the company's annual shareholders meeting to announce a new plan for corporate expansion. The company *publicly announced* it had identified several hundred prime locations to be developed as new company-owned Jack-in-the-Box restaurants. Foodmaker further designated another group of locations of somewhat lesser quality to be targeted for franchise development.

The practice of reserving the best locations for company-owned stores, and selling off the lesser offices as franchise locations, has long been a franchising practice. Because most franchisors refuse to make earnings claims with respect to specific locations, the inferiority of franchise locations versus company-owned locations would not be generally recognized.

More than any other instance of exploitation of multiple distribution chains, the development of a company-owned chain alongside a franchisee network has the potential for serious conflicts. Franchisees frequently suspect and complain that franchisors favor their company-owned counterparts. Even though the franchise outlet may outgross the comparable company-owned unit, the company-run store is likely to be more profitable to the franchisor. Although it was the franchisee's capital that financed the franchisor's success, once success is achieved, the franchise operator is seen as the "expensive" alternative.

When franchisors lose their dedication to their franchise distribution chains, the entire system can unravel. A well-known restaurant chain, which grew through franchising, now has more company-owned restaurants than franchised, and the franchisor aggressively sells frozen products in supermarkets and discount stores. Franchisee sales are down. Franchisees complain they are ignored by their franchisor, are denied training, and that company-owned stores are not paying a fair share of advertising expenses.

Such complaints are often registered in systems that have significant complements of company-owned and franchised outlets. Rarely do the franchisees

131

work in harmony with company-owned outlets. Franchisees perceive company-owned offices as threats and as cannibals—which, in many instances, they are.

Encouraging Conversion of Franchise Locations to Company-Owned Stores

A group of franchisees of a very large East Coast automotive tune-up and lubrication franchise system recently complained the franchisor had systematically used franchising for the purposes of financing the growth of a company-owned chain of tune-up shops. According to the complaining franchisees, the company systematically engineered its franchise system so that most franchisees are ready to get out of the business within two years.

The franchisees claim the company has a separate subsidiary organized for the purpose of buying out franchised units. Poor performing franchises are allowed to fail, and the better franchises are bought out on terms that include a general release of claims between the parties. In effect, the franchisor comes to own only the most successful units and the franchisees serve as the franchisor's financing system.

In the natural life span of a franchise system, profitable franchise operations will be converted to company-owned operations over time. Unprofitable company-owned locations, on the other hand, are frequently sold as franchises. As often as possible, it is the franchisee who provides the risk capital, and the risk taking. Unsuccessful franchisees fall by the wayside. Successful ones are bought out or taken over by the franchisor wherever possible.

As franchise systems mature, it is most common for company-owned and operated units to increase in number compared with franchise locations. For example, Marie Callender restaurants, which was once substantially a franchise chain, now has over 300 company-owned stores, exceeding the number of total franchised units.

The phenomenon of converting successful franchise locations to company-owned operations is present throughout the franchising industry. Once a franchise unit has established itself as profitable, the franchisee appears to the franchisor as a very expensive manager earning far more than a store manager would command in salary and benefits. Some years ago, Manpower Temporary Services (which no longer sells franchises) publicly indicated its intent to convert all its franchised offices into company-owned offices over time.

Manpower is accomplishing its goal through natural attrition and has continued to support its franchises. Other temporary employment services chains have effected significant conversions of franchise offices to company-owned offices far less gracefully, effectively maneuvering franchisees out of business. At least one of these companies has developed a frightening pattern of converting an existing independent operator to a franchise, encouraging the operator to overexpand, and then assuming the business assets when the operator fails. (This practice is described in greater detail in the next section.)

The practice of maneuvering the conversion of franchisees into company-owned outlets is not unique to employment services franchises. Similar trends have been documented in many industries as diverse as gasoline service station chains, electronics retailers, and restaurants.

Setting a Franchisee Up for Failure to Facilitate Conversion to Company-Owned Businesses

As a practical matter, and a matter of logic, it is difficult to fault a franchisor for converting profitable franchises into company-owned businesses. On the other hand, the practice employed by some franchisors of setting franchisees up for failure is very hard to justify.

In my recent litigation involving temporary services franchisees, I discovered a troubling and recurring business practice. The franchisor segmented its temporary employment services business by geographic territories and industrial classifications. For example, the company sold temporary employment services franchises for clerical businesses, industrial businesses, medical businesses, and other individual specialties. Additionally, the company would award franchises by geographic territory and would encourage franchisees to open multiple offices. Thus a typical franchisee might have a clerical franchise, an industrial franchise, and a medical franchise, and might operate several offices in different territories. It was common to discover an individual franchisee owning three to five franchises, and more.

133

It was also common to find the franchisee being successful in one or more of its units, but unsuccessful in the others. A provision in the franchise agreement provided that the franchisor could offset the profits of one franchise unit against the losses of another unit owned by the same franchisee. If one out of every four franchise locations proved successful, the probability existed that the multiple franchise owner would have one profitable office for every three unprofitable offices.

On investigation, I suspected this franchisor had actually grown its business on the premise that its franchisees would have one successful office for every three or four offices opened, and that the failure of several offices would offset the gains of the profitable offices. A franchisee with three failing offices against one successful one would soon be out of business. The franchise agreement allowed the franchisor to assume the operation of the profitable business. With the franchisee out of business, the franchisor wound up owning and operating only the profitable offices.

The Great Franchise Clearance Sale

A few years ago I was approached by the owner of a small chain of pizza restaurants to help franchise his business. On investigation, I discovered the pizza restaurants, though a well-known local chain, supported their managers but were not producing an attractive bottom line for the owner. My would-be client was looking to convert his pizza chain to franchises to effectively sell the business because, as a whole, it did not present an attractive investment.

The conventional wisdom states that a franchisee should always try to purchase a well-known and well-respected trademark. On the other hand, the conventional wisdom in the investment world is never to purchase in a market on its way down. Nevertheless, some businesses are able to sell off assets by liquidating company-owned stores as franchises. Frequently, the unlucky franchisees are left holding the proverbial "empty bag."

Selling off franchises to liquidate an unprofitable chain, or a chain in need of cash, is the converse of the conversion of franchises to company-owned stores. The two mechanisms are spurred by opposite motivations, but each tactic develops capital and maximizes profits at the expense (rather than for the benefit) of the system's franchisees.

Reselling Franchises Is Good Business: The Churning Issue

As I write this, I am representing a system of several hundred franchisees in a distressed weight control business franchise system. The franchisor is in dire financial difficulties and has admitted to having only 2 cents of current assets for every $1.00 of liabilities. Over a 24-month period, the company lost more than $154 million. In a 3-year period more than 1,000 franchisees have gone out of business.

As part of an overall workout of its debt, the franchisor has proposed a new, tougher, franchise agreement to replace all its existing agreements. In offering its new agreement, the franchisor has argued to its franchisees that the new (more expensive) contract is necessary to solve the franchisor's financial troubles.

My clients' response to the unilaterally offered franchise agreement was, in my view, compassionate, sympathetic, fair, and realistic. Many of the individual franchisees of my client's system are also losing money. The franchisor's proposed increase in royalties was financially impossible. Nevertheless, my franchisee clients responded to the franchisor that they were appreciative of the franchisor's problems, had been loyal and faithful operators within the franchise system, and were willing to open a negotiating dialogue to come up with a compromise agreement in everyone's best interests.

The franchisor's response was intransigent and adamant. Sign the new agreement or face withdrawal of support by the franchisor of the existing relationship. No discussion, no dialogue, no negotiations!

Quite honestly, my clients were baffled and bewildered by the franchisor's response. How could the franchisor be so intransigent when it was in so much trouble? Wasn't the franchisor's primary asset its long-developed system of several hundred franchised offices?

Unfortunately, the answers to these questions are fairly obvious. The franchisor did not see the existing franchise network as an asset. Rather, the franchisor saw the ability to abandon existing franchises and to begin selling new franchises as the hidden gold mine in the franchisor's arsenal. Quite simply, if all the existing franchises went away, the franchisor had a potential $20,000 to $25,000 in new franchise fees that could generate the immediate cash needed by the franchisor. Reselling franchises was the franchisor's business plan to salvation.

The preceding example is not isolated. Many franchisees have suspected their franchisors were guilty of churning franchise sales. Every time a franchise is resold, a new franchise fee or transfer fee is generated to the franchisor. It is like found money. Franchisors certainly will attempt to retain franchisees who are generating substantial gross revenues and, therefore, substantial royalty income. However, franchisors have a double incentive to dump low-producing franchisees, rather than to help them. Obviously, to find a better operator is always in the franchisor's interest. But a second receipt of fresh new franchise fees provides a silver lining.

In the securities industry, stockbroker churning of securities in an investor's account has long been considered one of the most onerous and despicable of fraudulent practices. On the other hand, churning in franchising is only recently being recognized. No specific state laws have been enacted to address the problem. The only way to prove franchise churning is to establish the franchisor knew the franchisee could not possibly succeed when the franchisee was accepted into the system.

Oddly, the very act of franchise churning appears to the public as a symbol of a franchisor's success. A high volume of franchise sales, without comparing the net gain of franchisees in business, seems to indicate a successful franchisor. Churning allegations have been leveled at such giants as Subway, Mail Boxes, Etc., Popeye's Fried Chicken, Snelling & Snelling, and even McDonald's. These organizations are all highfliers, whose claims of rapid growth and phenomenal franchise sales support their claims of success.

THE VICIOUS LIFE CYCLE OF FRANCHISORS

The various manifestations by which franchisees become expendable to their franchisors suggest there is an unsettling life cycle for franchisors that is fraught with franchisor-franchisee conflicts of interest at every turn. Far from being the self-protecting safe path to business ownership, franchisees must beware of their parents as well as their competitors.

Whether the franchisee buys at the beginning of the franchisor's life cycle (when the franchisee is the soldier in the franchisor's battle of attrition to establish a foothold and market), the middle glory years (when the franchisor is on top and aggressively looking for opportunities to capitalize on multiple markets and opening or converting company-owned stores to maximize profits), or at the end of the cycle (when the franchisee may be discarded or sold as an asset to yield urgently needed liquidating cash), the franchisees discover they are a pawn or a tool to achieve the franchisor's objectives.

COMBATING THE EXPENDABILITY OF FRANCHISEES: THE CASE FOR A FIDUCIARY RELATIONSHIP

That a franchisor may abuse its franchise network by exploiting the expendability of its franchisees is a harsh reality. Most of the abuses described in this chapter are perfectly legal. Franchisors are in the business of turning a profit, and they cannot be blamed for trying to get the most value from the commodities they have to sell. On the other hand, as long as franchisees remain ignorant of the true value of their franchise systems; as long as franchisees fail to investigate their franchise opportunities; and as long as they lack the knowledge to investigate their franchise opportunities, franchisors will continue to be able to spin off their losing stores and offices to an unsuspecting public.

The only way for franchisees to curb the abuse of making franchisees expendable is to achieve market power, and knowledge of the market. In the absence of substantial franchisee advocates, and in the absence of franchisees having a sense that they can negotiate franchise agreements, or avoid "take it or leave it edicts" from franchisors, it is not likely there will be any significant improvement in the economic structure of franchising.

Legislation was introduced in Congress in 1992 by Congressman John LaFalce that would require franchisors to pay franchisees the fair market value of their businesses on termination. Congressman LaFalce's legislative proposals, which are described in detail in Chapter 11, would provide an economic benefit to a franchisee who is being terminated. But the LaFalce proposals will not help a franchisee who buys a failing business.

To achieve franchisee protective legislation, the public must be aware of the industry abuses. Only when the public is educated and savvy will market forces begin to coalesce into formidable negotiating and political units capable of bringing the franchising industry back into balance.

When the marketplace comes into balance, as inevitably it must, I predict a new wave of truly successful franchise systems. I perceive contracts with economic and legal balance such that franchisors and franchisees have strong incentives to work together toward a common profit motive. I also perceive, by legislation or by contract, the long-awaited recognition that franchisors and franchisees must be mandated to deliver the highest standards of good faith, fair dealing, competence, loyalty, and trust that the law imposes. These are all standards of performance and care—duties of performance and care—that franchisees have long presumed and assumed were part and parcel of the franchise promise.

The law calls such standards of performance "fiduciary duties." When two people have a fiduciary relationship, they owe one another the highest degree of trust and loyalty, and the duty to look out for each other's interest even before their own. Parties can agree to be fiduciaries. Often, however, the law imposes fiduciary relationships in circumstances where there is opportunity for natural conflicts. Thus a stockbroker is legally bound as the fiduciary of his or her customers and is obligated to put their investment needs over the personal need for commissions and income.

Franchisees are not fiduciaries with their franchisors by contract or by law. But only when the industry comes to accept the confidence reposed in a fiduciary relationship will franchising begin to deliver all that the industry now promises.

Chapter 9

Separating the Wheat
from the Chaff

This chapter examines what a prospective franchisee should look for in trying to identify and isolate good franchise opportunities that will deliver the substantial promise of franchising. On the other hand, a franchisee is given practical advice on how to identify franchise systems that do not offer valuable services.

Against the backdrop of all the things that can go wrong in a franchise system and the current economic climate that allows a franchisor terrific negotiating advantages, I am frequently at a loss when I am asked to recommend franchise opportunities. In the existing franchising climate, there are virtually no franchises I can recommend wholeheartedly. Franchisees simply are at a serious disadvantage in the franchising equation. Even when a franchisor is both ethical and paternal in its dealings with its franchisees, there are no safeguards protecting franchisees from potential abuse.

When a would-be entrepreneur invests in a franchise opportunity, he or she is making a substantial economic investment in the franchisor's business enterprise. The franchisee is making a determination about the quality of the franchisor's products *today* as well as the quality of the franchisor's existing management. Invariably, the franchisee is counting on continued growth of the franchisor's enterprise.

The purchase of a franchise opportunity can be compared with an equivalent purchase of a growth-oriented common stock on the public securities exchange. When a cautious investor determines to invest in a stock with growth potential, the investor looks for certain important elements:

1. Quality business operations and performance by the targeted company.
2. Quality management.
3. Initial indications the stock is likely to perform well.
4. Attractive price compared with potential yield and growth in value.

Ideally, a prospective franchisee will make some of the same evaluations for a franchise selection. Indeed, franchisees should take even greater care because they bear significantly greater risks than does an investor in common stock.

Most investors in growth stocks claim to take a long-term approach to their investments. They don't expect quick results, and they expect to hold their shares over a long term to realize their hope for growth potential. Nevertheless, the stocks are publicly traded, and the shareholders have no vested interest in the performance of the companies in their stock portfolios. Equally important, investors in stock can diversify their portfolios by purchasing interests in several companies having apparent potential.

To the contrary, a franchisee is putting most, if not all, his or her investing eggs in one franchisor's basket. More importantly, the franchisee is making a "can't turn back" investment in the franchisor. There is no "free trading" of a franchise opportunity on a public market. As shown in Chapter 7, the termination provisions in most franchise agreements can be lethal, and therefore a franchise purchase is truly a commitment.

I guess the comparison comes down to saying that an investor in stock is somewhat "involved" with the future of his or her publicly traded company, while a franchisee is "committed" to the performance of the franchisor. I can't help but be reminded of the analogy I once heard comparing the difference between "involvement" and "commitment." Comparing the two terms to a breakfast of ham and eggs, it has been suggested that the chicken who laid the eggs was "involved" in the breakfast, while the poor pig who gave up the ham was "committed" to it!

If franchisees are, then, "committed" to their franchised businesses, extreme care is essential in selecting an appropriate franchisor. And when we take into consideration that the economic and legal scales are tipped heavily in favor of the franchisor, extreme care becomes too mild an admonition.

THE EIGHT CRITERIA FOR FRANCHISE SELECTION

Given the extent of the risks involved in franchising today, I am unwilling to make specific recommendations. But acknowledging that many would-be entrepreneurs will plunge headlong into franchising, the following list provides my personal eight essential criteria for selecting a franchisor:

1. The franchising company is primarily interested in distributing quality goods and services to ultimate consumers.

2. The franchising company is dedicated to a franchise system as its *primary* mechanism of product and service distribution.

3. The franchising company, in fact, produces and markets quality goods and services for which there is an established market demand.

4. The franchising company enjoys a substantial reputation and acceptance (this is frequently identified with favorable trademark recognition).

5. The franchisor has an established, well-designed marketing and business plan, and offers prospective franchisees substantial and complete training.

6. The franchisor has developed good relations with its franchisees, and the franchisees have a strong franchisee organization that has negotiating leverage with the franchising company.

7. The company has suitable earnings claims such that the investment in the franchise opportunity provides sufficient economic benefits to justify the cost of buying the franchise and starting the business. In other words, the economic rewards must justify the price.

8. The franchise agreement is consistent in promising to honor most, if not all, of the provisions of the Franchisee Bill of Rights described in Chapter 13.

The first two criteria are absolutely critical to a franchise selection process. Although the other criteria are important, any prospective franchisee should immediately abandon consideration of an opportunity unless completely satisfied the prospective franchisor is dedicated to selling goods and services through its franchise system. The following sections describe each criterion in greater detail.

Criterion 1. The Franchising Company Is Primarily Interested in Distributing Quality Goods and Services to Ultimate Consumers

In the preceding chapter, I have called this criterion the cardinal rule of franchise selection. Whatever a prospective franchisee does, he or she *must* be satisfied a prospective franchisor is *primarily* in business to produce quality goods and services for distribution to ultimate consumers. Although this prime directive may seem obvious, there are more franchising companies in business to sell franchises than in business to sell quality goods and services.

A prospective franchisee must understand that the fundamental purpose of franchising is to function as a distribution network for the sale of goods and services. When it works as intended, franchising is no more than a mechanism for product and service distribution. Franchisors intent on selling their products to the consuming public are most likely to protect and nurture their distribution systems.

Fortunately, prospective franchisees are able to make a reasonable evaluation of a franchisor's dedication to selling quality products and services. Initially, the prospective franchisee can make a personal judgment as to the quality of the franchisor's products and the quality control maintained by the franchisor. As much as possible, however, franchisees should not rely solely on their personal tastes. Wherever possible, consult consumer rating systems that have judged the franchisor's product line. Find out if any market research has been done about the franchisor's products.

An important mechanism for evaluating the franchisor's dedication to selling products (as opposed to franchises) is to demand the franchisor provide a breakdown of its gross revenues from the sale of goods and services as compared with the sale of franchises. Many franchisors will object to providing such information. Some may even tell you they are prohibited from providing revenue data by law.

The refusal of a franchisor to provide factual data about the company's actual sales should make a prospective franchisee most suspicious. The representation by a franchisor that it is not allowed by law to provide such data is an outright lie. You are not requesting projections (although you might like to see projections as well); you are merely asking your prospective franchisor for historical data that can demonstrate the franchisor's success in selling the products the franchisor is asking you to represent. You should accept no less than full compliance with such requests.

Criterion 2. The Franchising Company Is Dedicated to a Franchise System as Its Primary Mechanism of Product and Service Distribution

This criterion is the corollary to my first cardinal rule for franchise selection. Although I have discussed this principle earlier, its importance bears repeating again and again. A prospective franchisee should steer clear of a franchise network that is in competition with its franchises. When a franchising company is dedicated to the sale of products to consumers and also is dedicated to franchising as its primary mechanism for product distribution, its franchisees stand an excellent chance of having a franchisor who fully supports its franchises and nurtures them. In essence, the franchisees should rely on the old adage, "If you put all your eggs in one basket, watch that basket very carefully."

Although the cardinal rule is to select a franchisor *primarily* dedicated to its franchise network, the franchisor need not be *solely* reliant on its franchises. I personally believe that a franchisor needs to have some company-owned stores to ensure the franchisor understands the trials and tribulations of operating a profitable retail outlet. Otherwise, it is unlikely the franchisor will appreciate the plight of its franchisees, or will be able to provide necessary solutions as operating problems arise.

Although no studies have been performed, it seems to me there has been as much friction in franchise systems that are 100 percent franchised as in franchise systems with dual chains of distribution. At either extreme, the franchisor can be unresponsive to the needs and problems of its franchise network.

When a franchisor engages in multiple distribution chains, its interest in any particular distribution mechanism is diluted. And when a franchisor does not appreciate the difficulty of earning a profit in the operation of the franchise business, its sensitivity to the franchisees cannot help but suffer.

Criterion 3. The Franchising Company Produces and Markets Quality Goods and Services for Which There Is an Established Market Demand

This criterion constitutes a slight nuance of difference from criterion 1. It is, however, a very important nuance. While a franchisor's dedication to the sale of products and services is critical, a major attribute of franchising is the opportunity to invest in a proven commodity. Every prospective franchisee should seek to represent the very best products and services available.

Criterion 4. The Franchising Company Enjoys a Substantial Reputation and Acceptance

A recognized quality trademark is an important criterion in the franchise selection process. After all, a franchisee is primarily interested in obtaining an immediate market. The franchisee's bet is placed on the quality of the trademark.

Although The Franchise Fraud represents that franchising per se guarantees success, do not be fooled or victimized. A recent study by the American Association of Franchisees and Dealers found a whopping 70 percent of franchisors listed in *Entrepreneur* magazine's Franchise 500® in 1987 were out of business in 1992 (see Chapter 1). So much for a 95 percent success rate. The *safe* franchisees are the proven ones—recognized by their trademarks for quality and success.

Many franchise commentators will list trademark recognition as the number one criterion for franchise selection. While I certainly agree that choosing a quality trademark is most valuable, there have been significant examples of successful franchise systems whose trademarks were not household names. In fact, virtually every franchise system started from humble beginnings. Consequently, I would not completely rule out a franchise opportunity simply because it was a relatively new and unknown system. However, the lack of a recognized trade name would certainly play a dominant factor in what I was willing to pay for the franchise opportunity.

Incidentally, one of the strongest (and oldest) franchise systems in the United States today is E.K. Williams & Co. (also sometimes known as Edwin K. Williams & Co.). Although most people have never heard of E.K. Williams at all, it is a large network of accounting and bookkeeping franchises that have developed a long and successful bookkeeping and management service for gasoline service station businesses and automotive garages. While E.K. Williams is not a household trade name, it has built a reputation on providing a quality service.

Criterion 5. The Franchisor Has an Established, Well-Designed Marketing and Business Plan, and Offers Prospective Franchisees Substantial and Complete Training

The most common complaint of franchisees is that their franchisor has provided little or no viable support. Frequently, franchisees claim their franchisors have failed to provide any training or support whatsoever.

Along with a recognized trademark, the promise of an established marketing and support system is the most important benefit generally attributed to franchising. It would be difficult to find any definition or story about franchising that does not tie the word "support" to the concept of a proven and established marketing system and an established recognized trade name.

A franchisor's support of its franchisees, including training, is critical to the delivery and performance of the franchisor's marketing and business plan. The quality of a franchisor's training program is a significant indication of a franchisor's support of its franchise network.

Surprisingly, many franchisees fail to investigate and verify either the existence or quality of the franchisor's marketing plan and business plan. I say surprising because the evaluation of the franchisor's marketing system and training programs is comparatively easy to undertake.

As the first task in the evaluation of any franchise system, a prospective franchisee should make an evaluation of the franchisor's marketing system by simply observing an existing franchisee's operations. By visiting two or three franchised outlets, a franchisee can determine the uniformity of products and services, as well as the uniformity of employee training and service.

Invariably, franchisors and franchisee counselors recommend franchisees talk to existing franchise operators before making a purchase decision. The problem with this recommendation is most franchise owners do not like to air their dirty linen or "tell on" their franchisors. Prospective franchisees often can penetrate the natural aversion of existing franchisees to talk about problems within the franchise system by asking specific questions about training and the marketing system.

For example, a prospective franchisee should simply say, "Tell me about the training program." Instead of asking a franchisee whether he or she received adequate training, it is more productive to ask for details about the training, and specific aspects about the training.

With respect to the franchisor's marketing system, a prospective franchisee should ask to review the franchisor's confidential operating procedures manual. If the franchisor balks at showing the manual prior to signing the franchise agreement, the prospective franchisee can offer to sign a confidentiality agreement. If a franchisor still refuses, extreme caution should be taken before purchasing.

A prospect who cannot make a fair determination over the quality of the franchise business should require a money-back guaranty if he or she is not happy with the marketing plan following 90 days ownership of the franchise business.

The importance of the franchisor's business plan and marketing plan cannot be overemphasized. Even more than the franchisor's trademark, the lure of franchising is to acquire a proven and established business system. The whole idea behind buying a franchise is to reduce the risks of business start-ups, to buy into a system that has already proven to be workable and profitable. Consequently, it is essential that franchisees enter their enterprise understanding the franchisor's business processes and being proud of the opportunity to embrace the franchisor's program wholeheartedly.

Criterion 6. The Franchisor Has Developed Good Relations with Its Franchisees, and the Franchisees Have a Strong Franchisee Organization That Has Negotiating Leverage with the Franchising Company

As best you can, attempt to determine the franchisor's attitude toward its franchisees. Does the franchisor deliver more than is promised in the franchise agreement? Is the franchisor supportive and genuinely interested in the success of the franchise system? This is a difficult task during the franchise selling process, because it is unlikely that most existing franchisees will be willing to say anything bad about the franchise lest they tarnish the value of their own units.

Clues to the benevolence of the franchisor will be found in the franchise offering circular. The UFOC is required to provide a list of lawsuits the franchisor has experienced. Franchisees should also attempt to inquire of *all* franchises who have left the system (not just terminations) during the preceding five years. Unfortunately, most terminated franchisees (and many people who have litigated with a franchisor) have signed confidentiality agreements in the process of buying their peace with the franchisor. When this occurs, it is again difficult to find individuals who will talk. However, the existence of substantial litigation, and a substantial number of franchisees who have agreed to these contractual gag orders, is not a good portent for your future relationship with the franchisor.

Make sure you join a franchise system with a strong operating franchisee association. As will be seen, a viable franchise association provides negotiating leverage for franchisees, and the ultimate solution to the need of greater balance within the franchising industry. With all the problems in franchising today, it is finally the emergence of franchisee associations that provide some hope for the future.

Stay away from franchisors that have bent over backward to destroy the efforts of franchisee associations, and have refused to negotiate with them. Where a franchisor has a laudable record in dealing with its franchisee association, you have some hope for an egalitarian enterprise that puts the interest of the system ahead of personal profit.

Many promising and profitable franchise opportunities have arbitrary and autocratic franchise systems; the presence of these factors does not mean the franchise businesses are poorly run and unsuccessful. Indeed, some business tycoons have been noted for their autocratic business styles, ruthlessness, and even tyrannical behavior.

Nevertheless, an autocratic franchise system may not mix well with a prospective franchisee's notion of being in business for himself. If a franchisee is an individual with an independent spirit, buying into an autocratic franchise system will not be a happy experience.

Depending on each prospective franchisee's objectives, an evaluation of the "feel" of the franchise system should be made to determine whether or not the business opportunity and system provide a good fit. For most franchisees, having an accessible franchisor who is interested and respectful of the views and input of its franchisees is indicative of a franchising network where teamwork and the feeling of family create a positive business force.

Most franchisees want to feel good about their businesses, feel proud of their franchise networks, and have a warm feeling and trust in their franchisor's attitudes and intentions. Although a franchisor being responsive to franchisee concerns is not a mandatory element in a successful franchise system, I nevertheless urge that good franchisor-franchisee relations are critical to the happiness of most franchise owners, and therefore place franchisee relations high on my list of quality franchise attributes.

Criterion 7. The Company Has Suitable Earnings Claims Such That the Investment in the Franchise Opportunity Provides Sufficient Economic Benefits to Justify the Cost of Buying the Franchise and Starting the Business

In other words, the economic rewards must justify the price. My last two criteria for effective franchise selection are by far the most difficult to achieve. The vast majority of franchisors refuse to make any earnings claims, and further refuse to divulge data about the actual performance or earnings of existing franchises. Indeed, most franchisors have no idea about whether their franchisees are earning a profit or not, because franchisors only require reporting of gross sales.

Consequently, at first blush, it may seem very difficult to obtain sales and earnings data during the franchise selection process.

I urge prospective franchisees not to be deceived by the apparent refusal of franchisors to provide sales and earnings data about their franchise opportunities. More importantly, proceeding to buy any franchise opportunity without having an opportunity to review critical financial information should be avoided as a cardinal rule.

I can't imagine an attorney, CPA, or other business advisor allowing a client to purchase an existing business without a thorough review of the business's performance record for the past two or even three years. Indeed, the price established for most businesses is frequently tied to the sales, earnings, or performance of the business enterprise. Stated simply, franchisees should never purchase a franchise opportunity without having some careful validation of the business's ability to generate sufficient economic rewards to justify the purchase of the business.

Incredibly, a large majority of franchisors refuse to provide relevant financial data to prospective franchisees. Most always, these franchisors claim they are prohibited by applicable law from making projections and earnings claims to prospective franchisees. In fact, no state or federal law prohibits franchisors from making earnings claims. The suggestion that earnings claims are unlawful misrepresents both the intent and purpose of the various franchise disclosure laws that exist throughout the United States.

The truth is that all U.S. franchise disclosure statutes *allow and encourage* franchisors to provide relevant financial data, operating projections, and earnings claims for prospective franchisees. *However, invariably franchise disclosure laws do prohibit the use of projections and earnings claims that cannot be substantiated as reasonable and justifiable by the franchisor.* In essence, the laws prohibit franchisors from making false or unsubstantiated claims.

On the other hand, franchisors are told they will be held accountable for the truth and accuracy of any operating projections made to prospective franchisees. In effect, most franchising disclosure statutes *dare* franchisors to make earnings claims. While a few franchisors accept the dare and make formal projections to their prospective franchisees, most franchising companies utilize the statutory dare as an excuse not to provide important financial disclosures.

In fairness, most franchisors who refuse to make projections or earnings claims do so on the advice of their legal counsel. Because of the structure of franchise disclosure laws, a franchisor can be held accountable for any errors in

149

operating projections and earnings claims. Accordingly, a franchisor can avoid liability for errors in earnings claims by making no projections at all.

Prospective franchisees should be aware that many franchise salespeople will make projections notwithstanding disclosures in the franchisor's uniform franchise offering circulars denying the use of earnings claims. Franchisees should be distrustful of informal earnings claims (frequently written out on the back of a napkin in a restaurant). *Always insist on seeing the background data for which an earnings claim is computed.*

Additionally, most franchise agreements contain a clause whereby the franchisee acknowledges and agrees he or she has not been told anything outside of what was represented in the offering circular, and that only information contained in the offering circular was utilized by the franchisee in making the purchase decision. These clauses have been upheld in some jurisdictions, and rejected in others. Consequently, franchisees should exercise substantial caution when they are given an informal projection or earnings claim that has not been specifically authorized by the franchising company.

My best advice is that prospective franchisees should require earnings claims from any franchising company under serious consideration. Only when franchisees are adamant in demanding proper and relevant financial data will the franchising industry respond by providing relevant data necessary to encourage sales.

In fact, a growing number of franchising companies are putting their performance on the line by providing financial data, operating projections, and earnings claims for prospective franchisees. If their performance is attractive, these companies will be rewarded by attracting quality franchisees.

Many franchisors also claim they are unable to give earnings claims because they do not know the financial performance of their franchisees. Following criterion 2, prospective franchisees should stay away from franchisors who are not dedicated to the profitability of their individual franchisees. How can a company be dedicated to a franchisee's success when it fails to monitor the franchisee's performance?

Several franchising guidebooks are available, including a publication called the *Franchise Sourcebook,* that indicate whether or not a franchisor makes earnings claims. Additionally, there is an excellent publication called *Franchises: Dollars & Sense,* by Warren Lewis, which is a compilation of nearly 150 franchisors who make earnings claims. Mr. Lewis's book is a valuable resource that not only lays out the earnings claims of many franchising companies but also helps a prospective franchisee read and understand the financial data produced by the franchising companies that are willing to make claims.

In any event, a prospective franchisee's elimination of franchise opportunities for which no earnings claims exist provides the safest protection from unethical franchising conduct.

Criterion 8. The Franchise Agreement Is Consistent in Promising to Honor Most, If Not All, of the Provisions of the Franchisee Bill of Rights

This last criterion is truly my personal pipe dream. If this rule were followed in today's franchising world, there would be very few franchise opportunities worthy of anyone's interest.

In Chapter 13, readers will be introduced to the Franchisee Bill of Rights, which was promulgated by the American Association of Franchisees and Dealers in June 1992. These rights seek an equitable and balanced relationship between franchisors and franchisees. In today's franchising marketplace, few (if any) franchising companies could satisfy the requirements of this bill of rights. However, any franchising company that is respectful of the vested interests of its franchisees, and is sensitive to the franchisee's profitability and performance, is well worth serious consideration by a prospective franchise owner.

THE FRANCHISE TERMINATION TRAP

Of all the clauses in a franchise agreement, the termination provisions perhaps should be reviewed with the greatest care and caution. In most instances, on termination of the franchise, the franchisee is out of business, and frequently has little to show for his or her investment.

As is discussed in detail in Chapter 7, under most franchise agreements the franchisee goes out of business on termination of the franchise. Moreover, the terminated franchisee invariably agrees not to compete with the franchisor for two or three years. Frequently, the outgoing franchisee loses his or her location, identity, and any rights to the goodwill of the business.

At the very least, every franchisee should be aware of the termination provisions of the franchise agreement. When very restrictive termination provisions are encountered, a prospective franchisee should only purchase the franchise after substantial soul searching. The franchisee should look inside his or her own business practices and do a thorough investigation of the franchise opportunity. Evaluate the franchisor's humanity toward franchisees, and don't allow your emotional attachment to the franchise system blind you to the very serious forfeiture that may occur if something goes wrong.

Although it is a rare occurrence, it is possible to find franchise opportunities that will allow a franchisee to withdraw painlessly. Some distributorship opportunities even allow the franchisee to change brands when necessary. This is also true in the hotel industry, where the changing of affiliations is relatively common. In any event, heed the termination provisions of your franchise agreement and avoid going into a relationship from which you cannot withdraw without the greatest pain and difficulty.

COMPARISON OF BUSINESS FORMAT AND PRODUCT FRANCHISES

Although business format franchising is the growth area of franchising, more often than not, business format franchisors do not score well on my preference tests. There are significant blue chip business format franchise opportunities that make very desirable investments (Yes, McDonald's makes the list). On balance, however, I find product franchises, old line as they may be, make the most attractive franchise purchases.

As noted earlier, the line drawn between a business format franchise and a product franchise has become blurred in recent years. Most Chevrolet dealers have as much of an established identity and business format as do any restaurant chain I have ever seen. But a Chevrolet dealer exists as part of the distribution network to sell Chevrolet cars and parts. Historically, car manufacturers depend substantially on their dealership network to market their automobiles.

Car manufacturers exist to sell products (not franchises) and strive to maintain quality and trademark identity. Coincidentally, most automobile franchisees belong to strong local and national franchisee associations that, over time, have gained considerable influence and negotiating leverage with their franchisors. Additionally, there is substantial precedent for auto dealerships to change brands under appropriate circumstances.

While not intending to single out automobile franchises, it has been my experience that my criteria for franchise selection are more often met with product franchises. The elements present in automotive franchises are also found in soft drinks, liquor distributors, beer and wine distributors, petroleum products, and other product driven chains.

Unfortunately, it is the business format franchises that are more heavily marketed and are generally available to the investing public. Good financial opportunities exist, provided the franchisee is willing to give up the freedom and assume the financial, contractual, and legal risks described elsewhere in this book. In selecting a business format franchise, however, pay careful attention to the eight criteria outlined in this chapter. In franchising, be particularly wary of ground-floor opportunities, unless the attendant risks are mollified.

Keep in mind, no matter what the franchise salesperson may tell you about the inability to negotiate your franchise agreement, new franchisors most often *do* negotiate, because they need to make sales. Accommodations can be made, and frequently should be made.

Franchisors who claim not to finance franchise opportunities frequently do finance franchise opportunities. Franchisors have been known to negotiate royalties, to relax restrictions on products and services, and even to modify the difficult termination provisions in their franchise agreements. New franchisors are frequently hungry for sales; they need your dollars and are willing to make a deal.

But if you are in the process of casting your lot with a new unproven franchisor, remember you are a pioneer. You are a marine making an assault on a new beachhead and part of the advance guard. The marines who go into war zones get combat pay; so should you. Otherwise, you may well end up being another franchisee victim.

Chapter **10**

For the Want of
Market Power

This chapter explores franchisees' lack of negotiating power and lack of collective bargaining, which have resulted in completely one-sided and adhesive franchise agreements. The chapter also explores the failure of the American legal system to protect franchisees from abuse. Court decisions have allowed adhesion contracts to be enforced solely because franchisees had the right to refuse to sign them, or to select some other franchise in its place. The chapter begins to explore the civil courts' complete lack of empathy and sympathy for the plight of franchisees.

We Americans are proud of our free market economy. The entire fabric of our economy is based on a free market and freedom of contract. And it is fundamental to a free market economy that contractual commitments are honored and enforced. When contractual obligations can be ignored or avoided, the confidence and willingness of the public to make agreements is lost, and lawlessness and anarchy will be the result.

The success of the U.S. market economy is premised on the equality of bargaining power among citizens. It is assumed in every contract that a willing buyer and a willing seller, each free of duress, will come together in the marketplace and negotiate fair and reasonable contracts. Contracts thus negotiated establish what we call the "fair market value" of American products and services.

At times, however, the presumption of the existence of equality of bargaining strength is false. Frequently, one party has superior bargaining strength over another. One party may have superior knowledge; the other party a critical need. Relative bargaining strength is usually affected by the demand for a particular product and service. Frequently in our history, the U.S. *free* market has been *less* than free. Groups of individuals have often been caught in the attempt to combine efforts to control the marketplace, to fix prices, to control supply and demand, and to divide the market so that competition will not put downward pressure on market values.

In the course of American history, we have frequently recognized the necessity for the government and the court systems to monitor our market system and make sure it is working as intended. Thus, over time the courts and legislature have chipped away at the once sacrosanct market principle of caveat emptor (let the buyer beware) so that in most (but not all) areas of our market society, sellers of goods and services must fully disclose all problems and defects of the goods and services being sold. In essence, sellers may still extol the qualities and virtues of their products and services (the law calls this "salesman puffing"), but we cannot make false claims for the products and services, nor can we misrepresent or conceal material information that would likely affect a purchaser's decision to buy.

At one time, a written contract was enforced irrespective of the harshness of its terms. Today, courts frequently refuse to enforce contracts that are not fairly negotiated. The courts have said that where one party can dictate the terms of a contract to another, and the subservient party had no choice but to accept the terms imposed by the party with superior bargaining power, such contracts will not be enforceable to the extent the contract provisions are unconscionable.

Additionally, Congress and our state legislatures have recognized that certain industries are particularly susceptible to fraud and abuse. Moreover, for public policy reasons, certain classes of individuals are especially deserving of protection with respect to their purchase decisions. Consequently, Congress and all 50 states have passed strong laws requiring that sellers of securities disclose all material information about investment opportunities. These laws have been enacted because of the strong public policy concerns that our citizens be able to save, invest, and protect themselves for their retirement, and protect the American economy in the process.

The legal restraints on freedom of contract and freedom of the market have been enacted in an effort to blunt the tyranny of the marketplace when unequal bargaining strength is involved. In essence, our investor protection laws are intended to make the free market work the way we expect it to.

But our free market is not stagnant. It is a human institution, and therefore it lives. It is the nature of the free market that participants in the marketplace will always vie for superior bargaining position. Those seeking to sell will always seek a higher price, a greater benefit, and more control. Buyers always look for the best bargain. Consequently, market forces constantly evolve.

CYBERNETICS AND THE FREE MARKET

The free market is governed by the principles of *cybernetics*. Cybernetics is an engineering or scientific term that describes the mechanics of maintaining any system at optimum efficiency. For example, the heating system in your home is controlled by a *cybernetic* mechanism, your thermostat. You set your thermostat to a desired room temperature. The thermostat constantly measures the temperature in the room and turns your furnace on when the room is too cold and off when the room is too hot.

The same simple cybernetic process that is employed for managing the temperature in your house is applied conceptually to the management of the U.S. economy. Thus, you constantly see newspaper articles talking about how the Federal Reserve Board is acting to heat up or cool down the economy by controlling the money supply. The government's use of the taxing process and spending programs are also used as devices, albeit unpredictable ones, for turning the economy off and on with the goal of cybernetically maintaining a constant level of sustained and acceptable growth.

The U.S. economy is really no more than a gigantic marketplace driven by the principles of supply and demand. When demand is great, prices go up, supplies tighten, and poorer quality goods and services are more easily sold because of the high demand. Theoretically, higher prices soften demand forcing suppliers to keep price and quality in line. In theory, the effect of supply and demand will, over time, create a market balance of fair prices and acceptable quality.

Sometimes, the market gets out of balance and out of whack. There may be so much demand for a product, or a false perception of the product's value, that normal market forces, which are expected to soften demand, simply don't work. The "go go" 1980s presented such an overheated economy in the home-buying market. Hundreds of thousands of Americans bought homes that were overpriced and realistically out of the buyer's reach. Normal pricing pressures were ineffective to hold unreasonable demand in check because the government made financing unrealistically high prices easy, and made the high price of housing seem affordable. When inevitably the market slowed, homeowners couldn't pay their mortgages. Loan defaults have occurred in massive numbers, creating the savings and loan crisis and scandal of the past few years.

Like a pendulum, market forces swing back and forth in favor of seller and buyer, supplier and user, and in favor of those who have the supply and those who create the demand. Many economists claim the market will always correct itself. Others believe that sometimes the market needs help. In my view, the laws we enact are merely part and parcel of the very market forces that control our economy. A legislative act, therefore, is simply a part of the process by which the market is self-correcting.

The foregoing lesson in macroeconomics is important because it is the fundamental premise of this book that the marketplace in the franchising industry is enormously out of balance. In fact, the imbalance of power between franchisors and franchisees is so staggering that none of the traditional corrective influences have succeeded in achieving a correction in the market.

THE FRANCHISING MARKETPLACE

The franchising marketplace is subjected to traditional market pressures. Fueled by powerful and well-financed franchise marketers, the public has been educated to believe that franchising is worthwhile irrespective of price. Along with owning a home, business ownership has long been part of the American Dream. And the rush to own a business has been almost as impressive as the house-buying explosion of the mid-1980s.

As explained in Chapter 12, franchising is one of the last major industries in which the principles of caveat emptor (let the buyer beware) still prevail. Largely because of strong seller's market, franchise agreements are non-negotiable form agreements offered to prospective franchisees on a take-it-or-leave-it basis. In most instances, such agreements that are dictated by a party in a superior bargaining position are labeled as "contracts of adhesion," and are not enforceable to the extent they have unreasonable provisions. Although some inroads have been made in a few states, generally purchasers of franchises are not identified as a segment of the investing public worthy of special protection, and most franchise agreements are enforced according to their written terms.

In essence, the superiority of bargaining strength residing in franchisors has overwhelmed the ability of a purchaser of a franchise to negotiate a bargain. The bargaining strength of franchisors is so superior, in fact, that some state franchise laws mandate that franchise agreements cannot be negotiated!

Franchisors set the price of franchising and have set the terms in franchise agreements. Moreover, the franchisor's superior economic strength has overwhelmed the meager attempts by franchisee advocates to achieve market corrections through legislatures or the courts.

The degree of the franchisors' control of the marketplace is truly mind-boggling. The nature of that control bears close examination. As with most market aberrations, the problems start with a great idea, product, or service. Franchising works. Create a superior product or service, and smart enterprising businesspeople will want to sell it. Attaching yourself to a rising star makes all the sense in the world. *"Build a better mousetrap and the world will beat a path to your door,"* so the saying goes.

The premise of buying a business that somebody else has proven can work and operating under a trademark with an established and proven market makes good logical and economic sense. The fact that there is a strong market for the purchase of franchises in the United States is good and expected.

Nevertheless, the market should set the price and terms of franchise agreements. When the market is working properly, one franchisor will offer a better deal and more favorable terms, and prospective franchisees will gravitate in that direction. Such would be the expected result absent some collusion on the part of franchisors to hold the line on prices, on contract terms, and on competition.

THE AMERICAN LEGAL APPROACH TO BALANCING THE MARKET: ANTITRUST LAWS

The American response to collusion in the marketplace has been the enactment over many years of a broad spectrum of laws to promote competition and outlaw restraints on competition. We call these laws antitrust laws because they were aimed at breaking up the industrial trusts and cartels that inhibited the marketplace at the turn of this century in such important commodities as oil, steel, railroads, and automobiles (and more recently, telephone service).

Without going into a detailed explanation of American antitrust laws, it is important to note that our laws recognize two fundamental rules with respect to anticompetitive forces and activities:

1. Some activities and contrivances are considered to be per se undesirable and illegal. Consequently, most kinds of price fixing are outlawed, as are attempts for several competitors to get together and divide up a market (so-called horizontal restraints).

2. On the other hand, not all anticompetitive conduct is considered to be bad. Some activities and conduct limiting competition may have very good reasons and positive benefits. For example, a company's right to protect its trade secrets and its patents is very important to the encouragement of research and development efforts, and is directly embodied in the American entrepreneurial spirit. However, a powerful patent for a computer chip or a superior computer disk operating system can have substantial anticompetitive influences. Such anticompetitive forces with positive benefits to our society must be judged by a different rule that our courts have called "the rule of reason." By the rule of reason, a court must balance the positive purposes of an activity against its anticompetitive aspects and fashion rules and compromises that are acceptable in our society.

Unfortunately for those who would balance the scales in the franchising industry, many if not most of the anticompetitive influences that impair the franchising industry involve franchisor conduct that can be well justified under the rule of reason. In particular, the franchisor's strong right to protect the integrity and quality of a trademark and trade name has been deemed sufficiently important to outweigh most anticompetitive consequences of the franchisor's exercise of its protective powers. And for reasons that will be discussed, the courts and legislatures have shown anemic ability to achieve compromises respecting the interests of both franchisors and franchisees.

THE LEGAL SYSTEM AND THE MARKETPLACE

Without getting into a theological debate, in franchising, at the very least, money has been the root of all evil. And as much as I hate to admit it, the focus of much of franchisors' money has been on lawyers, and those able to afford them and pay them. Although I hope I am not writing my own epitaph, if Shakespeare's prescription were carried out, "The first thing we do, let's kill all the lawyers,"[1] the imbalance in the franchising industry might well disappear overnight.

The vast majority of franchising's brightest legal minds (present company excluded, of course!) work for franchisors. Franchisors have the money to hire the franchise specialists, and have the money to lobby for franchising laws.

The franchisors' market power translates into legal power and legislative power as well. The American Bar Association has a special study section called the Forum on Franchising. This study section includes several thousand members, all of whom consider themselves to be specialists in franchise law. Within the Forum on Franchising, there is an informal (and unofficial) subgroup of attorneys who represent the interests of franchisees. We have a mailing list of only 35 lawyers all told, who have expressed an interest in participating in a *franchisee counsel* committee. While I don't claim this information constitutes a scientific sampling of whom franchise attorneys represent, it appears fairly obvious that most franchise attorneys work for franchisors and not for franchisees.

It doesn't take a study to understand why the bulk of franchise attorneys represent the interests of franchisors. Most franchisees are independent private businesspeople, whose need of an attorney is infrequent and whose legal questions cross a broad range of subjects. On the other hand, a franchisor's business is so concentrated on the legal aspects of franchising that expert legal counsel on the subject is an everyday occurrence.

Whatever the reason, most of the attorneys who draft franchise agreements, or write articles about franchising, or participate in the legislative process to draft franchising laws, see the industry from the franchisor's perspective. And do these expert franchising minds share information? You bet. The Forum on Franchising holds a well-presented annual conference that tracks the trends of franchising law. This conference does not intend to be collusive, but it is an explicit opportunity for franchise counsel to compare notes on what's hot and what's not.

The International Franchise Association also holds an annual conference on franchise law. The IFA Conference hosts many of the same attorneys who attend the ABA Annual Forum program, but it is more blatantly profranchisor.

More important than that franchise counsel can hone their skills through networking and conferencing is that franchisors simply put substantial legal resources into drafting and defending their contracts.

Again no statistics are available, and I must draw on personal experience. Rarely do I represent clients who can afford justice (legal fees) as compared with the franchisors they take on. For every client who retains me, several others who seek my advice go elsewhere (or nowhere) simply because they cannot afford the price of our legal system's brand of justice. More about our legal system in the next two chapters.

The important thing here is that the franchisor's economic ability to afford the better lawyers gives franchisors an advantage in the legal system that pays huge dividends in the marketplace. U.S. courts have uniformly held that franchisors have no fiduciary obligations to their franchisees, even though the conventional wisdom (indeed, the industry's promise) holds that the franchisor-franchisee relationship is a fiduciary one.

Perhaps even more shocking, most law courts have held that franchise agreements are not adhesion contracts for the simple reason the franchisee had the choice "to sign" or "not to sign." By denying franchisees protection under two of our legal system's major doctrines of investor and consumer protection, franchising remains the only significant consumer industry where caveat emptor—in this instance, "let the franchisee beware"—still is the law of the land.

LEGISLATIVE ANEMIA

Usually, when the law courts fail to effect a market correction, the legislatures will fill the void. Such was the case when the courts were unable to curb the monopolistic business activities at the turn of the century. Congress and most of the states passed important antitrust laws giving the courts important powers to force market adjustments.

Here again, the franchisee's pathetic lack of market power has translated into an anemic legislative effort to provide franchisee protection. In 1971, the state of California passed its Franchise Investment Act. This was the first law that required franchisors to disclose material information to prospective franchisees. Since 1973, only 14 other states have followed suit. Congress has never passed a franchise disclosure act. Indeed, not until 1992 was a franchise disclosure act even introduced in Congress. Part of the reason Congress has not acted, however, is that the Federal Trade Commission promulgated a rule in 1979 requiring franchisors to provide a prospectus or offering circular to all prospective franchisees. The federal rule on franchising has been perceived by many members of Congress as satisfying the need for franchise regulation.

A few states, but not Congress, have passed so-called franchise fairness laws. For the most part, franchise fairness laws deal with franchisees' rights on termination of a franchise agreement. Most states do have antifraud protections built into their laws curbing unfair business practices. Franchisees have received some protection from these statutes, which are commonly referred to as Little FTC Acts, because the statutes have been modeled after the federal Fair Trade Commission Act.

A cursory review of legislation to protect franchisees shows an anemic record. Closer inspection, however, reveals the legislative response has been abysmal. Leaving the specifics to the next chapter, suffice it to say that the legislative efforts of franchise regulation have done more to protect and insulate franchisors than to deter franchise fraud and abuse.

Why have we suffered such an anemic legislative response to the problems in franchising? The answer is simple and cumulative: Money. Franchisors' money and market power have catapulted franchisors to become a major influencing factor in state legislatures and in Congress.

According to the magazine *Restaurant News,* at the IFA Convention in February, 1988, 900 cheering franchisors were addressed by the Association President, William Cherkasky:

> Cherkasky extolled what he called a 1000% batting average "in decimating numerous anti-franchising measures in 1987." Another IFA official reported that 27 restrictive legislative measures were introduced in 20 states last year, "and our government relations staff prevented any of them from being enacted."[2]

If anything, the IFA has been a magnificent lobbyist for pro-franchisor causes. Part of the reason is that the IFA has presented exceptional advocates. Another part of the reason is that the IFA had no competition from the franchisee side of the issues.

The story is told that the IFA was created in a restaurant in Washington, D.C., when the chief executives of a handful of powerful franchisors started throwing money on the dinner table to fund the operating budget for the fledgling organization. However its beginnings, the IFA has grown to be an organization with a $6 million annual budget. The IFA claims representation of several hundred of the nation's premier franchisors.

The IFA's business is to market the franchising industry; to monitor its trends; and to educate its members, their legal counsel, and the legislatures. The IFA has been the mouthpiece of the franchising industry. Indeed, until only recently, the IFA has been the only source of franchising data.

Chapter 4 detailed the Department of Commerce study on franchising. Officially, the study was conducted under the auspices of the Department of Commerce, but many believe it was orchestrated by and for the IFA. As previously noted, the study has been the source of the statistics that claim that only 5 percent of all franchises fail within five years of business. The statistic, though disbelieved by most franchising commentators, is still widely used by the press in extolling the virtues of the franchising industry.

When the Department of Commerce gave up keeping records on the franchising industry in 1986–1987, the IFA took over the responsibility publicly. The good news is that IFA data must now be presented under the IFA letterhead rather than as an official report of a department of the U.S. government.

Quite simply, the IFA has had dramatic legislative clout, has had a sympathetic ear from the Department of Commerce, and has cooperated with and courted the Small Business Administration in its efforts to promote minority businesses. This is not, however, an indictment of IFA activities. I applaud them. The IFA has a right to do what it does, and it does its job very well.

The franchisors' constitutional right to petition, to lobby, to influence legislation, to have all the due process it can afford through the courts is not the issue. The issue is that the IFA's ability to accomplish all these things is indicative of its power in the marketplace. The franchisor's power is absolute, and the industry has been corrupted absolutely.

By its strong legislative influence, the IFA has managed to drastically affect the legislative process. Primarily, IFA-influenced franchise legislation has centered on the enactment of statutes that require franchisors to disclose material information to prospective franchisees.

California's initial franchise law was a registration and disclosure statute. It puts most franchisors to the expense of an annual registration with the state of California and requires that franchisors provide audited financial statements in order to sell franchises in the state. The process of registration and of auditing financial statements is expensive. The IFA's tactic has been to applaud the requirement of disclosure, but to resist the requirement of registration and audited financial statements. Of the 15 states that have passed disclosure laws, only 2 require registration. The remaining have a disclosure requirement that is no more powerful than the Federal Trade Commission rule which is applicable throughout the United States.

It is important to understand that disclosure statutes serve as insurance policies for franchisors. Disclosure laws specifically detail what information must be disclosed (and frequently it is not the most pertinent information). If the franchisor discloses all that the law requires, it is insulated from claims of fraud. Consequently, a franchisor can blatantly conceal material information not required in the disclosure statement and be insulated from any punishment or civil liability because the franchisor has complied with the statutory requirements. What seemed like a victory for the franchisee, in reality, benefits the franchisors.

Even the California statute, which is touted as one of the strongest, has major benefits for franchisors. Most importantly, the California Department of Corporations has historically construed the California law as denying franchisors the ability to negotiate franchise agreements once they have been registered. Until recently, the California Department of Corporations required that any changes in a franchise agreement must be set forth in an amendment to the registration statement. Anytime a franchisor wishes to negotiate a contract, theoretically, the franchisor must "go public" with the negotiated change and even amend the registration statement. Recently, the state has backed off from this difficult posture and has produced new regulations allowing franchisors to negotiate changes. Still there is substantial procedural red tape if you want to negotiate a franchise agreement in California.

Personally, I have never understood the California rule. The statute says the franchisor must register any offer or sale of a franchise. Once the offer is made, it should always be subject to negotiation. However, you won't hear franchisors arguing about the rule. Hiding behind it, yes; arguing against it, never. Why? Quite simple. Under California's rule (and the rule has been adopted in other states as well), franchisors can truthfully claim they are not allowed to negotiate franchise agreements. The franchise agreement is a take-it-or-leave-it proposition—so mandated by statute and the rules of the state. Consequently, if the franchise agreement is an adhesion contract, it is only so because of governmental mandate!

There should be little surprise, therefore, that whenever new franchisee protection legislation is proposed, the IFA shows up and says more disclosure, more disclosure, more disclosure. Don't misunderstand me, I am in favor of disclosure—provided the disclosure includes all the material information a franchisee needs to make an intelligent investment decision; and provided the franchisee is given a private right of action to redress any claims of false disclosure; and provided the franchisee is given access to litigate claims in the courts of his or her home state where justice is accessible and most affordable.

Just how does the franchisor's power in the marketplace translate to power in the state legislature? The simple answer is "access." Dollars hire lobbyists and legislative educators who provide information and legislative assistance as well as other favors to legislators. The IFA is ever active; whereas franchisees, who are not well organized or endowed, are not. But there is a greater, more pervasive franchisor weapon: the power of industry, and the power to remove it from a state's borders.

I was recently contacted by a legislative analyst from the state of Kentucky who was doing a study for the state legislature regarding abuses in the franchising industry. At first, I was excited about a potential new franchise fairness bill. Unfortunately, on further inquiry, I discovered a telling example of the franchisor's market power in the legislative context.

It seems that the state legislature had conducted hearings on the problems in franchising, and those hearings had led to proposed legislation. It also seems that certain important Kentucky franchisors, including Kentucky Fried Chicken, didn't like the proposed legislation. The suggestion was made that enactment would lead to the expatriation of the industry from the state. Not surprisingly, the Kentucky state legislature tabled the legislation and referred the matter for further study. In essence, the legislative research and analysis was no more than a legislative "dog and pony show" designed to allow the legislation to die a quiet death.

THE CHALLENGE TO ACHIEVE
A BALANCED MARKET

And now comes the tragedy. The IFA's $6 million budget emanates from approximately 600 franchisors. Although funding comes from many sources, including publications, conferences, associate members, and other business activities, each franchisor member represents about $10,000 per year for the Association's budget.

As will be discussed in more detail in Chapter 14, there are approximately 500,000 franchise businesses in the United States, and perhaps an equal number of independent distributors whose businesses are very similar to franchises. The arithmetic is not too difficult to work out. Each franchise business would have to put up a paltry $6 per year, or 50 cents a month, to match the operating budget of the IFA. Indeed, if only 10 percent of the franchise businesses in the United States plunk down $120 per year per unit, franchisees would double the annual budget of the IFA.

The simple truth is that market power in the franchising industry is available for the taking. Franchisees merely need to organize and coordinate, and be willing to step to the line.

Many think the shift of the pendulum is already at hand. In the past 10 years, the number of franchisee associations for particular franchise systems has probably increased more than tenfold. Many of these associations spend the bulk of their time focusing on internal issues. More and more, however, franchisees are beginning to recognize there is strength in their numbers, and that franchisees can yet have the ultimate victory in the marketplace.

Chapter 11

Whom Do the Laws
Protect Anyway?

*Numerous statutes that purportedly regulate the franchising industry give investors a
false sense of security and protection. In truth, most states have no laws regulating franchising, and the statutes that do exist, for the most part, have been greatly influenced
by special interests representing franchisors.*

A recurring theme of this book is that The Franchise Fraud is a "systemic
fraud." It is the misrepresentation by an entire industry that franchising is a
safe and secure means to achieve the American Dream of business ownership.
The notion of franchising as a relatively safe method of owning a business has
become a fundamental part of the American conventional wisdom, and this
notion has been fanned by a comforting impression that franchisees are protected by a fabric of state and federal laws.

Representations that investors are protected by a uniform system of government regulation are false on several counts. Initially, there is no federal
law protecting franchisees generally.[1] At the state level, only 15 states have
passed laws regulating the offer and sale of franchises. More importantly,
only 16 states have laws regulating the franchise relationship. Of these, with
the exception of one state (Iowa), the so-called "Franchise Relationship
Laws" affect only the circumstances under which a franchisor may *terminate*
the relationship.

In 1992, Iowa passed the Iowa Fair Franchising Practices Act, the country's first effort to legislate "across the board" franchisee protection.

It is apparent the conventional wisdom that franchising is a regulated industry is simply not true. More importantly, the laws on the books have frequently served to provide more protection for franchisors than franchisees. Franchise disclosure laws, for example, are generally condoned by the franchisor community, and have long been used by franchisors as a means of insulating themselves against charges of fraud. Franchise relationship (termination) statutes, likewise, have effectively created safe harbor standards that guide (and even protect) a franchisor's right to invoke a franchise termination.

The plain truth is the franchise industry is not effectively regulated, and the existing regulations frequently protect franchisors more than franchisees. Additionally, as will be examined more closely in Chapter 13, to the extent franchisees have the ability to seek protection under existing state law, most franchisees lack the economic resources to obtain protection through the courts.

The failure of Congress and the state legislatures to provide effective franchise regulation is but another manifestation of the superiority of franchisors in the franchising marketplace. Like it or not, ours is a government of special interests and a government motivated by the strength of public opinion. Thus far, franchisors have been able to mold public opinion and have provided the only voice of franchising before Congress and the state legislatures. Franchisors have effectively controlled the contours of American franchise legislation.

THE FEDERAL GOVERNMENT'S IGNORANCE OF THE FRANCHISING INDUSTRY

As pervasive and invasive as our federal government has become, until recently Congress and the executive branch of government have comparatively ignored the franchising industry. As already noted, there is no existing federal franchising law. Until 1991, Congress had not even discussed the subject for many years. About 25 years ago, Congressman Abner Mikva introduced legislation to regulate the industry. Congressman Mikva's franchise fairness bill died in committee and never made it to the floor of Congress.

In 1990, Congressman John LaFalce (Democrat, N.Y.), Chairman of the House Committee on Small Business, decided to take a close look at the franchising industry. LaFalce hired a new staff member who was a specialist in franchising, Mr. Dean Sagar. Providentially for those who would like to see a congressional effort to protect the interests of franchisees, Mr. Sagar came to his position with substantial understanding of the undercurrents of serious problems within the franchising industry. Sagar was able to interest Congressman John LaFalce, the Chairman of the House Committee on Small Business, in the problems of the industry.

LaFalce directed Sagar to research the trends in the franchising industry, and to prepare a thorough report for the benefit of the Committee. The result was the report *Franchising in the U.S. Economy* published by the House Committee on Small Business in August 1990. This well-regarded report was the first *critical* examination of the franchising industry ever undertaken by any office or department of the United States government.[2]

Following the publication of *Franchising in the U.S. Economy,* Congressman LaFalce conducted several hearings on franchising designed to identify problem areas that federal legislation could help correct. Staff member Sagar was directed, in particular, to bring forth witnesses who understood franchising from the franchisee's perspective. Heretofore, franchising had only been seen and heard through the eyes and mouthpieces of franchisors.

As a result of what have become known as the LaFalce Hearings, in 1991, Congressman LaFalce introduced two separate pieces of legislation, H.R. 5232, proposing the "Federal Franchise Disclosure and Consumer Protection Act" and H.R. 5232, introducing the "Federal Fair Franchise Practices Act." These two important legislative proposals mark the first serious effort on the part of Congress to address the problems of the franchising industry, and to attack many of the abuses discussed in this book. Neither LaFalce bill was taken up for consideration during the 102nd Congress. However, the bills, in a slightly amended form, were reintroduced in the 103rd Congress in 1993.

The legislative process is cumbersome. Rarely is legislation maneuvered into law unless it is pushed by a terrific impetus of public opinion, the power of special interests, or the President's personal legislative program. In that the new Clinton Administration never once mentioned franchising in the 1992 presidential campaign, the only hope that Congress will seriously consider major franchising legislation is if franchisees are able to coalesce into special interest groups or motivate public opinion to bring the issue of franchising into government's limelight.

EARLY FRANCHISE LEGISLATION EFFORTS

In the 1950s, automobile dealership associations were able to develop suffi-cient political strength to achieve the enactment of an automobile dealership protection law, both at the federal level and in many states. At the federal level, Congress passed a fairly weak statute that essentially prohibited an automobile manufacturer from terminating a dealer without good cause, and without the dealer having an opportunity to be heard in his or her defense. Commonly known as the "Automobile Dealer's Day in Court Act," this first-ever federal franchising law was not as strong as laws passed in the various states and has not provided significant protection for automobile dealerships.

In 1978, Congress passed the "Petroleum Marketing Practices Act." Once again, the major thrust of the legislation was to prevent petroleum manufac-turers from unfair franchise terminations. Commonly referred to as the "PMPA," the new law prohibited petroleum manufacturers from terminating a franchisee without good cause. The PMPA was the first, and perhaps only, congressional legislation to have a meaningful impact on the franchising in-dustry. However, over time, petroleum manufacturers have found loopholes in the law and have created mechanisms to avoid the PMPA's protections for in-dependent petroleum dealers.

From the perspective of franchisee protection, the most important lesson from the enactment of both the Automotive Dealer's Day in Court Act and the PMPA is the recognition of the political forces necessary to achieve a new law. In each instance, franchisees effectively generated significant political influ-ence through strong and well-organized franchisee associations.

In the 1950s, the National Automobile Dealers Association, with the support of many local and trademark-specific dealer associations, brought significant political influence to bear in lobbying the enactment of a dealer protection law. Similarly, in the early 1970s, the Petroleum Dealer's Asso-ciation amassed substantial political strength to achieve strong protective legislation.

To date, no generic franchisee legislation has emerged. There can be lit-tle dispute that the lack of legislation can be traced directly to the lack of a national organization representing the interests of franchisees generally. The lessons of history tell us that a meaningful franchise protection bill will not become law until franchisees are well enough organized to engineer a successful legislative campaign.

THE FEDERAL TRADE COMMISSION TO THE RESCUE

In the absence of Congress acting to provide legislative protection for franchisees, the executive branch of government has attempted to provide a modicum of regulation.

In 1971, following a public outcry over a rash of franchising horror stories in California, the California state legislature responded to widespread claims of franchise fraud by enacting the California Franchise Investment Act. About the same time, the Federal Trade Commission announced its intent to adopt regulations pursuant to the Commission's rule-making authority under the Federal Trade Act.[3] Although the Federal Trade Act was not established with franchising in mind, the Federal Trade Commission's authority under the act is broad enough to cover most kinds of fraudulent business practices. Therefore the act gave the FTC the ability to create franchising regulations even in the absence of specific law.

After eight years of public hearings and comment, which generated more than 30,000 pages of testimony and documented more than 5,000 consumer complaints about the franchising industry, the Federal Trade Commission finally promulgated the FTC Rule on Franchising in October 1979.

The FTC Rule on Franchising required all franchisors to provide a disclosure document to prospective franchisees and further required that franchisors disclose all material information that a prospective franchisee would reasonably rely on in making a franchise purchase decision.

The good news was that the FTC rule, for the first and only time, created a uniform minimum standard of franchise disclosure applicable to all franchise sales throughout the United States. Without the FTC rule, in 35 states there would be no franchise sale protection whatsoever.

The bad news was that the FTC, as a practical matter, had wholly insufficient resources to monitor franchisor compliance or enforce the rule against violators. More importantly, the Federal Trade Act does not provide a right to individual citizens to bring private lawsuits if they are damaged by violations of the rule. Despite the FTC's best intentions, the FTC rule is, at best, a law without substantial enforcement.

The FTC rule has been a very mixed blessing. On the one hand, most franchising companies attempt to comply with the rule by providing required disclosure to prospective franchisees. Assuming the disclosures made by franchisors are relevant, the FTC Act has made it possible for franchisees to investigate franchise opportunities before they buy. And when I say *assuming the disclosures are relevant,* the value of current franchise disclosure is an issue of considerable debate.

On the other hand, with wholly inadequate resources to properly enforce the FTC rule, prospective franchisees are given a grossly inaccurate illusion that federal law has created a veil of protection within the franchising industry. The illusion of federal protection has encouraged many thousands of would-be business owners to buy franchises, more often than not without even seeking outside professional advice and counsel.

I certainly am not claiming there was any intent by federal regulators to foster franchise fraud and abuse. However, notwithstanding the FTC's best intentions to provide a modicum of protection, the unintended effect of the FTC rule may have been to perpetuate The Franchise Fraud by giving an erroneous impression and delusion that the franchising industry was regulated by the federal government. Franchisors who comply with the FTC rule by making required written disclosures may be insulated from liability for oral fraudulent conduct of franchise salespeople who overzealously oversell their franchise systems.

STATE LAW REGULATIONS: THE 30 PERCENT SOLUTION

State legislatures have done a better job than the federal government in regulating the franchising industry, *but not much*. In fact, only one state, Iowa, has enacted a true franchisee protection law, the Iowa Fair Franchising Practices Act of *1992!*[4] Since 1971, when California was the first state to pass a franchise investment law, only 15 other states have followed suit. Thus only 30 percent of the country's state legislatures have made an attempt to curb franchise fraud and abuse.

Three broad categories of laws affecting franchising have been enacted at the state level:

1. Franchise registration and disclosure acts.
2. So-called franchise relationship acts.
3. Little FTC Acts.

With the introduction of the Iowa Franchise Relationship Act, a fourth very important category has been created, fair franchising practices acts. The Iowa legislation served as a model for the Federal Fair Franchising Practices Act introduced by Congressman LaFalce in 1992. Other states are currently investigating the Iowa law.[5]

State Franchise Disclosure Statutes

The first statute enacted in the United States to regulate franchising generally was the California Franchise Investment Law, adopted in 1970 and effective on January 1, 1971. The statute was aimed at preventing fraud in connection with the offer and sale of franchises within the state of California.

Under the statute, any franchisor desiring to sell a franchise in California is required to give prospective franchisees full disclosure of all material facts concerning the franchise, including an offering circular that requires the disclosure of 21 specific items set forth in the statute. Additionally, companies that do not have an established record in franchising are required to register with the California Department of Corporations before they are authorized to sell franchises in the state. Large established franchisors are exempted from the registration requirements of the statute, but must still provide material disclosure.

The California statute set a precedent for the Federal Trade Commission franchising rule and several other state statutes that have subsequently become law. However, only 14 states (plus the District of Columbia) have followed

California's lead to enact some form of franchise disclosure act. The following states have enacted franchise disclosure statutes:

California	Rhode Island	Indiana
Michigan	South Dakota	Virginia
New York	Illinois	Hawaii
North Dakota	Wisconsin	Washington
Oregon	Minnesota	Maryland

Although the purpose of franchise disclosure laws is to protect investors, the strength of the franchisor special interest lobby (the IFA) has rendered these statutes a mixed blessing.

Indeed, although the franchising industry initially fought the passage of registration and disclosure laws, the industry has discovered these laws create an impression of investor protection while insulating franchisors from substantial liability.

Twenty years after the enactment of the California statute, the franchising industry now sees disclosure as *the panacea* for all of franchising's ills. Whatever problem is raised by franchisee advocates, the industry comes forward to suggest greater disclosure. For example, when franchisee advocates complain a franchisee's ownership rights in his or her business have been eroded through decades of inferior bargaining power for franchisees, the franchising industry merely suggests that the franchisee's eroded equity should be disclosed in uniform franchise offering circulars.

The problem with disclosure statutes is that they allow the franchisor to set forth the details of the franchise opportunity, including details that are unfavorable to the prospective franchisee, and therefore escape any responsibility for any injustice created in the franchise contract. Once a franchisor has made disclosure and the franchisee has received disclosure, the franchisor has met its obligations, no matter how unfair the franchisee relationship. It also doesn't matter whether or not the franchisee has read the disclosure statement, understood it, or sought experienced legal advice who has explained it. Since "full disclosure" is contained in the fine print of the offering circular, the franchisor cannot be charged with fraud.

More importantly, because any *unconscionable provisions* in the franchise agreement have been disclosed by law, the franchisee can no longer reject the unconscionable portions of the contract as a mandated form contract that was not truly "agreed to" by the franchisee. As will be seen in Chapter 12, generally the law allows one-sided contracts (called "adhesion contracts") to be avoided to the extent the provisions of such contracts are unconscionable and not understood by the party disadvantaged by the unsavory contract provisions. However, a key element to an adhesion contract is a lack of knowledge. This element is missing once a franchisor has complied with required FTC disclosure.

After 20 years of franchise disclosure laws, it appears franchisors reap more protection than franchisees. Moreover, several states have ruled that a franchisor may not negotiate changes in a franchise agreement once it has been registered with the state without amending the registration application. Consequently, many franchisors utilize state registration laws as an excuse for refusing to negotiate franchise agreement terms, thus placing franchisees in a truly *take-it-or-leave-it* position.

As was seen with the Federal Trade Commission Rule on Franchising, state franchise disclosure statutes actually contribute to The Franchise Fraud. While these statutes insulate and protect franchisors, they are perceived by the public as evidence of investor protection and give rise to the public's sense of security in making franchise investments.

Franchise Relationship Acts

In addition to franchise registration and disclosure statutes, some 16 states, plus the District of Columbia, Puerto Rico, and the Virgin Islands have passed statutes called "franchise relationship acts." These statutes generally limit a franchisor's powers with respect to termination and renewal of franchise agreements. Chapters 7 and 8 dealt extensively with problems frequently encountered on termination of a franchise. The purpose of franchise relationship laws is to ensure that terminations only occur with due process and for reasonable cause. For the most part, however, franchise relationship acts are seen by franchisee advocates as *validating* the franchisor's ability to terminate. Many states, including California, allow the franchise agreement to override the provisions of the franchise relationship statute.

Business Opportunities Laws and Little FTC Statutes

Most states have enacted business opportunities statutes and other laws intended to prevent a whole variety of fraudulent and unfair business practices. These laws are frequently called "little FTC acts" because they are, generally, patterned after the Federal Trade Act. Business opportunities laws and little FTC acts are not technically franchising laws. For the most part, these statutes were enacted for the purpose of consumer protection. However, they have been effectively utilized as a deterrent and punishment for franchise fraud. Indeed, many states have not enacted specific franchise legislation, because they have relied on their business opportunities laws and little FTC acts to protect against fraud and abuse.

The Need for Franchise Fairness Statutes

Franchise Disclosure Acts, business opportunities laws, and little FTC acts can all be effective deterrents against flagrant fraud. Unfortunately, none of these statutes really deal with the many unique core problems in franchising. Moreover, none of these laws deal with the fairness of the relationship between franchisors and franchisees.

As of this writing, only Iowa had passed a comprehensive statute attempting to regulate many of the unfair franchising practices discussed in this book. The Iowa statute has established a limited fiduciary duty between franchisor and franchisee, prohibits franchise termination or nonrenewal without the payment of fair compensation for the franchise enterprise, limits the ability of the franchisor to encroach on a franchisee's territory without just cause, and provides other areas of franchisee protection.

Not surprisingly, the Iowa statute came into existence due to the efforts of the Iowa Franchisee Association. Once again, it took the efforts of an organized franchisee population, making known their special interests to achieve passage of a major piece of franchise protective legislation. Thus, the message is becoming clearer and clearer: Franchisees must organize to provide a united voice demanding legislative protection at both the state and federal levels.

WHAT IT WILL TAKE TO GET A STRONG FEDERAL FRANCHISE LAW

As previously discussed, in June 1992, Congressman John LaFalce of New York introduced two major franchising bills into the 102nd Congress, the Federal Franchise Disclosure and Consumer Protection Act and the Federal Fair Franchising Practices Act. If passed as introduced, these two pieces of legislation would constitute a significant swing of the pendulum back toward franchise fairness.

The Federal Franchise Disclosure Act is an attempt to provide a true federal *law* to replace the Federal Trade Commission rule. The proposed legislation seeks to incorporate most of the successful provisions of existing franchise disclosure rules. More importantly, the law seeks to enforce relevant and meaningful franchise disclosure, and to make sure that prospective franchisees are truly protected by the disclosure law.

Most importantly, the proposed legislation provides a private right of action that allows individual citizens to enforce the proposed law's provisions. The proposed disclosure law would provide a dramatic improvement for prospective franchisees in the 35 states where no private right of action now exists.

Although the proposed Federal Disclosure Act is a dramatic improvement over the disclosure laws existing today, disclosure statutes generally do nothing to solve the most important problem in franchising—the unjust nature of the franchise relationship. As previously documented, disclosure statutes have been effectively utilized by franchisors as a protective screen or mechanism to limit their liability, rather than improve the quantity, quality, and delivery of promised performance to franchisees.

Many franchise advisors and commentators compare franchise disclosure statutes to the blue sky laws applicable to the securities industry. However, many blue sky laws establish minimum standards of quality in a security to be sold before disclosure ever becomes an issue. For example, the state of California requires that any proposed sale of securities must meet a minimum test for being "fair, just, and equitable" for prospective purchasers of the security. No such tests are applicable in the franchising arena.

If you accept the premise that many prospective franchisees are mom-and-pop investors who lack the requisite experience to determine the fairness of a proposed franchise opportunity, then it stands to reason there should be guidelines and minimum standards of what constitutes a reasonable franchise opportunity.

From the perspective of franchisee protection, the Federal Fair Franchising Practices Act should give existing and prospective franchisees cause for enormous excitement. This proposed law establishes standards and duties of performance on the part of franchisors. The law creates a limited fiduciary duty owed by franchisors to franchisees. The law would expand the franchisor's duties of good faith and impose a standard of care that should be applicable in all franchise agreements.

Most importantly, the proposed law recognizes the enormous difference in economic strengths in most franchisor-franchisee relationships. Accordingly, the law grants franchisees the right to resolve disputes in the franchisee's jurisdiction (where the franchisor has chosen to do business). Additionally, the law does not permit franchise agreements to dictate dispute resolution procedures that may limit important procedural rights available to franchisees under their local laws.

As enamored as I am with the proposed legislation by Congressman LaFalce, I am coldly aware that the introduction of legislation does not create a law. Without substantial grassroots support of the franchisee community, neither of these proposed laws will ever make it to the floor of Congress, let alone the desk of the President.

As has been documented in this effort, franchise fraud and abuse is a virtually unrecognized problem in this country. Franchisees have long been aware of their lack of genuine bargaining power and of their inability to protect themselves from abusive franchise relationships. But until franchisees muster public opinion and push their message into the halls of Congress, protective legislation has no chance of becoming law.

Once again, franchisees must recognize their enormous need for increased market power and bargaining strength. More importantly, franchisees must recognize their enormous collective potential to achieve such power. As with all crusades and battles for independence, franchisees must sacrifice to achieve their goals. But as will be seen in the following chapters, the potential for franchisees to level the playing field and achieve a true balance of negotiating power with franchisors is a readily obtainable goal.

Chapter 12

A New Perspective on Blind Justice

This chapter looks at the failure of the U.S. legal system to protect franchisees and explores the growth of legal precedents in the United States that have protected franchisors more than franchisees. The chapter explains why and how a legal and political system can be controlled by an industry that has substantial market power over franchisees.

We have this picture of the Goddess of Justice, blindfolded and ignorant of favoritism, and holding high the Scales of Justice to fairly weigh the evidence and decide the truth without bias.

It is an idyllic picture of hope and faith, and of confidence in the American system of justice. In fact, it is this very picture that led me to a career in law, as a way of fulfilling my dreams about pursuing the cause of truth and justice.

Unfortunately, in my more than 20 years in the practice of law, I have developed a new perspective on Blind Justice. I still see justice as blind. But the blindfolds no longer represent the lack of bias. Rather the presence of it.

I have often heard it said that each of us carries our own special baggage—our own special biases and prejudices, standards, and ethics. I believe this is true of every judge and juror, of every client and advocate. And I believe we are each *blinded* by our personal baggage. This is a blindness that our system of justice must accept.

Our legal system is a human institution, and God willing, it will always be so. For this reason, attorneys worry about the candor and appearance of their clients, the draw of the judge who hears their cases, and the makeup of the juries or arbitrators who determine the facts that will apply to each case in dispute. These are parts of justice I can accept and live with, though often I find the humanness of the system most frustrating.

But there is a more exasperating aspect to our system of justice that causes me grave concern, even despair. For the most part, our courts lack the time to determine studiously the merits of the cases before them. The caseloads are simply too large. In these circumstances, the courts lean heavily on the attorneys who appear before them to ease the court's case burden. Too often, the thoroughness of case preparation wins out over truth and justice.

In Chapter 11, we examined the influence of market power on our legal and legislative systems of government. In this chapter, we continue the investigation, with a closer examination of the laws that have been developed by case authority through the influence of extraordinary market power.

In the law, we give much credence to weight. We talk about the "weight" of the evidence tilting the scales of justice in favor of one side or the other. We talk about the "weight" of authority as establishing the general rule of law versus contrary decisions of opposing points. And an instruction commonly given to jurors says that the trier of fact is to give more "weight" to the quality of evidence than to the accumulation of evidence. Evidence is to be "weighed" for its probative value, and not because one side presents more facts than the other.

Notwithstanding legal theory, extensive case preparation and cunning frequently overcome truth and just results. Cynics have restated the Golden Rule as "He who has the gold, makes the rules." This statement frequently rings true of our legal system.

Our courts are overcrowded. In San Diego, each of our more than 40 superior court judges has a case load of 300 to 500 cases at any given time. The ability to stop long enough to dispense careful justice is more the exception than the rule.

As frustrated as most clients are with lawyers (hopefully, most frustration is really at the legal system and not the individuals who practice within it), clients would feel even greater irritation if they recognized that the 10 to 20 hours their attorney spent researching and carefully drafting a probative brief supporting their claim would receive a 1-hour reading by a research attorney and a 10-minute briefing with the judge.

I have sat in law and motion courts and watched 40 cases being called out and decided in a 2-hour period. I feel for the judge and staff, who must deal with 30 to 40 different disputes every day. I feel worse for the attorneys who have toiled long hours for 10 to 20 minutes of legal review. But I especially feel for the clients who look to our law courts for a *thorough* dispensing of justice. We are all shortchanged by a court system so taxed that it can do no better.

In the environment of a court system swollen with disputes, it is to be expected that our judges will find solace in lawyers who appear before them better prepared and more thorough. How difficult it must be to wade through a never-ending litany of documents that say "I am right and he is wrong" and somehow come up with the truth. It is therefore not surprising that confident and authoritative legal counsel can often win the respect and attention of an overwhelmed judge.

Before I apply all this information to the franchising industry, as is my purpose, I will digress just a moment longer, to suggest a better way. I part company with those who believe our adversarial system of civil justice, with its greater emphasis on winning than on finding the truth, is the best system of justice yet devised. From my perspective, this is a smug and inaccurate notion. I personally prefer the European approach (at least to the extent I understand it) where the trier of fact participates in the effort to achieve truth.

If I had my way, all trial attorneys would truly be officers of the court, and advocates of justice, not of particular clients. Clients could choose their legal counsel from an available list much as we choose arbitrators today. Counsel for the plaintiff and counsel for the defendant would each choose an attorney from that list, and the two attorneys would then select a judge, or have a judge appointed to serve as a referee. The attorneys and the judge, working together, would then depose witnesses, request and demand the production of evidence, and act as the initial fact finders.

I would not do away with the jury system—I believe it still is important to have trials by our peers—but I would change the method of presentation. The panel of the lawyers and the judge would present the evidence to the jury at trial, the lawyers laying out the portions of agreement and those portions in dispute, and the clients would have the opportunity to take issue with the panel's presentation.

I happen to think my proposed system of justice would be more efficient than what we have today. But more importantly, I believe our orientation would be toward finding the truth, rather than winning.

Enough of my personal digression—although I might add that if society's litigants could all learn to assume some responsibility for their deeds, and misdeeds, we lawyers would be in need of new work very quickly.

THE INABILITY OF OUR LEGAL SYSTEM TO DEAL WITH FRANCHISING ISSUES

I haven't made a study of all areas of law, but time and again I find that franchise law, both statutory and decisional, has been dramatically dominated by the more thoroughly prepared advocates. The well-built case, taking advantage of the cumulative effect of massive evidence, is frequently indicative of the meticulous case preparation characteristic of most large law firms.

I don't mean to indict our judicial system, but the following maxim certainly is a fated truth: *Money buys better justice.* Our judges appreciate the thorough presentation that a well-heeled law firm can bring to a dispute. Judges tend to be short with attorneys who are less prepared even though the attorney may have lacked sufficient economic resources to properly build his case.

Although many judges don't understand, or remember, a lack of preparation frequently results from inadequate funding rather than from the lack of a just cause.

In the practice of medicine, the widespread use of health insurance has helped (but not solved) the equitable dispensing of medical care to our population. Most of us who have adequate health insurance finally get all the treatment our doctors recommend, and we rarely see or recognize the bills.

In the practice of law, however, clients are faced with many hard choices. Frequently, franchisors believe they need to establish legal precedents to keep entire franchise systems in line. It is not uncommon for a franchisor to invest $300,000 in a $30,000 dispute. The sheer expenditure of such sums is usually adequate to break the financial back of most franchisee clients.

How can you expect a client to withstand the expense of seeking out all witnesses, taking their depositions, doing document requests, thoroughly researching the law in local and distant jurisdictions, hiring investigators, discovering the location of assets, meeting mandatory scheduling conferences and settlement conferences, and dealing with law and motion disputes? How many clients can appreciate and afford the expense of a legal profession that requires highly skilled and well-compensated support staff?

It is particularly distressing when I think that five out of every six franchisees who have an honest dispute with their franchisor cannot afford justice and must roll over and accept whatever the franchisor dishes out. (Honestly, I'm not sure that rolling over isn't a better fate than what awaits my clients who have the initial wherewithal to stand and fight, and who attempt to protect and defend their causes and claims.)

The clients I see mostly live in California. They enjoy a significant advantage because California has a unique public policy in favor of preserving a person's right to engage in a trade or profession. I can usually assure my franchisee clients that they can stay in business notwithstanding prohibitions in their franchise agreements to the contrary.

THE IMPACT OF CASE LAW ON FRANCHISEES

As providence would have it, the day I sat down to write this chapter I was visited by a new client who told me a rather typical story: For the past few years my client has been a franchisee of a large tire store chain; the store has been a good producer and has provided a good living.

My client did not purposely purchase his business to become a franchisee. Rather he bought an existing tire store (from one of the founders of the franchise system, as it turned out), and becoming a franchisee was incidental to the business acquisition. Nevertheless, my client was given a uniform franchise offering circular before he bought and was required to sign a franchise agreement like any other franchisee.

The franchise agreement extended my client an exclusive territory of a three-mile radius from his store. Additionally, the franchise agreement provided my client would have a right of first refusal to purchase and operate any proposed store to be built outside of the three-mile exclusive territory, but within five miles of his existing location.

San Diego County already had 11 of the more than 300 tire stores in the chain. My client contended San Diego could probably sustain as many as 20 stores, and that there were numerous excellent locations for new stores without encroaching significantly on any existing businesses. In other words, according to my client, there was no reason for the franchisor to open a location that would impact my client's natural market territory. Indeed, my client pointed out that no company-owned chain would consider positioning two stores so close together as to affect both stores' sales and profits.

Nevertheless, a few days earlier, my client had received notice from his franchisor that a new franchise location was being proposed just outside my client's exclusive territory, and within the five-mile area with right of first refusal. My client immediately complained to the franchisor that the proposed location would adversely impact both his store as well as the proposed store, and that there were numerous suitable locations available within San Diego that would help build overall system sales without adversely impacting any existing store.

My client pointed out that while the proposed store was outside his three-mile exclusive territory, the store was clearly within his logical target market. My client further complained he had continuously advertised his existing store throughout the market territory for the proposed store. Indeed, my client contended the original owner and former president of the franchisor had also marketed the business directly into the territory now targeted for the new location.

When my tire store franchisee left my office, I couldn't help thinking how applicable his story was to the message of this chapter. My client had signed a franchise agreement that granted him an exclusive territory of a radius of three miles from his store. Indeed, my client's franchise agreement is generous compared with the "location only" franchises that are popular today. Nevertheless, my client had no right to negotiate the size of his exclusive territory. He was presented with a standard form franchise agreement and given the option to sign it or find another business opportunity.

Courts in the United States have fairly routinely enforced the territorial restrictions in franchise agreements, no matter how harsh. The courts have reasoned that because prospective franchisees receive a disclosure document that provides an ample opportunity to understand the provisions in the franchise agreement, the contracts are not adhesion contracts, and the franchisee should be held to the strict enforcement of the franchise agreement.

My client would respond that the franchisor has an *ethical duty* to perform under the franchise agreement in the best interests of the franchise system and all the franchisees. My client would also argue that opening a location which would negatively impact the performance of existing locations (as well as the new location) is acting against the interests of the franchisees *and* the entire system. Unfortunately, the courts in the United States have responded that in most instances franchisors do not owe fiduciary obligations to their franchisees. Moreover, commercial good faith is rather limited in the commercial context.[1]

Finally, even if my client wanted to contest his franchisor's right to allow another franchisee to encroach on my client's territory, the franchise agreement required any litigation to take place in the franchisor's home state, some 2,000 miles away.

Then there was the subject of attorneys' fees, and the problem that my estimate of probable costs to litigate my client's claim was well beyond his means. In the typical franchise lawsuit against a well-established franchisor, litigation costs are extremely expensive. Franchising companies will usually pull out all the stops to avoid adverse precedent among the franchisee community. And as will be seen, franchisors tend to hire batteries of franchising attorney specialists, who are armed to the teeth with technology's finest litigation support systems. The sheer costs of defense are usually all it takes to cause a franchisee to throw in the proverbial "towel."

Although there have been important instances when a franchisee "mouse" has successfully roared and brought the franchising "lion" to its knees, such occurrences probably have longer odds than a progressive slot machine jackpot in Las Vegas. Believe me, I have gone into litigation with a "popgun" defense against the franchisor's row of howitzers, and the experience has not been fun.

STACKING THE FRANCHISOR'S DECK AGAINST THE FRANCHISEE

The point of this none-too-blunt discourse is that "Blind Justice" is *blind to justice* in most franchise litigation. Quite simply, the deck is almost always staked against the franchisee. In our American legal system, more often than not, "He who has the gold *does* make the rules," or, in this instance, "He who can *afford* justice *gets* justice."

It is not that the court system is philosophically tainted or intentionally biased. Rather, the court system is overburdened by the previously described crippling case load. Judges simply do not have the luxury of carefully deciding each dispute based on complete evaluation and well-reasoned jurisprudence.

Under the enormous pressure of time, the better-prepared, better-researched law briefs have a distinct advantage. For the most part, franchisors have the financial resources to develop data, to conduct discovery, and to investigate all the factual nuances of a case.

Franchisors are able to throw so much "mud" at a dispute, even the most discerning jurist would be confused. On numerous occasions, I have litigated with franchising companies who have been willing to spend in defense of a claim 10 and 20 times what my client would have accepted in settlement.

The franchisors' exhaustive resources, combined with the limited time a court has to decide most issues, is usually lethal to franchisees in court. Moreover, forcing franchisees to extend their meager resources by coming to a franchisor's home state merely adds insult to injury. What brand of justice can a franchisee obtain in such a mismatch?

Occasionally, however, I have had the good fortune of representing groups of franchisees who, acting together, were able to battle a franchisor toe to toe. On a few occasions, my franchisee clients were even able to muster substantially more financial resources than their franchisor. Oh, what a pleasant experience! How nice to walk into court armed with deposition transcripts of all relevant witnesses and a battery of analyses by experts, after having had the opportunity to properly investigate and prepare my client's case!

Just as in the marketplace, equal strength in the courtroom makes for a fair fight. Like it or not, our court system is not about truth or justice. It is about winning; it is about who can bring the most resources to bear and who can purchase the most "justice." It is about who can afford the price of a "day in court." And just as we have seen before, when franchisees are able to collect their inconsequential individual power into a cohesive united front, the strength to join the battle and gain a victory is well within grasp.

A MISMATCH OF LEGAL COUNSEL

Another major contributing factor to the franchisor's superiority in the court-room emanates from the plain truth that franchisors are able to hire better, more experienced legal counsel.

Let's face it. The very best attorneys attract the highest salaries and are available to the highest bidders. This is not to single out lawyers as being money conscious. This economic fact is true of all professions from accountants, to engineers, lawyers and doctors, and baseball players. In fact, anyone with half a brain wants to earn top dollar and have the security of knowing he or she is going to be paid for services rendered. Inevitably, the best lawyers will go where the money is.

As has been documented in these pages, if not obvious to the naked mind, the money in franchising is with the franchisors. Consequently, it is not surprising that of the more than 2,000 franchise law specialists in the United States, fewer than 100 claim to earn their livings predominantly from service to franchisees.[2]

Most of the small but mighty band of franchisee attorneys are highly skilled practitioners. A few represent large trademark-specific franchisee associations that are able to provide competitive compensation. Others have made a moral commitment to the cause of franchisees and frequently must be innovative in order to get paid.

Just as there are country doctors, there are fine attorneys in all fields who are dedicated to their craft above and beyond their desire for top dollar remuneration. But the legal profession, like most any other, is a numbers game, and most of the top franchising legal minds gravitate to the clients who can pay the bills.

THE MYTH OF CONTINGENCY CASES

An extremely high percentage of the injured franchisees who see me in my law practice are hopeful I can represent them on a contingent fee basis. They have seen the late night television ads for personal injury attorneys who will work on a straight contingency, and believe franchise lawyers will (or can) work on the same basis.

Unfortunately, the practice of contingent fee legal services can rarely be employed in the franchising context. Indeed, the perception that contingent fee attorneys are taking risks for their clients is a myth. No attorney will accept a case on a contingency if there is a risk of losing. The vast majority of contingent fee cases are settled quickly out of court, and those that end in lawsuits are inevitably the result of an attorney's misjudgment in accepting the case.

Most franchise disputes involve complex and document-intensive litigation requiring the interpretation of contracts as well as the tedious review and evaluation of business records. More often than not, franchise litigation involves allegations of fraud that require a wrongful intent in the mind of the perpetrator.

Contract disputes and fraud claims are difficult to prove, and require substantial case preparation. Quite simply, such lawsuits are almost never suitable for a contingent fee arrangement for the simple reason that the costs of preparing the suit are beyond the affordability of most legal counsel.

Although most franchise disputes are not susceptible to handling on a contingent fee basis, a few law firms in the United States do specialize in representing large groups of clients on a contingency basis. These firms have managed to accumulate substantial amounts of capital that will allow them to invest in a franchise dispute in appropriate circumstances.

These "public interest" law firms are usually looking for a big kill—a major monetary claim suffered by a substantial group of potential plaintiffs. More importantly, public interest law firms are only interested in cases that have a deep-pocket defendant(s) capable of paying a *megajudgment*. Needless to say, most franchisee complaints would not whet the appetite of a firm hoping to generate a seven-figure income against the risk of six-figure expenses.

THE FRANCHISEES' PATHETIC SCORECARD

In the absence of sufficient resources to challenge franchisors through our legal system on an equal footing, franchisees' success rates in court have been most discouraging. In the wake of the franchise industry's legal juggernaut, throughout the United States there has developed a mountain of judicial precedent adverse to the interests of franchisees. With an enormous investment in the American legal system, franchisors have successfully turned the scales of justice to their advantage. Statutory laws that were drafted to protect franchisees have been honed and interpreted to the franchisor's ultimate advantage.

I know the great body of American franchise attorneys who are dedicated servants to the franchise industry will charge that I am a poor loser, or that I am pleading "sour grapes." It will be argued that maybe, just maybe, this supposed mountain of unjust and ill-founded precedent exists, in reality, because it is grounded in sound justice in the best traditions of American jurisprudence.

I readily admit I have no patent on truth and justice. Reasonable men may fairly differ as to what constitutes "right." I further have confidence my colleagues in the Bar who represent the franchising industry are motivated by their personal conviction for the causes they espouse. I am also quite certain that most of the judges who decide franchising cases diligently attempt to dispense justice and to apply our laws with justice.

But notwithstanding the good intent of our legal system, the advantages of economic muscle will more often than not carry the day in court. And notwithstanding allegations that I am a poor loser (which may be correct), I have utmost confidence in the truth of the message presented on these pages.

To my critics, my response is quite simple—I have been on the winning side. For most of my legal career, I have represented the interests of franchisors: I have enjoyed the privilege of being able to pull out all the stops in the preparation of a lawsuit against franchisee defendants who are unable to afford even an "inadequate" defense.

However much I have enjoyed winning in court and (getting paid for my efforts), several years ago I started to become concerned that the growing imbalance between franchisors and franchisees was creating a very bad climate for the franchising industry. Indeed, my growing concern over the inequity of the franchise relationship caused me to tell a reporter for *The Wall Street Journal* that I had "never written or read a franchise agreement I could recommend a franchisee to sign."[3] The reporter used my quote to conclude an article that produced dozens of inquiries from around the country and redirected my career to its current focus on efforts to protect franchisees.

Over time, I have become convinced, whether representing franchisors or franchisees, that the swing of the pendulum in favor of franchisors is counterproductive to the franchising industry. I have become convinced, whether on the winning or losing side, that the legal precedents being established in franchising do not serve the true needs of justice, or the industry. I fervently believe that a balanced industry, providing all the promise of franchising to franchisor and franchisee alike, is in the best interests of the parties to a franchise relationship, as well as the interests of the American economy.

In Chapter 11, we witnessed how statutory efforts to protect franchisees have frequently been turned to the advantage of the franchising industry. However discouraging the record of statutory efforts to protect franchisees, the effects of legal decisions impacting franchisees have been far worse.

In the 1960s and early 1970s, many legal precedents in franchising were favorable to the cause of protecting franchisees. Over the past 20 years, however, the franchising industry has mustered its enormous financial resources to win numerous legal battles in virtually every U.S. jurisdiction. The extraordinary trend of pro-franchisor legal precedent has extended to virtually every significant aspect of the franchise relationship. The growth of pro-franchisor legal precedent has grown to the point where most franchisee counselors are loath to recommend the purchase of franchise opportunities in today's legal and economic climate.

The following sections, which survey important trends in the judicial interpretation of the franchise relationship, will read like a review of many issues already treated in these pages. Nevertheless, this review is important in understanding why the current legal climate is disadvantageous for prospective franchisees.

Franchising as a Fiduciary Relationship

In my judgment, the most distressing aspect of The Franchise Fraud is the false representation of the franchising industry that franchisors are benevolent guardians and benefactors of their franchising networks. The conventional wisdom regarding franchising is that franchisors are looking out for the interests of their franchisees. Franchising is generally sold by representing that franchisors and franchisees are in a partnership to advance system sales and the franchise network. In selling a franchise, franchisors tout the substantial support of the franchise system. The franchisor usually represents itself to be a friend, advisor, mentor, protector of the faith, and solver of system problems.

In court, however, franchisors describe franchising as a far different phenomenon. Franchisors have long denied they owe any fiduciary duties to their franchisees. Rather, franchisors claim the franchise relationship is a traditional commercial relationship where each side is responsible for looking out for its own self-interests. Franchisors have long argued their only responsibilities are set forth in the "promises" contained within the "four corners" of the franchise agreement.

A fiduciary is generally held to a high standard of loyalty to those to whom fiduciary duties are owed. Fiduciaries are required to act in the best interests of those with whom the fiduciary relationship exists. Fiduciary duties are required of trustees, corporate directors, partners, lawyers, doctors, bankers, and stock brokers. In each instance of a fiduciary relationship, there is found to be the placing of trust and confidence in the fiduciary to act in the best interests of the person relying on the "trusted" advisor.

Notwithstanding the conventional wisdom (supported by the franchising industry) that franchisors are partners to their franchisees and maintain a sacred trust to promote the interests of the franchise system, the U.S. courts have uniformly concluded that no fiduciary relationship is implied in a franchise agreement. Rather, the courts have held that franchise agreements, like most business contracts, involve two parties respectful of one another while bargaining in good faith at arm's length. Consequently, many courts have denied the existence of a fiduciary relationship because the franchise agreement does not include the elements of a fiduciary relationship. Other courts have found that the very existence of legislation protecting against fraud in the franchising context implies there is no fiduciary relationship.

It may be the cruelest irony in franchising, but franchisees continue to buy franchises in the belief they are owed the highest duties of care and support by their franchisors. In fact, most courts have ratified the paucity of support provided by nearly all franchise agreements.

The "Community of Interest Doctrine" in Franchising

In the absence of finding that franchisors are the fiduciaries of their franchisees, many courts have recognized that there is a special "community of interest" in the franchising relationship. The courts that have adopted community of interest standards seem to recognize franchisors and franchisees join together in a common enterprise with a mutual purpose and goal.

On its face, the community of interest doctrine would seem to be a logical compromise between those who expect a fiduciary relationship and those who believe franchising is no more than a common commercial enterprise.

Unfortunately, while courts have held that a special community of interest exists, to date no court has defined any special duties that may arise from the franchise relationship. No judicial effort has been made to set forth what duties of loyalty, support, and good faith are owing between franchisors and franchisees. Consequently, the community of interest doctrine has provided little in the way of benefit to the franchisee cause.

Franchise Agreements as Adhesion Contracts

As noted in Chapter 11, a contract of adhesion is a contract whose terms are dictated by one party in a superior bargaining position and offered on a take-it-or-leave-it basis. The terms of most adhesion contracts are usually not enforceable if they are considered to be "unconscionable."

Franchise agreements are rarely deemed to be adhesion contracts because franchisees have the option of not signing them. Moreover, courts have held that by virtue of the various state and federal disclosure laws and rules, franchisees are apprised of all the provisions in franchise agreements (including onerous provisions) before the contract is signed. In that a critical element of an adhesion contract is that the unconscionable terms are not fully disclosed to the party being bound, courts find that franchise agreements do not meet the requirements. Statutory disclosure rules out adhesion, and because of disclosure, the franchise buyer is subject to the archaic doctrine of caveat emptor (let the buyer beware).

Similar arguments have been used by courts to deny that franchise agreements are unconscionable. The courts also tend to note that franchisees always have the right not to sign the agreement, and therefore franchisees are never acting out of duress. The courts assume franchise agreements, like most commercial contracts, are made between businesspeople who are familiar with bargaining and the process of allocating risks. Once again, courts have held that a standardized franchise agreement, even though nonnegotiable, will not usually be unconscionable since the franchisee was not required to enter into the agreement.

The Covenant of Good Faith and Fair Dealing

It is said that there is an implied covenant of good faith and fair dealing in every commercial contract. Franchisees have frequently attempted to use the implied covenant of good faith and fair dealing to require franchisors to provide the support and protection that had been anticipated from the franchise relationship. As we have seen, the representations of support and service made in the franchise selling process are conspicuously absent from most franchise agreements. Unfortunately, courts have been more interested in the contractual promises than in the presale representations. Mere sales "puffing" is not unlawful.

For the most part, courts have limited their use of the covenant of good faith and fair dealing to instances of contractual ambiguity. In other words, if the contract says a franchisee has no exclusive territory, the courts have, until recently, refused to apply any restrictions in the franchisor's ability to build a second office nearby.

In 1992, a federal district court case in the state of Florida caused shock waves throughout the franchise community by applying the covenant of good faith and fair dealing to restrict the franchisor from encroaching on an existing franchised territory.[4] This recent Florida lawsuit is a dramatic departure from the traditional usage of the implied covenant of good faith in a franchise context and may bode well for greater franchisee protection in the courts.

Franchising and the Antitrust Laws

Franchisors have also been treated very kindly with respect to the American antitrust laws. For the most part, the public policy in the United States is against such anticompetitive influences as price fixing, the vertical or horizontal control of markets, and the "tying" of the right to sell one product to the requirement to sell another (called a "tying arrangement"). Franchisors, however, have long enjoyed a virtually exempt status with respect to the proscriptions of American antitrust law.

The courts have reasoned that franchisors have a vested interest in the protection of their trademarks and trade names. In the interest of trademark protection, franchisors have been allowed considerable leeway in establishing systemwide pricing and tying the right to use the franchisor's trademark and trade name to the requirement to offer specific products and services. Consequently, practices that are deemed unlawful or "predatory" in most commercial settings have been approved when the franchisor applies the practice to its franchisees.

The Availability of Injunctive Relief

One of the franchisor's most powerful weapons for keeping franchisees in line is the ability to obtain injunctive relief from the courts to prevent a franchisee from continuing in business following termination of the franchised business. Because of the ability of a franchisor to enjoin a terminated franchisee from staying in business, most disgruntled franchisees are dissuaded from terminating the franchise relationship and trying to go independent.

Courts have struggled mightily with the question of who owns the franchise business. Most franchise agreements claim the franchisee is an independent contractor, and is not an employee or agent of the franchisor. On the other hand, most franchise agreements also claim the franchisor's operational system and customers are trade secrets of the business, and virtually all franchise agreements restrict franchisees from competing with the franchisor upon termination of the franchise.

For the most part, courts have merely enforced the provisions of the contract irrespective of the public policy decisions of who really should own the business. California, as has been previously discussed, is a notable exception to this rule because California has decreed that noncompetition clauses are inconsistent with the state's public policy guaranteeing its citizens a right to conduct a trade or profession.

195

Throughout the United States, the ability of franchisors to restrict franchisees from post-termination competition has created an enormous lever of power to keep franchisees in line. Virtually every franchisee who comes to my office seeking to get out of an untenable franchise situation is petrified he or she will not be able to leave the franchise business without getting out of the industry completely.

As I have hopefully made clear, a franchise relationship should continue in existence only if it works. Both the franchisor and franchisee should respect the relationship and have the highest duty of good faith to make the relationship work. If it doesn't work, it should be allowed to dissolve, with both parties allowed to go their separate ways.

The franchisee has a vested interest in the business enterprise, and so does the franchisor. On termination, both should be able to continue to apply their chosen trade and profession, and both should have equal access to the customers and trade secrets that they have jointly developed.

Notwithstanding what ought to occur on the termination of a franchise, U.S. courts, seemingly perplexed by how to divide the business goodwill, merely enforce the language of the franchise agreements, which usually give the businesses to the franchisors and prohibit franchisees from post-termination competition. The effect is to put the franchisee out of business. In most instances, the franchisee forfeits all goodwill in the business enterprise, and the franchisor carries off the entire prize of the business entity.

Enforcement of Boilerplate Contract Provisions

The cutting edge of franchisor control is the utilization of the so-called "boilerplate" provisions in franchise agreements. Innocuous looking clauses which set forth seemingly mundane specifications such as the jurisdiction of lawsuits and what law the court must follow have been effectively used by franchisors to force franchisees to resolve disputes far away from home. Because such boilerplate clauses are common in negotiated agreements, courts routinely enforce such provisions and thereby enable franchisors to usurp substantial contractual advantages even though franchise agreements are almost never negotiated.

The ability of franchisors to dictate where disputes are resolved is perhaps the most intrusive clause routinely imbedded in most franchise agreements. The practical advantage of defending a dispute at home may save the franchisor thousands of dollars, while requiring the franchisee to seek unknown legal counsel and bring his or her dispute in a foreign jurisdiction. Another frequently used clause provides that the law of the franchisor's home state, or some state that is favorable to the franchisor, will be applied to govern the enforcement of the contract and the relationship between the parties. Often, though not always, these clauses are honored by courts, but the mere inclusion of choice of law clauses can serve to confuse an issue and cause travail and expense to a franchisee who is trying to resolve a problem.

Another typical boilerplate provision in most franchise agreements is the "integration clause." This clause provides that the language of the agreement represents all of the understandings of the parties, and that nothing that happened, or was promised, prior to the signing of the agreement should be considered by the court in deciding any disputes. In essence, the court cannot look beyond the agreement to decide if a wrong has been committed. Frequently, the franchisee is upset over promises that were made by franchise salespersons, or other agents of the franchisor. Unless the promises were written into the agreement, the franchisee cannot have such promises even considered. Such clauses are routinely enforced in most states.

Other clauses that routinely work against franchisees include provisions acknowledging that the franchisee has read and understood the contract and the offering circular, and further acknowledging the right to seek legal counsel. Most franchise agreements include a clause in which the franchisee acknowledges he or she has received no prior oral promises or representations other than those contained in the agreement. Another common clause provides that each clause in the contract is severable, and if one provision is unenforceable, the remainder of the contract still stands.

The practical effect of these boilerplate clauses is often to deny franchisees access to justice. The ability of franchisors to litigate on their home turf makes most franchise litigation prohibitively expensive for franchisees to prosecute or defend. The acknowledgement by a franchisee that no oral promises have been made, or the agreement that such promises are not binding, can literally throw the franchisee out of court.

197

The Judicial Preference for Arbitration Clauses

Arbitration clauses are also highly favored by the courts as an effective means to lower the cost of franchise disputes. Unfortunately, arbitration clauses have the practical impact of substantially reducing judgments. In fact, proponents of arbitration argue this is a very important justification for the procedure. The problem is that civil suits provide (and exposure to large jury judgments establishes) a deterrence to a franchisor's abusive practices.

I find arbitration a mixed blessing. In many instances, I believe arbitration is in everyone's best interest, such as when there is a legitimate commercial dispute that the parties want to resolve as efficiently as possible. On the other hand, in cases of alleged franchisee abuse, the existence of arbitration frequently encourages abusive practices. Even more importantly, most arbitrators will not allow the joinder of multiple franchisee plaintiffs in a single arbitration, thus completely blunting the franchisee's ability to level the playing field by joining forces with other franchisees who have shared a similar injury.

The foregoing trends in decisional law have led me to dissuade prospective franchisees from acquiring a franchised business in all but the most exceptional business opportunities. When those who are counseling franchisees are recommending against a purchase, the future of the industry is in great jeopardy. When stockbrokers are recommending that investors sell their stocks, a bear market is the invariable result. The same is true in franchising.

Only when the franchising climate is more reasonable for franchisees—when the legal climate is more balanced in the interests of franchisor and franchisees—will the "Buy" signal be rung again; and only then will the franchise industry regain the opportunity to achieve its enormous promise.

Chapter **13**

The Franchisee
Bill of Rights

This chapter compares the problems facing franchisees with the events leading to the American Revolution. The Franchisee Bill of Rights is intended to be a rallying call for franchisees in the United States, and a key to gaining economic balance within the franchising industry to allow it to achieve its enormous potential.

This is a time, I believe, when American franchisees are near their breaking point. The United States does not even know a problem exists, and yet we are on the verge of a revolution by franchisees.

Although deep undercurrents of serious problems were brewing in America 220 years ago, the vast majority of American colonists were still loyal to the king of England. These problems emanated from the taxation and exploitation of the colonies without due respect for the colonists and their rights as free citizens. "No taxation without representation!" was the cry that rang out to lead the charge toward revolution. In the early days of the colonial revolt, the purpose was not to gain independence and sovereignty so much as it was to achieve respect for the rights of the citizens of the colonies.

And what were the 13 American colonies? If you think about it, you will realize that each of the colonies arose from a franchise granted by the King of England. Several of the colonies were *corporate* enterprises—literally commercial ventures *franchised* by the king of England to bring profit to the crown. The Massachusetts Bay Company, Virginia, and Pennsylvania all were corporate franchises, as were Maryland, New York, New Jersey, and others.

History has told us the king of England was a royal franchisor who failed to respect the rights and individualism of the colonists. The enfranchisement of the colonies evolved into the indenture of the colonists, and this eventually led to outright rebellion.

The colonists were able to test and defeat the king of England because they joined their grievances in a strong union. The American Revolution began with timid whispers and grew into a bold Declaration of Independence by men too angry to be timid any longer. And when the War of Independence was won, a new Constitution was formed and was immediately emboldened by a dramatic document guaranteeing the very individual rights for which the colonists had fought during the seven-year war.

In a very real sense, the Declaration of Independence grew out of a revolution of "franchised" colonies that became independent states and formed a union. With striking similarity, franchisees of individual franchise systems are beginning to challenge their franchisors for representation; for rights of equity, ownership, and sovereignty; and for a share of the franchised enterprise.

THE PURPOSE OF
THE FRANCHISEE BILL OF RIGHTS

Inevitably, franchisees will come to recognize their generic common goals and will organize. The process has already begun—frequently with great resistance from franchisors. The emergence of independent "trademark-specific" franchisee associations is a growing trend.

The starting point, the call to action, will most likely be a list of goals and demands. In essence, it is time for franchisees to identify a Franchisee Bill of Rights and to demand that the franchisors recognize and honor these rights. Those franchisors who respect the rights and the contributions of their franchisees will be so much the better for it. I do not believe the Franchisee Bill of Rights to be a destructive list of demands. Rather, these rights, if equitably applied, will foster more productive and profitable franchised relationships. I am confident the result will be franchised systems that are stronger, more powerful, and economically viable.

Many franchise systems already have organized franchisee associations. Sometimes the franchisee association is controlled, directly or indirectly, by the franchisor. But over the past several years, trademark-specific franchisee associations have begun to make their mark. For the most part, even franchisors would agree the efforts of franchisee associations have been more positive than destructive. As yet, most franchisee associations have shied away from openly challenging contractual restrictions in franchise agreements that deny franchisees important measures of independence.

Several years ago, a group of dissident McDonald's franchisees created the McDonald's Operators' Association with the purpose of effecting dramatic changes in McDonald's franchising program. The group failed, and most of its members were forced out of McDonald's system. But in the wake of the McDonald's Operators' Association, McDonald's allowed the creation of a new franchisee association. Over time, with less militancy, many of the goals of the early McDonald's "rebel faction" have been achieved.

For the most part, existing franchisee associations have tried to keep a low profile. Franchisee associations rarely engage in political debate and rarely seek to collectively bargain franchise agreements. Rather, existing franchisee associations have provided a communication link between franchisor and franchisee, and among franchisees. Many associations have achieved significant inroads with respect to marketing issues and in fostering concessions from systemwide suppliers. Subtly, franchisee associations have effected moderation from franchisors and fostered respect for franchisee members.

The Midas Dealers' Association is an example of a strong franchisee system. One of the oldest American franchisee associations, Midas dealers have developed considerable power and influence with their franchisor. Over time, the association has become a major partner in developing policy and marketing development for Midas. It is an indication of the power of a collective voice, and a lesson well worth learning for franchisees throughout the United States.

As a committee of one, I have brazenly assumed the mantle for suggesting a list of universal franchisee rights. The list itemizes basic protections for which all franchisees can and should aspire. Franchisors who honor the rights of franchisees should be rewarded, promoted, and proudly recognized by the franchisees of their system, and by franchisees generally.

The franchise revolution will be fought in the marketplace, and not in the streets. Once franchisees identify and recognize a bill of rights, and franchisors that honor these rights are properly placed on a pedestal of good faith and high ethics, entrepreneurial Americans will flock to these enlightened franchisors

The Franchisee Bill of Rights

The Franchisees of America, representing the best of the American entrepreneurial spirit, hereby recognize and demand a basic minimum of commercial dignity, equity and fairness. In recognition thereof, the franchisees of America do proclaim this franchisees' Bill of Rights as the minimum requirement of a fair and equitable franchise system:

* The right to an equity in the franchised business.
* The right to engage in a trade or business.
* The right to a fiduciary relationship with the franchisor.
* The right to trademark protection.
* The right to market protection.
* The right to full disclosure from the franchisor.
* The right to initial and regular training.
* The right to ongoing support.
* The right to marketing assistance.
* The right to associate with other franchisees.
* The right to representation and access to the franchisor.
* The right to local dispute resolution and protection under the laws and the courts of the franchisee's jurisdiction.
* A reasonable right to renew the franchise, and the right not to face termination, unless for cause.
* The reciprocal right to terminate the franchise agreement for reasonable and just cause.
* The post-termination right to compete.

©The American Association of Franchisees and Dealers has developed The Franchisee Bill of Rights and works to promote awareness and acceptance of it among the franchising industry and the general public.

whose good reputations precede them. I urge my readers to seek out franchisors that respect these important rights and protections and to recognize that the best franchise systems are the ones for whom these rights are sacred.

ANALYSIS OF THE FRANCHISEE BILL OF RIGHTS

The Franchisee Bill of Rights is a dramatic enunciation of many major concerns recognized by franchisees for years. On close examination, however, it is apparent that this Bill of Rights clashes monstrously with rights and privileges long claimed by franchisors. When carefully analyzed, the Franchisee Bill of Rights really represents a checklist of negotiating issues of fundamental importance to franchisors and franchisees alike. Given equal bargaining power in contract negotiations, franchisees would address each issue contained in the Franchisee Bill of Rights in bargaining for a relationship of equity and fairness.

In the existing franchising marketplace, franchisors can completely ignore the franchisee's legitimate interests in these 15 important negotiable issues. With the exception of the right to trademark protection (which is generally acknowledged by franchisors) and the right to full disclosure (which has been legitimized by statute and franchisor acquiescence), the rights are almost always dictated in favor of the franchisor's best interests.

The time has come for franchisees to understand their right to negotiate franchise agreements. More importantly, the time has come for franchisees to understand and demand the basic protections that a franchise relationship should always include as part of the conventional wisdom. With this in mind, I will analyze each of the essential rights proclaimed in the Franchisee Bill of Rights.

The Right to an Equity in the Franchised Business

Every franchisee should be guaranteed an equity interest in the franchised business. On termination of the franchise, the franchisee should be entitled to retain the business, or to continue in business. At the very least, the franchisee should have the right to sell the business (to the franchisor or an independent party) for its fair market value.

Most readers may assume that a franchisee's right to an equity in his or her business is so obvious and so basic that it does not need to be addressed as a specific right. To the contrary, the franchising industry generally denies that business ownership is an automatic component of the franchised relationship. The cutting edge of franchise design provides that the right to engage in a trade or business is granted by the franchise agreement, and the right is extinguished on termination of the franchise. Most franchisors believe they own the franchised business on termination and the franchisee has no ongoing rights in it. Even though the franchisee has paid for the right to enter the business and has established the business, developed it, and built its customers and goodwill, franchisors believe all these efforts are for their benefit and not for the benefit of the franchisee.

Most franchisees, on the other hand, have always understood that they were going into business for themselves, that they own their franchised businesses, and that even if the franchise terminates, the franchisee would nevertheless continue to own the business or a significant value in its equity.

Certainly, the franchisee's vision of business ownership is supported by the historic notion of a franchise. The franchisee's right to an equity in the franchise business has been eroded over many years by the lack of negotiating leverage on the part of franchisees. The right needs to be retained, or reinstated, as the case may be. More than anything else, a franchisee's right to an equity in the franchise business enterprise must be preserved.

The Right to Engage in a Trade or Business

By legal definition, franchisees acquire the right to engage in a trade or business in acquiring a franchise. Usually franchisees pay for and receive specific training in connection with the trade or business purchased. Franchisees deserve the right to ply their selected trade whether or not they continue in business with the franchisor.

Once again, the evolution of franchising has continuously eroded a franchisee's right to engage in a trade or business that he or she is trained to perform by virtue of the franchise. Noncompete covenants, trade secret clauses, control of the franchise premises, and other devices have all been used effectively by franchisors to prevent franchisees from continuing in their established trade or business on the termination of the franchise.

Above all else, franchising is praised as supporting the public interest by accomplishing job training. The value of job training is lost, however, if the people trained in a profession are restricted contractually from participating in that profession. Accordingly, the right to engage in a trade or business is a critical right of franchisees that must also be preserved and maintained.

The Right to a Fiduciary Relationship with the Franchisor

The relationship between franchisor and franchisee necessarily involves an extremely high standard of good faith, fair dealing, confidentiality, loyalty, and full disclosure. By its very nature, the franchise relationship involves a high degree of confidence and trust. Uniformly, franchisors and franchisees speak of the relationship in terms of partnership and as a joint effort toward a common goal.

The franchise relationship should be a fiduciary relationship in the strictest sense of the term. But it is a mutual right, to be shared equally by franchisor and franchisee. Both parties to the relationship owe one another the highest standard of trust, confidence, loyalty, good faith, and fair dealing. As much as a franchisee has a right to rely on the franchisor for support, so should the franchisor be able to rely on its network of franchisees as an extension of the company's business and marketing plan.

The Right to Trademark Protection

Of the entire list of the Franchisee Bill of Rights, trademark protection is the only right conceded by franchisors. Indeed, a careful review of a typical franchise agreement readily reveals that most franchisors promise little more than the license to use a valid trademark.

Accordingly, it is incumbent on a franchisor to represent that it owns the trademark and will protect its licensees from improper infringements by pretenders to usage.

The Right to Market Protection

In most instances, franchisees should be entitled to an exclusive area; where no exclusive area is granted, franchisees should nevertheless have protection against overcrowding of the market area.

In the beginning, there were protected territories. And by my reference to the beginning, I am going all the way back to feudal times when a serf became a freeman, thereby receiving independent ownership rights to a particular parcel of land and all its produce (subject to the royal tithes or taxes, which came to be known as royalties).

In the beginning of modern franchising, the "right" of a protected territory was carried on as a fundamental right and privilege of a franchised relationship. Market protection went hand in hand with the licensing of a trademark and marketing plan.

With the franchise explosion of the past 20 to 30 years, franchisors have discovered that protected territories diminish the supply of franchises to be sold. Moreover, with the great popularity of franchising, and with the franchising image of a foolproof, risk-free path to independent business ownership, franchisors have discovered exclusive or protected territories are not necessary to sell franchises.

Today, we live in the age of the "location only" franchise. Most franchise agreements license the franchisee to do business at a specified location and prohibit anyone else from doing business *at the franchisee's location*. However, the franchisor reserves the right to grant an additional license across the street.

Franchising's new policy against exclusive territories is probably the second most prevalent franchisee complaint. It is called many things, including encroachment, oversaturation, and unfair competition. McDonald's franchisees call it "impaction"—the practice of building new units that interfere with existing market areas. The impaction issue has become one of the major disputes between McDonald's and its franchisees in recent years.

Market protection is another one of those sticky issues involving valid concerns of both franchisors and franchisees. The franchisor is in business to sell product, including goods, services, *and franchises*. The more units the franchisor opens, the greater its sales and the greater the franchise fees and royalties. Franchisors further argue that the more units in existence, the greater the advertising and marketing dollars available to build ongoing demand for the franchisor's products. Franchisors claim the more marketing dollars spent, the greater demand and the greater sales and profits.

Franchisees, on the other hand, are locked into their product and their business. They literally are limited to the franchisor's product line and their territorial protection. For franchisees, their market territory is as much their lifeblood as is the franchise name and products that they sell. Territorial encroachment can only result in the reduction of the franchisees' market and lower profits.

The Right to Full Disclosure from the Franchisor

The right to a full disclosure of all relevant and material information necessary to make an informed franchise purchase decision is the only franchisee right currently embodied in existing franchise protection law. Further, the right to full disclosure is alone among the list of the Franchisee Bill of Rights to be endorsed by the franchising industry. Why? The answer is really quite simple. Full disclosure has been the franchising industry's sacrificial lamb.

The franchising industry has been willing to trade the promise of full disclosure for all the other claimed rights of franchisees. The industry does not want to give franchisees an equity in their businesses but is willing to disclose that no equity accrues to the franchisee. Franchisors are more than willing to disclose posttermination restrictions in their franchise agreements as long as they are able to impose the restrictions.

Disclosure is important. But it is a *right* of a consumer and investor, not a bargaining chip. Disclosure should come without trading away other important rights and privileges of business ownership. The duty of full disclosure does not replace the duty of fairness, the duty of loyalty, and the duty of competent performance by franchisors.

More importantly, franchisor disclosure provides more protection for franchisors than for franchisees. Think about it. Franchisors disclose all the bad news of their franchise contracts in their uniform franchise offering circulars, and the documents become veritable insurance policies against lawsuits. How can a franchisee claim he or she has been defrauded when the claimed misrepresentation was described in full detail on page 39 of an offering circular in 8-point type? It is no wonder that disclosure has become a mainstay of the franchising industry. It is expensive to provide full disclosure, but it is very good business.

Standing on its own, a disclosure document is an impressive exhibit that legitimizes the franchisor's enterprise. At a cost of $20,000 to $30,000 to prepare the disclosure document, disclosure costs the franchisor a few dollars to a few hundred dollars per franchise sold. The insurance protection gained by the franchisor far outweighs the cost of disclosure.

Most regrettably, the information in most disclosure documents is not the information the franchisee really needs to make an intelligent business decision. Indeed, disclosure documents rarely contain any kind of operating projections for franchisees. Taking advantage of a loophole in franchise regulations large enough to drive a truck through, most franchisors refuse to disclose sales history, projections, or provide any type of information that will give the franchisee an understanding of potential earnings.

Disclosure documents are equally deficient when it comes to spelling out what the franchisee gets for the franchise fees. Rather, most disclosure documents describe what the franchisee is required to do and what services the franchisor *may* provide but is not required to provide. Franchise disclosure should be presented in a simple, straightforward manner. For example, there ought to be one section that says, "*What we do for you,*" and perhaps another section that says, "*What we do not do for you, but is routinely provided in other franchise systems*"!

Also *absent* from franchise disclosure documents is a section on risk factors. Complete disclosure of known risks has been a mainstay in securities offerings for many many years. Franchisors should be required to state everything that can go wrong in the franchise operation—a disclosure of all the negatives the franchisor can think of as to why a franchisee should not buy.

Mainly, disclosure without other fundamental rights is meaningless.

The Right to Training

Complete training in the franchisor's operational methods is almost always listed as one of the primary virtues of buying a franchise. And yet, franchisees *frequently* have no legal right to training, and rarely are franchisees granted a contractual right to training. Rather, most franchise agreements make the successful completion of the franchisor's training program *a condition, rather than a promise,* of receiving the franchise.

To those schooled in the law, the difference between a promise and a condition is much more than semantic. The failure of a franchisor to give complete and adequate training does not support a claim for damages if the franchisor has made no promise to train the franchisee. The vast majority of dissatisfied franchisees who have come through my doors have complained their training was worthless and the franchisor had not delivered its promise of training. You can imagine their surprise when I pull out their franchise agreement and offering circular and ask them to point out where the franchisor had promised to provide training.

While the franchisor may have promised training, that promise wasn't contained in the offering circular or the franchise agreement. The promise was implicit in the marketing materials, and the franchise salesperson had boasted about how great the training was. Virtually every article written about franchising in the past 20 years has touted training as a major attribute of the industry. Training has become synonymous with buying a franchise, and therefore the failure to disclose that complete training is not promised supports a reasonable assumption that complete training will be provided.

Although the right to training is essential, actual training is frequently unnecessary. Often, the franchisee is already experienced in the industry and is really only interested in acquiring a franchisor's product line or trademark recognition. An experienced hotelier may not require training when he signs on with Travelodge, or when he converts his Travelodge to a Hilton.

Since Century 21 popularized the development of conversion franchising, there has been a growing segment of franchised businesspeople who do not require general training in the franchisor's field. Nevertheless, learning the peculiarities of the franchisor's system and procedures will always be a requisite of franchise ownership.

The level of a franchisee's training should be the subject of individual negotiation between the franchisor and each franchisee. However, *the right to be trained* in the franchisor's methods and procedures is critical to the success of the franchise system and the individual franchisee. But although franchisees may have a right to be trained, they do not have a right to receive that training without charge.

As with the right to a fiduciary relationship, the right of training is to the mutual benefit of the franchisor and franchisee. Each has a vested interest in the franchisee's receiving and successfully completing competent and effective training.

The Right to Ongoing Support

Without question, the number one franchisee complaint is a lack of operational support from the franchisor. Conversely, whether or not franchisees have a right to their franchisor's support is open to considerable debate. Reduced to its most essential elements, a franchise grants only a right to engage in a trade or business under the franchisor's trademark and trade name. No more and no less. There is no implied or explicit duty or promise by the franchisor to stand in the franchisee's corner and provide training, assistance, nurturing, and moral support during the life of the franchise.

The promise of operational support is a glaring example of The Franchise Fraud. The industry perpetuates a *systemic fraud* by advertising, marketing, and promoting franchising as a substantial support system for franchisees. This industry-promoted image of the franchisor in the franchisee's corner has led every franchisee to assume that franchisors have their franchisee's best interests at heart.

Among the difficulties in pinning down the elusive right to ongoing support is the difficulty in understanding what the term "support" actually means. The definition of franchise support will vary from industry to industry, trademark to trademark, franchisor to franchisor, and franchisee to franchisee. It can mean providing a constant supply of quality products. It can mean the elimination of intrabrand competition and dual systems of distribution. It can mean ongoing training in new marketing techniques; it can mean provision of financing, or the relaxation of royalty payments during bad times. Franchise support, in the eyes of the franchisor, may mean cracking down on recalcitrant and poor-performing franchises for the purpose of keeping the quality up throughout the franchise system. In other words, it may mean being tough rather than being lenient.

I cannot recount the times a franchisee has told me, "I asked my franchisor to send somebody out to help me improve my sales, but all they did was send out an accountant to verify if I had paid my royalties." The franchisor's reaction might well be, "Unless we strictly adhere to our accounting procedures, all our franchisees would be trying to avoid their bills, and we would not have the facilities to support the system in general, let alone individual franchisees specifically."

In trying to understand and pin down the parameters of franchisee support, I can't help recall the famous words of U.S. Supreme Court Justice Potter Stewart when he tried to define pornography. Acknowledging the total frustration of the Court to develop a workable definition of "smut," Justice Stewart confessed that he couldn't define it, but he knew it when he saw it. Unfortunately, the existence of a franchisor's support may be "seen" very differently by franchisees and franchisors.

However difficult it may be to define ongoing support, we can agree that the franchising industry promises its existence. Accordingly, although a franchisee may not have a "right" to ongoing support from the franchisor, before entering the franchise relationship, every franchisee should have the inalienable right to clearly understand what kind of support and assistance can be expected from the franchisor.

As previously discussed, current franchise disclosure requirements act more as an insurance policy for franchisors than as a vehicle for meaningful disclosure. The quality and effectiveness of disclosure must be judged by the understanding of the franchisee. Perhaps each franchisee should be required to fill out a questionnaire acknowledging exactly what ongoing services and support are due from the franchisor on signing the franchise agreement. Franchisors would still have the benefit of liability exculpation, but we would have greater certainty that franchisees understand what they receive from the franchise relationship.

Moreover, franchisors' marketing materials must not be allowed to imply services that are not contractually delivered. The state of California has begun to monitor franchisors' advertising and marketing efforts. State regulators often prohibit implied representations and guarantees of success, as well as the use of suspect franchising statistics. California's efforts are laudable but should be extended to include a comparison of services implied in advertisements with the actual services promised in the franchise agreement.

Most importantly, franchisee protection should be understood in the context of consumer protection generally. The statutory framework for franchising should hold franchisors accountable for performance of those services and support obligations that are implied to the franchisee, whether or not such services are specifically promised in the franchise agreement.

Most franchise agreements, for example, start out with a series of recitals setting forth the reasons the franchisor and franchisee are getting together to form an agreement. The following recitals are typical:[1]

1. RECITALS
   A. COMPANY has certain rights to use and license the use of TRADE SECRETS (as hereinafter defined) relating to restaurants known as, CHICK'S NATURAL RESTAURANTS, featuring prepared food and restaurant services specializing in chicken pursuant to a uniform system developed and owned by COMPANY, all of which may be improved, further developed, or otherwise modified by COMPANY from time to time (the "System").
   B. The System has been developed as a uniform method and philosophy of operation, customer services, marketing, advertising, promotion, publicity, and technical knowledge relative to the restaurant business. In connection with the System COMPANY has certain rights to use and license the use of the name CHICK'S NATURAL RESTAURANTS and the service marks, trademarks, logos, and trade secrets now or hereafter used in conjunction with the System (the "TRADEMARKS").
   C. COMPANY grants to persons who meet COMPANY'S qualifications and are willing to undertake the investment and effort, franchises to establish and operate a CHICK'S NATURAL RESTAURANT at a specified location and a license to use the TRADEMARKS in connection with the promotion and operation of such Restaurant.
   D. FRANCHISEE desires a franchise to establish and operate a CHICK'S NATURAL RESTAURANT (the "RESTAURANT") and COMPANY is willing to grant such a franchise on the terms and conditions hereafter stated.

Such common recitals do not constitute promises contained in the agreement, but to franchisees, the words certainly imply a level of service. The same can be said of the marketing materials produced by virtually every franchising company touting the company's operating system and support capabilities. The promises in such literature are not contractual. It is urged that franchisors should be held accountable for performing the level of services implied to their franchisees.

In essence, franchisees may not have an inalienable right to ongoing support from the franchisor. But he or she should have a right to all the ongoing services and support that are implied by the franchisor. Moreover, the franchisor should have a duty to perform such services as are promised or implied in a competent and faithful manner. Anything less is to misrepresent the underlying promise of the franchising industry.

The Right to Marketing Assistance

The right to do business under and in accordance with the franchisor's marketing system and plan is a fundamental element, right, and privilege of franchising. However, the right to ongoing marketing assistance from the franchisor is vigorously contested by the franchising industry.

As with a right to ongoing operational support, the only inalienable right a franchisee has for ongoing marketing services is that all assistance promised by the franchisor is delivered in a competent fashion. Realistically, the duty of the franchisor to deliver marketing services and assistance is a function of the specific rights and duties set forth in the franchise agreement.

Systemically, the franchising industry promises marketing support as a key advantage of buying a franchise:

> So what can you do? How can a small business person finance a comprehensive advertising program? It seems a Catch-22 situation. You need advertising to grow. But you can't afford to advertise because you are small. Is there a solution? Certainly, and it is franchising. Virtually every major franchise company pools franchisee resources to finance regional or national advertising programs.[2]

Most prospective franchisees expect franchisors to provide substantial advertising, marketing, and general marketing assistance as part of their franchised packages. However, industry representations that franchising includes marketing assistance are *not* characteristically included as basic promises of most franchising companies.

As with the right to ongoing support, at a basic minimum, franchisees should have the right to be *apprised prior to entering into their franchise agreement* exactly what marketing assistance will be provided by the franchisor.

The Right to Associate with Other Franchisees

The right of franchisees to associate is *the key* to bringing a balance to franchising relationships. Indeed, the right of petition is constitutional. I am talking about the U.S. Constitution.

The specific right of franchisees to associate, and to organize themselves into franchisee associations has been recognized by several state legislatures, including California, Hawaii, Michigan, New Jersey, Washington, Arizona, Connecticut, Iowa, and perhaps others. These states have enacted laws making it unlawful for any franchisor to inhibit the right of franchisees to freely associate and communicate.

The right to associate implies the ability to collectively bargain. Association equates to a collective voice and collective economic strength.

The franchisee's right to associate is an anathema to franchisors, and for good reason. Franchisees outnumber franchisors by a ratio of perhaps as large as 300 to 1. The unbridled economic power of franchisees to demand an equitable balance in their franchise relationships is one well-organized association away from reality. Franchisors know it, and they have done their level best to prevent it ever happening.

The voice of franchisees has yet to be joined in a cohesive manner. In essence, the Franchisee Bill of Rights includes the all-important right of association. Thus far, and for the most part, it is a right that franchisees have merely left on the table.

The Right to Representation and Access with the Franchisor

The right of association, as important as it is, is merely a means to the end of franchisees' gaining market power and equity. The combined rights to representation and access inevitably will be the battle cry that will trigger franchisees to action. Historically, the demand for access and representation has spearheaded many great political revolutions. The American Revolution, the French Revolution, the events leading to the signing of the Magna Carta, and many other political struggles have evolved around the demand for access and representation.

It is said that history repeats itself. Throughout history, political and economic democracy has arisen from the servitude imposed by powerful oligarchies. The turning point occurs when the masses gain sufficient economic and political power to match the authority and muscle of the powerful few.

Franchisors represent a strong and unified oligarchy. The industry has managed to control the dynamics of the institution and to keep franchisees in a subservient role. Franchisors of today are much like the robber barons at the turn of the twentieth century, or the monarchies during colonial times. These historical epochs eventually led to the political organization of the masses and an inevitable balancing of economic power.

Some will read these words and claim I am fomenting rebellion. I simply do not agree. In our free market economy and democratic political system, we depend on economic and political power to achieve access and representation. Stated another way, access and representation are sure and certain results of the aggregation of economic and political power.

The essence of this discussion is that the franchisees' claimed rights of access and representation with franchisors are not inalienable. These are rights that must be earned and retained, even fought for.

Representation and access are most valid interests for franchisees. Moreover, enlightened franchisors have recognized their franchisees have a much better feel for the pulse of their communities and markets than can the corporate office. Joint access and representation among franchisors and franchisees will almost certainly bring positive benefits to any franchise system. This truth has been recognized by McDonald's whose franchisee co-ops have been responsible for many, if not most, of McDonald's marketing and product successes. Other franchise systems have made similar discoveries, and have given a wide range of marketing discretion to their franchisee cooperatives. Midas Muffler, Ramada Inn, Arby's, and Burger King are all excellent examples of franchisors that have listened to their franchisees and received major dividends.

It is critical for franchisors and franchisees to recognize that franchising can be a dynamic institution capable of fulfilling its enormous potential for business expansion and productivity. However, those who have a vested interest in the success of the franchise enterprise must communicate and work together for the greater good of the franchise system. The franchisee's claimed rights to representation and access, therefore, are not only politically critical for franchisees, but economically of benefit to the entire industry.

The Right to Local Dispute Resolution and to Protection under the Laws and the Courts of the Franchisee's Jurisdiction

The franchisor chooses to do business in the franchisee's locality. Moreover, franchisors are almost always in a stronger position to afford legal battles than are franchisees. At a basic minimum, franchisees should have the right to resolve disputes in their home jurisdiction, and under the laws of the jurisdictions within their home states where their franchise agreements are performed.

The right to local dispute resolution is perhaps the least appreciated and understood of the franchisees' claimed rights, but local dispute resolution is of vital importance to franchisees. Without fail, this right is denied in the back-page boilerplate of virtually every franchise agreement. Most franchisees are not even aware they have agreed to submit to binding arbitration in a faraway jurisdiction when they have a dispute with their franchisor.

The importance of dispute resolution, however, cannot be overemphasized. The ability to control where a dispute will be resolved, who resolves it, and what laws apply to the issues in dispute is a powerful weapon that franchisors have used deftly for many years. The few states that have passed laws regulating franchising have uniformly imposed rules requiring local dispute resolution, and for good reason. When a franchisor decides to do business in a foreign state, the franchisor is opting to come into that state and deal with citizens of that state. If a franchisor from New York decides to do business in Arizona, the franchisor must voluntarily also accept the jurisdiction of the courts of Arizona and the laws of Arizona. Certainly, the franchisor has superior economic ability to defend in a faraway jurisdiction than does the individual franchisee. A franchisor that had sufficient economic strength to open the market in Arizona surely can hire an attorney there. Equally important, Arizona has a vested interest in the welfare of its citizens and the state's public interest requires local resolution of disputes involving its citizens.

Historically, American law allows parties to a contract to determine issues of jurisdiction, the application of law, and the venue of disputes. Therefore, to claim a right to local dispute resolution for franchisees denies our long-standing rules in favor of freedom of contract. But there are many exceptions to our general rules promoting the rights of people to freely reach agreements. Whenever the public good suffers, the public good can make rules to deviate from our norms. In this instance, however, like most of the rights contained in the Franchisee Bill of Rights, the demands of franchisees are capable of free and compelling negotiation once franchisees have amalgamated sufficient economic negotiating power.

A Reasonable Right to Renew the Franchise, and the Right Not to Face Termination, unless for Cause

Too many franchisees do not understand their franchise agreements run for a finite term. Some franchises run for as little as 2 years, some 5, and others as long as 10 or 20 years. But when the franchise term expires, the franchisee must enter into a new arrangement. Frequently, he or she must pay a new franchise fee, and almost always the franchisee must accept the terms and conditions of the then prevailing franchise agreement no matter how onerous the new agreement is compared with the existing contract. Many franchise agreements, however, do not even address the franchisee's right to renew at the end of the franchise term. In many instances, the franchisor can merely say "Thank you, but I have other plans for your territory." At the time of termination, the franchisor can turn the franchised office into a company-owned office, say goodbye to the former franchisee, and pay no consideration for the franchisee's many years of hard effort.

Those who promote the cause of franchisees urge that as long as a franchisee is in good standing and is giving fair and appropriate effort to the franchised enterprise, franchisors should not be able to terminate the franchise, and renewal rights should be automatic. In essence, as long as a franchisee is performing, the franchise business should be his or hers in perpetuity.

From the perspective of law and logic, the claim that a franchise should run in perpetuity is difficult to justify. In effect, it is like saying a person who owns an apartment building can never evict a tenant at the end of a lease as long as the tenant is behaving responsibly. Those of us who own real property believe we have property rights including the right to utilize our land in the way we choose. Presumably, the same is true of franchisors.

Although I personally have difficulty accepting the concept of the perpetual franchise, I nevertheless appreciate the importance of assuring franchisees a committed permanent vested interest and equity in their franchised businesses.

The Reciprocal Right to Terminate the Franchise Agreement for Reasonable and Just Cause and the Right to Be Free from Termination unless for Cause

There is a curious similarity in most franchise agreements that truly exemplifies much of what is wrong in the franchising industry. Uniformly, franchise agreements have lengthy provisions describing in great detail the circumstances under which a franchisor may terminate the franchise relationship. It is common for the franchise agreement to set forth 10 to 15 independent items and conditions under which the franchisor may terminate the agreement "for cause," with or without some form of limited notice and opportunity to cure on the part of the franchisee.

Franchise agreements rarely make any provision whatsoever for the franchisee to terminate the agreement for cause. While many franchise agreements provide limited rights for franchisees to terminate with notice (usually by abandoning the business to the franchisor or selling it for book value), almost never does the franchise agreement accord the franchisee the right to terminate the agreement as a result of the franchisor's breach of contract or behavior that threatens the existence of the fruits of the contract. Franchise agreements uniformly give the franchisor the right to terminate the franchise agreement on the insolvency or bankruptcy of the franchisee. To the contrary, no such reciprocal right is given to franchisees when the franchisors declare bankruptcy, although the circumstances of a franchisor's bankruptcy may sound the death knell for the franchise system and the individual franchisee's business.

Many attorneys and legal scholars will protest my concern for the lack of a right of franchisees to terminate their franchise agreement for cause. They will rightly claim that a material breach of any contract can result in the discharge of performance by the party who is performing the agreement according to its terms. I have always found, however, that rights which may be awarded only by court decree prove to be very expensive and hollow rights indeed. Accordingly, the Franchisee Bill of Rights stresses that whatever right of termination is accorded to the franchisor, a reciprocal right of termination should also be available to the franchisee.

Franchising should not be the equivalent of indentured servitude. The joint enterprise entered into between a franchisor and a franchisee should continue as long as it is mutually beneficial, but either party should be able to leave the enterprise and continue to enjoy the fruits of the shared goodwill to the same extent as we accord dissolving partnerships. Partners may agree that on termination of a partnership one party continues with the business and the other does not; but almost always, negotiated counterbalancing consideration flows to the partner that leaves a partnership when the other partners get to carry on the trade or business.

Ideally, every negotiated franchise agreement will provide reciprocal termination rights for both franchisor and franchisee. Both parties should have the opportunity to retire from the enterprise, or to terminate the relationship, without having to give up the right to engage in their chosen trade or business, or to enjoy the benefits of each respective party's share of the formerly jointly operated business.

Another problem for franchisees, which is of perhaps equal magnitude and importance as the franchisee's right to terminate the agreement, is the right to prevent termination of the franchise agreement by the franchisor when the franchisor does not have good cause emanating from the failure of the franchisee to perform. For the most part, franchise agreements involve a substantial investment by the franchisee. I am not talking about an employee who invests many years of faithful service with an employer only to be replaced by a machine or younger employee, although such circumstances suggest a substantial investment indeed. Unlike the employee, the franchisee may put in those same hard years, the same dedication and loyalty, but he or she has also put in capital, has borne the risk of the success of the business, and has not been accorded substantial company fringe benefits such as health care, a pension plan, paid vacations, and other employee perks.

The Franchisee Bill of Rights makes claim to an important protection of a franchisee's right to maintain the value and equity of the franchised business. The requirement that the franchisor may not terminate the franchise agreement except for just cause is an important protection to a hard-working franchisee who has made a substantial investment in the business enterprise. At the very least, this right should be viewed in the context of our U.S. Constitution, which provides that our government may not take any of our property without paying just compensation.

The right of a franchisee to avoid franchise termination without just cause or without just compensation has been hotly disputed by the franchising industry. It is a right that has been suggested in some of the model franchising laws and has been incorporated into the most enterprising state franchise law to date, which was enacted in the state of Iowa in 1992.

The right to stay in business, and the concomitant right to receive just compensation when the franchisor takes the business, are crucial to the notion that a franchisee has an equity in the franchised business. It is the basis on which most, if not all franchises are sold.

The Post-termination Right to Compete

Franchise agreements uniformly restrict the right of the franchisee to compete with the franchisor on termination of the relationship. Post-termination covenants not to compete cut deeply against a franchisee's fundamental right to carry on the trade or business for which the franchisee has been trained at considerable expense. Indeed, one of the major reasons our society embraces franchising is for its job-training capacity. Undue restrictions on the former franchisee's right to stay in business following the termination of the franchise place an undue burden on the franchisee's right to engage in a lawful occupation and are against the public good.

On the other hand, the franchisor's interest in the goodwill built in a joint effort with a franchisee is substantial and should not be ignored. When the franchise relationship terminates, respect for both the franchisor's and franchisee's interests in the ongoing business is an important and sensitive issue.

Although the franchisee's post-termination right to compete should be the subject of careful and balanced negotiation at the commencement of the franchise relationship, post-termination rights and obligations are normally mandated by the franchisor in the franchise agreement. Noncompetition restrictions must be limited and supported by adequate consideration. The franchisee's ability to earn a living must never be taken away completely. To the extent that noncompetition clauses will be enforced, they must be supported by fair and adequate compensation.

Chapter 14

Bringing about a Balance

The franchising industry can deliver its enormous promise if the franchising marketplace can be balanced between the interests of franchisees and franchisors. Franchisees can balance the franchising market and level the playing field in franchising by developing a collective voice to demand fairer treatment in franchise relationships. Franchisees outnumber franchisors by almost 300 to 1. A national franchisee association can coalesce the collective strength of franchisees and create a persuasive and powerful bargaining force to achieve an equitable negotiated balance in franchising.

As this book has come together, so too has my personal perspective grown clearer and more focused. From the beginning, I saw this work as a rallying cry for the franchise business owners of the United States. More than an exposé of an industry that refuses to admit it has enjoyed too much power for far too long, my purpose has been to describe franchise abuse in human terms. I have not sought to blame the franchising industry for the accumulation and abuse of economic power because I believe the abuse of power inevitably flows from the lack of countervailing power and authority. Most of all, I have seen this book as a blueprint for balancing the franchising marketplace.

For several decades, the franchising marketplace has been critically out of balance, but until recently, few seemed to notice or care. The franchising industry has been able to perpetuate The Franchise Fraud because the public, the government, and (to an amazing degree) franchisees have been taken in by the captivating promise of franchising to deliver the American Dream of business ownership to a vast number of citizens.

EXPOSING THE MARKET

Indeed, as shameful as the existence of The Franchise Fraud is that franchisees have allowed unconscionable conduct to continue unabated. Franchising has succeeded because the public has been willing to buy a very inequitable and unsatisfactory product. Unfortunately, prospective franchisees have not been sufficiently educated or sophisticated to appreciate the real risks and hazards associated with buying a franchised business.

Over 20 years ago, attorney Harold Brown wrote a book called *Franchising: Trap for the Trusting,* which detailed many of the abuses I have discussed here.[1] Notwithstanding a captivating title, Brown's book was an intellectual treatise and not marketed to the general franchise-buying public. Whatever the reason, Brown's book was overwhelmed by legions of industry-supported articles singing the praises and security of buying a franchise.

As I write these pages, I am reminded of my favorite episode of a 1960s television series, *Outer Limits.* The episode was about cone-headed extraterrestrials who landed on Earth with a great show of advanced power and technology. The aliens descended on the United Nations with telepathic promises to rid the world of hunger, war, and pestilence, and to bring a new age of peace and prosperity.

One alien left behind a book written in the alien language. The volume was retrieved by American cryptographers who set about to break the code and translate the work. The first breakthrough brought signs of great promise as the cryptographers were able to translate the book's title: *To Serve Man.* A world eager for peace and plenty flocked to the aliens' protection, and people's trust was seemingly rewarded when the Earth's deserts were turned to gardens and the world prospered under alien management.

The world's population began to grow exponentially, and the aliens began to encourage human emigration to the aliens' faraway planet. As thousands of humans began to leave for the promised new land, the cryptographers finally broke the code: *To Serve Man* was a cookbook!

Many a franchisee has been "cooked" by blindly falling for the promise of franchising. By helping to break the code and expose the many inequitable practices that are commonplace in franchise relationships, I hope the public will be more discerning and refuse being ensnared in a dangerous trap from which there is frequently no escape.

DEMANDING AND NEGOTIATING
A BETTER PRODUCT

The solutions to unfair franchise practices begin with education. Only when the public understands what it is really being sold will buyers begin to say "No!" More importantly, as franchisees become better educated and organized, and the buying public more discerning and discriminating, better and fairer franchise opportunities will appear to meet the market. This is the basic law of supply and demand—a buyer's market demands and gets better quality, price, and value. By taking control of demand, buyers gain market power and can dictate and negotiate the quality and price of the available product.

Market power is a critical concept to anyone entering a market to buy or sell. Although we think of the steely tycoon, rich enough to control a market to satisfy personal greed, as the exercise of market power, market power is the critical tool *all* consumers need to protect themselves in the marketplace. Market power is *Consumer Reports* telling you what to buy and Ralph Nader telling you what not to buy. Market power is expressed in the buyer's or seller's ability to demand good value for a fair price.

Our economy is at its best in a balanced market—when a willing buyer and willing seller, each with equal bargaining power, negotiate in good faith for some product or service. The interests of both parties, and the economy in general, are well served, resulting in better products and balanced prosperity.

THE IMBALANCE IN FRANCHISING

Unfortunately, most franchisee-franchisor negotiations (and disputes) are David and Goliath affairs. I am frequently reminded that David won the battle with Goliath, and that my reference to David and Goliath augurs hope for franchisees. Fair enough, but remember—David's slaying of Goliath was deemed a miracle of Biblical proportions!

One on one, a franchisee is no match for the awesome economic strength of a franchisor. As has been seen, by combining awesome public relations, government relations, and the effective control of the best legal minds, franchisors have enjoyed the unbridled ability to dictate the terms of the franchise relationship.

The *cybernetics* of franchising have broken down—the mechanisms of market corrections have been sadly missing for decades. The seller's market in franchising has continued, in spite of growing reports of abuses, because there is no existing countervailing market force to balance the economic market strength of franchisors.

On the other hand, in the United States alone, franchisees outnumber franchisors by nearly 300 to 1. In the McDonald's system, franchisees outnumber their franchisor 8,000 to 1. If there is strength in numbers, it is amazing franchisees have not found the wherewithal or the rallying point to organize themselves into a cohesive unit to deter franchisors' abusive practices.

A good part of my law practice involves the representation of franchisees in disputes with their franchisors. Invariably, I encourage my clients to find other franchisees who have similar disputes in order to challenge the economic muscle of franchisors in court. Unfortunately, presenting a united front is usually a most difficult task.

ORGANIZING FRANCHISEES

There is a dramatic trend toward the organization of franchisees, and most large franchising systems have franchisee associations or franchisee advisory councils. Still, there are very few truly independent franchisee associations that have effectively mustered their combined economic strength to negotiate toe to toe with their franchisors for economic and contractual equity.

Many factors have inhibited the growth of franchisee associations. Such associations most often are formed to deal with marketing and operational considerations, and trademark-specific associations want to focus on the very important business of operating successful business enterprises. They naturally desire to stay on a positive focus within their systems and with their franchisors. Consequently, antagonistic issues dealing with the fundamental rights and obligations of the franchisor-franchisee relationship are frequently avoided within trademark-specific franchise associations.

Another important reason franchisees have been slow to organize is found in their very makeup. Remember, franchisees have chosen to be independent businesspeople. For the most part, franchisees are a conservative lot. Many franchisees are individuals who were unhappy in an employer–employee situation. In essence, many franchisees are antilabor and antiunion. They are not eager to accept that the franchisee's lot is much like an employee's. As this book evidences, in many ways franchisees have the worst of it.

The most important barrier to effecting a viable franchisee association, however, is the considerable efforts of franchisors to prevent association, or to control it.

Even today, many franchisors prohibit the association of their franchisees. In recent litigation with a major employment services franchisor, the franchisor refused to allow its franchisees to start a franchisee newsletter. The franchisor denied it even maintained a list of its franchises for the stated reason that it did not want its franchises to perceive themselves to be different from company-owned offices!

Over the past 20 years, there have been many battles within franchised systems to obtain the right to associate. In the 1970s, several McDonald's franchisees attempted to form a McDonald's operators' association; the ringleaders are no longer in the McDonald's system. Similar battles have been fought in other franchise systems, and the franchisor, inevitably, attempts to distance the mainstream of its franchisees from the rabble-rousers and the dissident few.

In the typical case, however, while the franchisor is able to expel dissident forces, the franchisor has also been forced or shamed into accepting the association of its franchisees. For example, the independent McDonald's franchisee association was banned, but McDonald's sponsored and engineered an operators' association of its own.

As is frequently the case in franchising, McDonald's set the trend. Using an age-old mechanism of oligarchic government, McDonald's and other franchisors have followed the maxim, "If you can't stop it, control it," to effectively emasculate and sedate the efforts of franchise associations to serve as truly independent bargaining forces for their constituencies.

A major problem inhibiting the successful organization of franchise associations is that most associations are trademark specific. Consequently, when franchisees seek to organize, they are perceived as antagonistic to their franchisor. This natural assumption of antagonism creates an immediate barrier and fosters oppressive tactics by the franchisor.

On the other hand, trademark-specific franchisee associations have been loathe to foster viable *generic* franchisee associations. Quite simply, the leaders of existing trademark-specific associations have developed their own power structures and do not want to lose their own accumulated power to a generic organization. As a result, until recently the International Franchise Association, the generic association representing franchisors, remained the sole voice of franchising in the United States.

I usually find three primary obstacles to joining franchisees in a common cause. Most prevalent by far is simple fear. Maybe if the franchisee keeps quiet, the franchisor will leave him or her alone. An unsettling apathy is the second most prevalent excuse—that same "I don't want to get involved" attitude that allows crime to go on in public view and has caused many a society to disintegrate. I cannot recount the number of times groups of franchisees have expressed anonymous sympathy and moral support but have been willing to stand idly by while a fellow franchisee is effectively brushed aside by a franchisor's legal juggernaut. The third reason is that franchisees are an independent lot. Their very entrepreneurial spirit dissuades teaming with others to form a cohesive unit. Most franchisees want to solve their own problems independently.

BALANCING THE MARKET—AN ASSOCIATION OF "EES!"

To me, the greatest frustration is that franchisees, collectively, constitute a sleeping giant capable of shifting the balance of power in the franchising industry in a moment. The prescription is simple and relatively painless, but for those three ever-present obstacles: fear, apathy, and independence.

The solution is to do just what the franchisors have done—create an industrywide trade association of "EES" to address the issues of franchising, only from the franchisees' perspective:

- To provide an educational link to franchisees and prospective franchisees.
- To educate the public as to the virtues and faults of franchising.
- To appear as friends of the court in vital litigation.

- To sponsor litigation where appropriate.

- Most importantly, to develop market power and bargaining strength for franchisees.

A franchisee association would provide a powerful lobby for franchisee interests at the state and federal level. More importantly, an association of EES can bring simple economic incentives to bear on the franchising industry to create an immediate negotiating balance.

Just imagine a national Association of EES promulgating the Franchisee Bill of Rights set forth in Chapter 13. Imagine further, the Association of EES offering accreditation for franchisors who agree to adhere to the "Franchisee Bill of Rights" and further agree to amend all franchise agreements, current and prospective, so that they comply with accreditation standards.

McDonald's, with its strong marketing position, may not be persuaded to alter its course. However, many of the more than 3,500 franchisors competing to sell franchises in the United States may well be economically compelled to beat their competition by earning the "Fair Franchising Seal of Approval."

What a simple maneuver. Relying on our free market system to do its job. No legislation, no court battles, just good old free enterprise. Allow the franchisees of the world to set the competitive standards, and let the franchisors meet the market. I may miss my bet (and I sincerely hope to see the day this script played out), but I can see the day when a *prospective franchisor* is told by legal counsel that the model franchi*see* agreement adopted by the American Association of Franchisees and Dealers is "typical" and therefore the accepted industry standard.

But at what price can an association of EES be achieved? The answer to this question is as frustrating as it is surprising.

Let's begin by mentioning that the International Franchise Association, the well-financed organization representing the interests of franchisors in the United States, has an annual budget slightly in excess of $6 million per year. In comparison, if each of the 1 million franchisees and dealers in the United States popped in $6 annually—*that's six dollars*—the IFA's budget would be met.

But forget about 100 percent participation; we all know it would never happen at any price. Instead, let's talk about an association representing only

10 percent of U.S. franchisees (the IFA claims about 60 percent membership of significant franchisors). And rather, let's ask each member franchisee to pay dues of $10 per month, or $120 annually. The result is an annual budget of $12 million—almost twice the budget of the IFA.

Even with such extraordinary numerical advantages, franchisees, thus far, have not pulled off the effort of organizing themselves nationally. On the other hand, over the past few years, there has been a proliferation of franchisee associations within individual franchise systems. More and more franchisors are assisting the establishment of franchisee advisory councils or franchisee associations, so as to prevent adverse organizations from challenging the franchisor's management.

With a few notable exceptions, internal franchisee associations have not achieved significant results. Invariably, the exceptions have involved associations large enough to have a significant dues base, with the ability to afford a full-time executive director. It also helps to provide compensation for the board of directors so that meaningful work can be accomplished on something other than a volunteer basis. The problem with most associations is that they require the volunteer efforts of a board of directors that meets sporadically (often bimonthly) and really doesn't have the opportunity or the wherewithal for concentrated effort.

Again, the focus must be on a national association where the volume of potential membership is so significant that a modest investment will generate a significant financial base.

Several years ago, I participated in an attempt to establish an association of EES. We started with six participants, who each advanced $5,000 to prime the pump. The group formed a corporation, set up bylaws, and hired an initial executive director. Unfortunately, all the founders were *former franchisees* who had successfully terminated their franchise relationships. Having escaped franchising, each of the founders went on to new projects, and their interest in forming the new association faded.

Over the past 6 to 10 years, my law practice has become increasingly dedicated to helping franchisees flee their systems and recover for the contractual breaches and false promises made by their former franchisors. It is truly unfortunate so much effort and expense is invested in "getting out" instead of making franchising worth "staying in."

Given my absolute conviction that a well-put-together franchise system has dramatic benefits for both franchisor and franchisees, I would much rather see resources aimed at correcting the imbalances in franchising and at bringing about an equitable industry that fulfills all the promises claimed by franchising proponents.

I often think too simplistically, but I am convinced the solution for the franchising industry *is* quite simple. Franchising needs an equitable balance; franchisees need a voice, an organization, an advocate, and the economic strength to support the cause.

THE AMERICAN ASSOCIATION OF FRANCHISEES AND DEALERS

Within the past two years, I have been involved with a new group of franchisees, and franchising advocates, in establishing the American Association of Franchisees and Dealers. Although I have been at the forefront of the organizational effort, I am not a franchisee, and I will be no more than an associate member. This time around, the organization will limit its voting membership to existing franchisees, although associate membership is available to suppliers, service providers, and prospective franchisees. Consequently, the potential membership base far exceeds the 1 million figure previously discussed.

The new association has already created a national 800-number, a Franchisee Info-line, to provide important information for prospective members. The association also created a Franchisee LegaLine™ to connect franchisees and prospective franchisees directly with legal professionals throughout the United States.

When I began this effort, the American Association of Franchisees and Dealers (AAFD) was a fledgling dream of an organization, literally only a few weeks old. A little more than a year later, the AAFD has already grown to represent thousands of independent franchisees.

This book has grown along with the AAFD. As the trade association has recharged the hopes and aspirations of its members, has achieved the focus and respect of the press, and has reached out across the United States to test the premises on which it was formed, the correctness of our purpose has become clearer and bolder.

In less than a year, the AAFD has already impacted the franchising marketplace. The association is promoting the Eight Criteria for Franchise Selection (see Chapter 9) and has advocated the Franchisee Bill of Rights (see Chapter 13). Franchisees are beginning to see that a strong trade association can achieve the crucial balance of *market power* necessary to return fairness to the franchising industry.

The Franchisee LegaLine™ has expanded to provide discounted legal services for franchisees in more than 35 states. Attorneys, accountants, suppliers, lending institutions, and franchising professionals have come forward in impressive numbers to offer discounted services to AAFD members in exchange for the right to market services through the trade association.

More importantly, as the final paragraphs are being added to this manuscript, the AAFD has nominated the first recipient of the Association's "Fair Franchising Seal of Approval." Without passing a law, or filing a lawsuit, the franchisee trade association has exhibited the most powerful statement of *market power*—rewarding fair practices and good products in the marketplace.

The Fair Franchising Seal of Approval is based on the satisfaction of two important criteria:

1. The franchisor must have collectively bargained a uniform franchise agreement that has been ratified by at least 75 percent of the franchisees of the system.

2. The franchisor must receive an 80 percent or better performance rating from at least 75 percent of the franchisees of the system pursuant to an independent franchisee satisfaction survey.

Taco John's International, a fast-food system with more than 400 units located throughout the Midwest, was nominated by the Taco John's Independent Franchisee Association to earn the AAFD's "Fair Franchising Seal of Approval" after the company had successfully negotiated a collectively bargained franchise agreement with its franchisees. The agreement is in the process of being ratified, and Taco John's must submit itself to a franchisee satisfaction survey. If the company meets the AAFD's requirements, and the indications are most positive, the AAFD will have the opportunity to reward Taco John's fairness in the marketplace.

Equally important, the AAFD is establishing the standards, the guideposts, by which prospective franchisees can measure quality franchise opportunities. With enough economic incentives to make fair franchising economically attractive, the AAFD seeks to encourage franchisors to moderate their practices to earn the Fair Franchising Seal of Approval. The blatant goal is to educate prospective franchisees to seek out the advice and counsel of the AAFD, and to ferret out the best, fairest, and most attractive franchise opportunities.

In the process, the association seeks to provide economic rewards to franchisors willing to negotiate—and more importantly, to renegotiate—bilateral and balanced franchise agreements within their franchise systems.

The AAFD is organized into trademark-specific sections for every franchise system the association represents. Thus there is the Baskin Robbins section, the Western Temporary Services Section, and the Mail Boxes Etc. Section of the AAFD. In the absence of an independently constituted franchisee association, AAFD trademark-specific sections will serve virtually as fully empowered franchisee associations capable of negotiating with their respective franchisors. Fundamentally, it is the purpose of the AAFD to provide the impetus for every franchise system of the United States to organize effective collective bargaining units capable of bringing equity to the franchising industry.

The process is working. Excitement is building on a daily basis for the members of the American Association of Franchisees and Dealers. We can sense the pendulum beginning to swing back toward a balance in the franchising industry.

Long term, the AAFD serves several very important functions: an organizational function, a legal support function, and a legislative function. But perhaps most important of all, the AAFD helps to develop and promote quality franchise products, while *exposing* those franchise opportunities that most exemplify The Franchise Fraud. As the AAFD grows, it intends to provide the authoritative expression of *what is fair and what is abusive* in franchising. To protect against the association itself being corrupted, the fair franchising standards for each franchise system will be developed and enforced by the franchisees of each respective system, and not by the association acting as independent arbiter.

As quality franchise products become available, the AAFD's voice will become ever stronger. Exhibiting a sense of reward and punishment, the association will continuously strive to honor all that is fair, just, and equitable in franchising. But for those who intend to perpetuate The Franchise Fraud, the AAFD has three simple words of rebuttal—"Just Say No."

The effort has begun. The opportunity is at hand for American franchisees to demand and achieve a balanced playing field in the franchising industry. The promise of franchising is very real. Only the lack of a market correcting mechanism has allowed the perpetuation of The Franchise Fraud. The development of vital market power for franchisees will, at last, provide the countervailing force to correct the franchising marketplace. The time has come for franchise owners to amalgamate their collective economic strength to bring an end to franchise abuse and reclaim the American Dream of business ownership.

Appendix

STAFF MEMORANDUM TO JOHN J. LAFALCE,
CHAIRMAN OF THE COMMITTEE ON SMALL
BUSINESS, U.S. HOUSE OF REPRESENTATIVES:
FRANCHISE INDUSTRY RESEARCH AND
DATA—AVAILABLE DATA ON
FRANCHISE FAILURES

Congress of the United States
House of Representatives
103d Congress
Committee on Small Business
2361 Rayburn House Office Building

Washington, DC 20515-6315

STAFF MEMORANDUM

TO: Chairman John J. LaFalce

SUBJECT: Franchise Industry Research and Data
                  Franchise Success/Failure Rates

I. Lack of Reliable Data on Franchise Performance

A number of academic papers have been published in recent years noting the lack of reliable statistics on franchising in general and a serious void of empirical research on the success rates of franchise businesses. The Department of Commerce ceased collecting national data on franchises in 1987 and much of the research undertaken by independent researchers either has sought to reinterpret the earlier Commerce Department data or has focused narrowly on selected franchise systems or franchises within limited market areas.

A 1992 study by two Oklahoma State University professors attempted to review and categorize all published academic research on franchising. The authors noted a "disturbing" lack of research on the operation of franchise systems, a deficiency they described as "inexcusable given the vast and growing significance of franchising" (Elango & Fried). The study also found that "little empirical work" had been done to measure levels of success among franchises in order to ascertain whether franchising tends to help or hinder small business growth.

An earlier paper by two Arizona State University marketing professors surveyed the published research on rates of success and failure among franchise businesses and concluded that "a large information void exists with regard to failures in franchising" (Walker & Cross). Describing a "complete lack of either 'hard' or 'soft' data," the authors observed "it is difficult (in fact, impossible) to ultimately locate statistics on franchise failures that are derived from broad-based, systematic examination." They noted further that "broad-based data and investigations related to causes of franchise failure are virtually non-existent."

(1/94)

The study goes on to state that "despite this void of reliable statistics, a large amount of information about franchise failures--particularly with respect to low failure rates among franchisees-shows up in talks and articles about franchising." The authors concluded that *"in the absence of reliable statistics, it appears that statistics on franchise failures are being created, misused, abused, and/or misrepresented"* (Walker & Cross).

Other writers who have surveyed the research on franchise failures have expressed similar concerns regarding the lack of reliable statistics. "One of the most difficult characteristics to assess about franchising is the rate of business failure" (Hadfield). A 1992 paper reviewing prior research on franchise failures noted that "different analysts have come up with markedly different estimates of the overall failure rate" and that a "fair amount of disagreement exists as to the rate of failure among franchisees and among the franchisors themselves" (English & Willems). An earlier 1986 research paper concluded that the data available on franchise failures was "only somewhat better" than when the first studies of franchise success had been attempted some fifteen years earlier. (Padmanabhan).

Concerns regarding the reliability of data on franchise failures have not been limited to researchers and have been expressed by persons more directly involved in monitoring franchising trends and growth. In his testimony to the Small Business Committee in 1992, the chairman of the American Bar Association's Franchising Forum, observed that "the information concerning franchisee success that is currently on the street is of dubious assistance to prospective franchisees." He observed that few in franchising "seem to be comfortable with the available data on franchising" and "we don't have a good handle on what is going on in the industry" (Barkoff, 1992).

Similar views have been expressed by publishers of two of the leading independent national directories of franchise opportunities. "We believe that there is a strong core of franchisors, that franchising continues to grow in many areas...but really, there are no valid statistics available on success rates of franchising" (Dixon). "The only available data on the success of franchising is clearly flawed, misused, self-serving and should be carefully updated and amended" (Bond).

II. Frequently Cited Data on Franchise Success/Failure Rates

Questions regarding the sources and the accuracy of industry data on franchise failures has been voiced for more than twenty years. In the first independent study of franchising failures undertaken for the Small Business Administration in 1971, Ozanne and Hunt observed that while many categories of turnover of franchises may involve failures, franchisors had tended to focus only on the less than 20 percent of franchisee turnovers that involve closed or "discontinued" outlets. This focus had produced failure rate figures well below what Ozanne and Hunt suspected were the actual failure rates of franchisees. The study also criticized the franchising industry for using misleading information in creating "erroneous comparisons" between success rates of franchises and non-franchised businesses "which would be completely misleading when read by potential franchisees" (Ozanne & Hunt).

The 1971 study identified a key problem with all franchise failure figures in use at the time--the fact that data on franchisee failures derived from information supplied by franchisors. It identified several factors that tended to understate actual failures and to make resulting failure rates "nonrepresentative" of franchising generally: that "ethical" or successful franchisors were more likely to respond to requests for information than franchisors operating troubled systems with numerous failures and the fact that failed franchise systems were not available to respond to surveys. The study also identified franchisor errors, "both intentional and unintentional," as further creating "bias" in industry failure rate figures.

Questions regarding the sources and reliability of industry data on franchise failures raised by Ozanne and Hunt in 1971 are equally applicable to failure rate figures used by the franchising industry since the early 1970s. While a variety of often conflicting claims have been made in promotions by individual franchisors and in industry data disseminated by the International Franchise Association (IFA), five figures or sets of data have appeared most frequently in franchise promotions--

(1) figures claiming only 3 percent to 5 percent of franchises fail annually (95% to 97% success rates);

(2) figures claiming only 1 percent of franchises fail in the first year of operation and 5 percent fail over five years;

(3) figures claiming a 94 percent success rate for franchises; and

(4) long-term success rate charts showing that 90 percent of franchises are successful over ten years, as compared to only 18 to 20 percent of non-franchise independent businesses.

All of these figures purport to show franchises as having extremely high rates of success and, therefore, only limited risk. But these figures suffer from a variety of problems relating to sources and accuracy. As explained below, each set of figures can be show to be based on incorrect or, at best, incomplete and inappropriate information.

A. 95 Percent and 97 Percent Annual Franchise "Success" Rates

The most commonly cited statistics on franchise failures have been those which claim that only 3 percent or 5 percent of franchises fail each year or, alternatively, that 95 percent or 97 percent of franchises are successful. These figures are attributed to data compiled by the U.S. Department of Commerce from annual surveys of franchisors and published in the Department's reports, *Franchising in the Economy*. An examination of these Commerce Department reports, however, fails to show any figures providing comparable failure or success rates for franchises or franchisees. On the contrary, the reports note specifically that "the number of failures is unknown" (*Franchising in the Economy*, 1988).

What the *Franchising in the Economy* reports do provide is data on the number of franchise outlets which franchisors report to have "discontinued". A "discontinued" franchise, as opposed to a failure, is generally understood to include only businesses or outlets which have been physically closed either due to the failure of the franchisee or a decision of the franchisor to withdraw from the market area. The number of "discontinued" franchises was reported as between 3 percent and 5 percent per year during the period covered by the Department surveys.

As Ozanne and Hunt first noted in 1971, discontinued outlets may account for only a portion of the total number of franchises that fail. The 5 percent figure "may be moot," one analyst explained in the early 1980s, "because troubled franchised outlets rarely go out of existence. They are often sold back to the franchisor or to another operator at fire-sale prices" (O'Donnell). "What that statistic doesn't reveal," one franchise industry expert admits, "is the number of franchisees who have failed, but have been bought out, either by another franchisee or by the franchisor" (Boroian).

Other researchers have noted similar flaws in the Commerce Department's data and with its use by the franchise industry to reflect franchise failures. In the Department's statistics, "neither 'terminations' nor 'nonrenewals' count officially as 'failures'" (English & Willems). "If a site survives under a different owner, supposedly no failure has occurred" (Walker & Cross). "From the standpoint of the franchisee," the resale of a franchise "could very well be considered a business failure, whereas from the standpoint of the Department of Commerce statistics it is not" (Boe).

Like the earlier SBA study, these researchers question the Commerce Department figures for relying solely on information supplied by franchisors without independent review or verification. This data was further weakened, these analysts maintain, by the fact that "the aggregate statistics are based on data the franchisors choose to submit" and the fact that the Department's surveys have gone only to a "select group" of franchisors rather than to all franchisors (Walker & Cross; Boe).

B. One Percent Annual Franchise "Failure" Rates

A second set of widely used success rate figures are those claiming that only 1 percent of franchises fail annually and, consequently, only 5 percent fail after five years of operation. These figures also are attributed to Department of Commerce statistics. Once again, however, review of the Department's *Franchising in the Economy* reports shows no directly comparable statistics on failure rates for franchises or individual franchisees.

What the reports do provide are figures for the number of reported failures of franchisors, not individual franchises or franchisees. Franchisor failures were reported as totaling 78 in 1986 and 104 in 1987, the last two years of the Department surveys. The number of failed franchisors in 1987, for example, represented 4.7 percent of the total number of franchisors in the survey. This figure, however, was not included in the survey reports. Instead, calculations were made to further reduce this figure for the reports, first by estimating the portion of sales represented by the failed franchise companies in comparison to estimated total sales by all franchisors, then by subtracting the sales of the company-owned outlets of these failed franchisors. The result, in terms of "lost" sales volume of the franchises of failed franchisors, was approximately 1 percent (Franchising in the Economy, 1988). This 1 percent figure for "lost sales" volume was reported relatively consistently throughout the 1973-1987 period of the Department's surveys.

This is the only place where the term "failure" appears in the Commerce Department reports. Again, the 1 percent figure does not apply to any broad measure of failures among franchises or individual franchisees, but only to the "lost sales volume" of franchises affiliated with franchise systems which were known to have failed. *[As noted below (see "Commerce Department Data on Franchisor Failures"), a significant number of franchisors were also identified as having "discontinued" franchising each year, but neither their franchises nor sales volumes were ever included in this "failure" calculation.]*

C. 94 Percent Franchisee "Success" Rate

The most recent figures purporting to show extremely high rates of success for franchises are those claiming franchises have "a 94 percent success rate" or, alternatively, that "94 percent of franchise owners are successful." While similar in substance to earlier success rate figures, this claim differs significantly in that it is said to derive from an "independent" study conducted by the Gallup Organization and from information gathered from franchisees.

Analysis of the 1992 Gallup report cited as the source for these claims reveals serious methodological shortcomings and misrepresentations. What is described in industry promotions as an "independent Gallup survey" is in reality a limited market research study done by Gallup under contract with the International Franchise Association. The study did not employ independent sampling techniques to obtain a scientific survey sample of franchisees nor did it seek to include any former or failed franchisees (Tannenbaum, 1993).

Gallup's study consisted of a telephone survey of 994 franchise owners to solicit their "attitudes and opinions" with regard to franchise ownership. Franchisee names were supplied by a consultant with close ties to the franchising industry. As part of the survey, respondents were asked to choose from among four responses that most closely reflected their opinion of the "overall success" of their franchise business. The listed responses used versions of the term "successful" ("very unsuccessful"; "somewhat unsuccessful"; "somewhat successful" and "very successful") without defining these terms.

An interesting aspect of Gallup's findings on this question, particularly in light of the survey's controlled sample, was the fact that more than half the respondents (52%) indicated that their franchise was, at best, only "somewhat successful." Respondents indicating either "somewhat successful" (47 percent) and "very successful" (47 percent) were combined by Gallup to produce a finding that "94 percent of respondents considered their franchise operation to be successful."

Despite the rather lukewarm response of over half the respondents, and the fact that no failed or former franchisees were contacted for the survey, this finding of the IFA/Gallup study began appearing in industry promotions as a "94 percent success rate" for franchises. In national advertising for the International Franchise Association's 1993 International Franchise Expo the study was described as an "independent survey" to support the broader claim that "franchise owners enjoy an incredible 94 percent success rate."

D. Long-term Business "Failure Rate" Chart

Another set of success rate figures used frequently in promotions and industry fact sheets during the past two decades involves detailed information in chart form which purport to compare, over a ten-year period, the success rates of franchises with those of non-franchised independent businesses. Almost uniformly, these charts show franchises as having success rates approach 90 percent over ten years while independent businesses are depicted as failing at rates exceeding 80 percent over the ten-year period. Once again, however, the sources identified for information included in the charts provide little or inadequate substantiation for the claims made.

One version of the chart purporting to show "failure rates among U.S. businesses" began appearing in franchise promotions in the 1970s. The chart is the most detailed version of the success rate charts, including multiple sources of failure rate data for non-franchise businesses as diagonal lines running over five and ten-year periods. The International Franchise Association is identified as the source of failure rate data on franchises, which are shown as failing at roughly a 3 percent rate in the first year, at an 8 percent rate after 5 years and 10 percent over ten years of operation.

The chart includes four lines representing failure rates for non-franchise businesses or businesses generally which it attributes to the Department of Commerce, Dunn and Bradstreet and the U.S. Small Business Administration (SBA). All four lines rise sharply to show failures of between 15 and 40 percent in the first year and rising to rates of between 66 to 77 percent after 5 years. Two of the lines representing Commerce Department data continue to show failure of between 80 and 90 percent over 10 years.

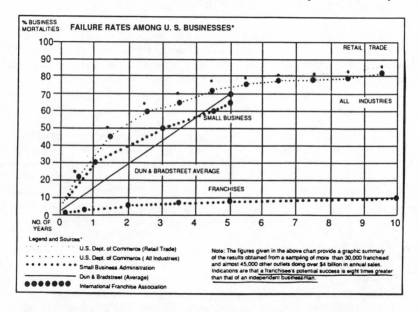

Critics have questioned the source and accuracy of much of the information in the chart, particularly the data on failure rates for non-franchise businesses. Neither the Department of Commerce, the SBA or Dunn and Bradstreet produced comparable data on business failure rates as those shown on this chart. The likely source of the information used for the chart is a 1968 study on franchise failures prepared by J.P. Atkinson and published by the International Franchise Association. In the study, Atkinson calculates an annual failure rate figure for franchises of 1.6 percent based on failures reported to the IFA by 70 franchisors. Using an assumption that 75-100 percent of the franchises that fail do so in the first 5 years of operation, he projected this 1.6 percent figure over 5 years to produce an 8 percent failure rate for franchises after 5 years and a 10 percent rate over 10 years.

The study compared these figures with failure rates for businesses generally, which are attributed to a Commerce Department report entitled "Age and Life Expectancy of Business Firms" and to Dunn and Bradstreet reports for 1967 and which are claimed to show "on the average, 65-75 percent of all business firms fail within five years." Comparing this failure data with his own five-year failure rate for franchises, Atkinson concluded "even if the actual franchise failure rate were eight times higher than reported, it would still pay an investor to be franchised rather than start an independent small business" (Atkinson).

Serious questions were raised almost immediately with both the sources and accuracy of Atkinson's findings. A number of researchers tried without success to locate the sources of the statistics on independent business failure rates claimed to have been used in the study (Levy). Other analysts criticized Atkinson's franchise failure figures as "based on arbitrary exclusions and highly selective, rather than random, testing" (Brown).

The strongest criticism of the study appeared in Ozanne and Hunt's 1971 SBA study which claimed Atkinson had presented "misleading information" in comparing failure rates for franchise and non-franchise businesses. They found that the Commerce data cited by Atkinson had provided data on business "turnover" and not business failures as Atkinson claimed. Moreover, the Commerce report had clearly distinguished between broader categories of business turnover and more limited numbers of business failures, stating that "many other reasons other than lack of profitability" can account for business transfers and turnovers. Ozanne and Hunt also found that the Dunn and Bradstreet figures used for the study were incorrectly cited as providing a 66 percent failure rate for all businesses over five years when, in fact, the study showed only that of companies which do fail, 66 percent do so within the first five years of operation (Ozanne & Hunt).

This misuse of data prompted Ozanne and Hunt to accuse Atkinson of making "erroneous comparisons" with overall business failure rates to produce conclusions they described as "completely misleading." This version of the failure rate chart continues to be used in promotions by a number of franchisors, including major franchisors like the Subway Sandwich chain, despite the fact the information on which it is based is now more than 25 years old and was repudiated in a federal report and Congressional testimony more than twenty years ago (Subway Concept).

E. Ten-Year Business "Success Rate" Chart

A different version of the franchise success rate chart gained widespread use in promotional materials after it appeared in *Franchising* magazine in 1987. This chart is a simplified version of the earlier chart using bar graphs to compare success rates for franchises over ten years with a single set of success rates for "independent" businesses. Like the earlier chart, this graph shows only 3 percent of franchises failing in the first year, 8 percent over 5 years and 10 percent over ten years of operation. The chart differs, however, in presenting these figures more positively as percentages of businesses "still operating" each year. Thus 97 percent of franchises are shown to be operating after the first year, 92 percent after 5 years and 90 percent after ten years of operation. The contrasting figures for independent businesses failures correspond generally with those attributed in the earlier chart to Commerce Department "failure rates" for retail businesses. Stated as percentages of businesses still operating, these figures show 62 percent of independent businesses operating after one year, 23 percent after 5 years and only 18 percent operating after 10 years.

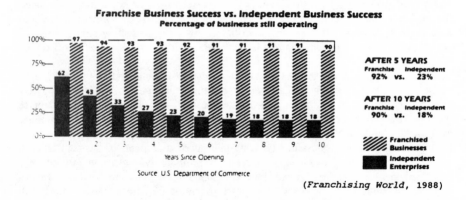

Franchise Business Success vs. Independent Business Success
Percentage of businesses still operating

AFTER 5 YEARS
Franchise   Independent
92%   vs.   23%

AFTER 10 YEARS
Franchise   Independent
90%   vs.   18%

Years Since Opening

Source U.S Department of Commerce

Franchised Businesses

Independent Enterprises

(*Franchising World*, 1988)

Differing versions of this chart cite the source of the data as the Department of Commerce, the Small Business Administration or both agencies. Once again, however, no comparable data for independent businesses failures can be found to have been produced or published by either agency. With regard to the figures on franchise failures, it is possible the failure rates used in the chart were simply extrapolated from the Commerce Department data described above, using the 3 percent rate included in Department reports for "discontinued" franchises to represent franchise failures in the initial years, with the lower 1 percent figure for lost sales of failed franchisors used to produce 1 percent annual failure rates over subsequent years.

A version of this chart used before 1987 presents essentially the same data but cites as its source a series of hearings conducted by a subcommittee of the House Small Business Committee in 1978 and published under the title, the *Future of Small Business in America.* The only reference to franchising in the hearing was provided in testimony by the Small Business Legislative Council, a business coalition whose membership included the International Franchise Association. The testimony cited data, attributed to the IFA, claiming "about 70 to 90 percent" of people who go into business independently "terminate" in the first 10 years, with "51 to 57 percent" terminating during the first year. In contrast, the testimony claimed, "less than 2 to 4 percent of franchised establishments were discontinued" (*The Future of Small Business in America*).

No comparable figures for independent business failures were provided in testimony by the Small Business Administration or any other witnesses. On the contrary, the testimony of SBA's Administrator, Vernon Weaver, acknowledged that the agency did not have data on ownership "longevity" or the age of failed businesses. The SBA did submit data from studies done by Dun and Bradstreet of selected businesses that had failed showing that "about 55 percent...do so during the first 5 years of business, and about 27 percent fail during the first 3 years." Again, like the Dunn and Bradstreet data used in the Atkinson study 10 years earlier, these figures represent percentages only of groups of known business failures, not percentages of all independent businesses.

A number of researchers have tried to reproduce the data used to compile this success rate chart with little success. "Due to the lack of citations," one paper notes, "it is not possible to track down the specific sources of the statistics pertaining to success and failure rates. When one is able to track down sources, the statistics often were drawn from another source, such as a congressional subcommittee hearing" (Walker & Cross). Another researcher explained he "could not replicate" the extremely low rates of failure for franchises as compared to non-franchises that are incorporated in the charts using both Dun and Bradstreet data and data from the Commerce Department (Balkin).

III. Franchises as "Risk Free" Investments

All these figures and charts have been used, individually and in combination, to portray franchises as uniformly successful and virtually risk free. These figures, according to one analysis, are used "to tell prospective franchisees that franchising is a good way to invest...that your chance of being in business five years from now are excellent in franchising" (English & Willems). These figures have also been used very successfully to hide the fact that objective or comprehensive data on franchise failures does not exist. This has made it possible for franchisors to extol the high success rates of franchisingwithout challenge and for individual franchisors to include low failure rate figures in marketing materials "even when their own company has much larger franchisee attrition" (Rager).

While widely accepted, the notion that franchises have substantially higher rates of success than independent businesses has little conclusive substantiation in research data. The review of available research on franchise failures by Walker and Cross found not only that "sloppy use of terms such as failure and turnover (was) common" but that "many of the statistics typically used are based on anecdotal information or are derived through unspecified methods." The researchers concluded "it is not possible to conclusively determine whether failure rates among franchisees are lower (or higher) than among independent businesses (Walker & Cross).

Research on attrition rates among restaurants by English and Willems also found little evidence to substantiate the broad claims of substantially higher rates of success among franchised restaurants. Where the researchers did find higher initial success rates among franchises, this success generally corresponded with other factors, particularly higher levels of initial capitalization and expenditures for advertising, which the franchise chains required of franchisees. But it is these "other factors," they concluded, that have "more to do with their greater success than their association with the franchising format" (English & Willems).

The Federal Trade Commission also concluded that "there may be less of a difference than is commonly thought" between rates of success of franchises and independent businesses. In testimony to the Committee in 1991, the Commission described the 5% failure rate figures attributed to the Department of Commerce as "an understatement" that had "never counted the hidden failures" of franchisees who resell or simply abandon their franchise. The testimony suggested that failures among independent businesses, on the other hand, were probably much lower than generally assumed, basing this conclusion on research data showing "the failure rate for such businesses may be as low as 27 percent after three years, or just 9 percent a year" (Cutler).

The figures for independent business cited by the FTC were the findings of a 1989 study of independent business owners by the National Federation of Independent Business and American Express Small Business Services. The study, which claimed to be the first study to track some 3,000 businesses during the critical first three years of operation, found that 77 percent of all new businesses remained in operation after three years. Even retail businesses, assumed to have the highest rates of failure, were found to have a 73 percent survival rate. While the study included a representative sample of franchises (12 percent) it found nothing to suggest differing success rates for franchises than for the other businesses studied. "No relationship existed," the study concluded, "between the possession of a franchise or operation under a franchise name and survival" (Cooper).

The Small Business Administration has also stated that little difference exists between franchises and independent businesses in the statistics it keeps on loan defaults on guaranteed loans to business owners. Responding to a Senate inquiry in 1992, the SBA reported roughly comparable default rates among loans made to franchisees and non-franchise business owners. Reported default rates on franchise loans ranged from 8.1 percent on loans made in 1987 to .4 percent on newer franchise loans made in 1990. Comparable loan default rates for non-franchise loans were reported as 7.5 percent and .6 percent for loans grated in these years (Sakai). The data reported by SBA represents a marked improvement from the findings of an earlier 1980 General Accounting Office audit which reported default rates on franchise loans as nearly 10 percent, more than twice the default rate for all SBA loans (Eschwege).

A recent analysis of Census Bureau data on independent businesses also tends to refute claims that franchises tend to be far more successful than independent business ventures and even suggests that franchises may be "less profitable and more likely to go out of business" than non-franchise businesses. The study tracked more than 7,000 non-minority businesses randomly selected from all business owners providing information for the Census Bureau's Characteristics of Business Owners data base. Among business owners who began operations between 1984 and 1987 and who identified their businesses as franchises, 34.9 percent were out of business by late 1991. Failures among comparable non-franchise businesses were reported as 28 percent (Bates).

The study provided more striking comparisons between franchise and non-franchise businesses when the findings are broken down by the age and type of business. The newest businesses included in the study (those opening in 1987) showed the highest rates of failure (43.4 percent for franchises and 39.3 percent for non-franchise businesses). Businesses in operation over three and four years showed lower failure rates, but greater discrepancy in failure rates between franchises and non-franchise businesses (29 percent failures for franchises and 19.6 percent for non-franchise businesses). Greatest discrepancy was found in failure rates for franchise and non-franchise retail businesses, with 46 percent of all retail franchises going out of business as compared to 23.6 percent of non-franchise retail businesses.

The study's author observed that "conventional wisdom regarding the attractiveness of franchising may have some historic validity" but was not evident in the operations of newer businesses in the late 1980s. He concludes that "despite their larger revenues, much greater capitalization, and their supposed advantages of affiliation with a franchisorparent firm, the franchisees lag behind cohort young firms in profitability and rates of survival" (Bates).

The inadequacies of available data on franchise failures and the misuse of this data in franchise promotions are best summarized in a letter to the Committee from the publisher of a national franchise directory. The letter describes how many franchisors have been able--

> to mask the fact that, in many cases, a large number of franchisees may have been unsuccessful, for whatever reason, in running a profitable franchise operation. The extent that he or she sells the franchise to a 'bigger fool' or back to the franchisor for 50 cents on the dollar, this is not considered a failure for reporting purposes. As far as the general public is concerned, by looking only at the historical growth in operating units, the franchisees and the franchisor are assumed to have been successful...

> This problem is compounded by the only industry statistics on franchisee success (i.e., a 5% failure rate over 5 years), unfairly attributed to the Department of Commerce. Again, failure is defined only as closing up the tent. No consideration is given to sales to third parties, downsizing the operation, the fact that the franchisee hasn't formally declared bankruptcy, etc. As long as a location continues in operation, it is not considered a failure, and, inversely, a success for marketing purposes.

> The end result is that the franchising industry uses this statistic very effectively in making the public in general and the potential franchisee in particular believe that success is almost guaranteed if he or she joins a franchise operation." (Bond)

IV. The Problem of Franchisor Failures

Franchise industry claims of success rates in excess of 90 percent over five and ten years have long been questioned on grounds that significant rates of failure among franchisors themselves make such claims virtually impossible. In their 1971 SBA study Ozanne and Hunt noted numerous franchise system failures among fast food franchisors in 1969-1970, stating that the failures they had been able to document represented "6.7 percent of all franchise systems in existence during this period." Given numerous reported franchise system failures in other market sectors, they concluded that actual rates of failure among franchisors "could easily be double or triple the number identified." Determining exactly how many franchise systems fail was described as a "challenge" by the authors "because it is difficult to locate something that no longer exists" (Ozanne & Hunt).

A. Commerce Department Data on Franchisors

While the Commerce Department reports published between 1973 and 1988 offer little in the way of direct substantiation for claims of extremely high success rates among franchises, they do provide information pertaining to franchisors that have either failed or ceased franchising. The reports present annual statistics on the number of known franchisor failures, together with a second, generally larger, figure for the number of franchisors who "discontinue franchising as a method of doing business". What constitutes a "failure" or a "departure" from franchising is not explained in the reports. But, as one analysis concluded, many franchisors who discontinue franchising could be construed to be failures "even if they were not business failures in the sense that the business ceased operations due to unsatisfactory financial performance" (Walker & Cross).

The combined number of failed or departed franchisors reported in the annual surveys is significant, amounting to 125 in 1985, 183 in 1986 and 184 in 1987. It is probable that the number of failed franchisors may have been even greater since, as one analyst noted, the Commerce Department surveys appeared not to have included many of the newer and smaller franchisors (Boe). Even as reported in the Department's reports, however, the combined figures for franchisors that failed or stopped franchising totalled 1711 for the 15-year period of the Department of Commerce surveys. This number represents **44 percent** of the total number of franchisors that were included in the Department's surveys through 1987.

This raises questions as to what happened to the franchises affiliated with nearly half the franchise systems included in the Commerce Department surveys? How many continued operation as independent businesses? And were any of these franchises included in any count of franchise failures?

The Commerce Department reports do not address these questions. Rather, they appear to have minimized the importance of these high franchisor "drop out" figures, as noted above, by taking only the estimated franchise sales of known franchisor failures and comparing them with total franchise sales to produce low (1 percent) annual sales "loss" figures. This minimizing of the high annual drop out rate among franchisors prompted one group of researchers to conclude, "the Department of Commerce apparently is not concerned about these rates of franchisor failure" (Walker & Cross).

B. Evidence of Franchisor Failures Since 1987

Although the Commerce Department did not collect national data on franchisors after 1987, there is evidence to suggest not only that high levels of franchisor failure have continued, but that the accelerating rates of franchisor failures observed by experts in the mid-1980s (Kreisman) have continued to the present.

A spokesman for the International Franchise Association, for example, was quoted in 1991 as saying that while the IFA did not specifically track how many franchise companies go out of business each year, "about 8 to 10 percent of the companies listed with the organization drop off annually" (Reynolds). This approximates the rate of failed and departed franchisors shown in the Department of Commerce surveys in the mid-1980s.

The American Association of Franchisees and Dealers compared the annual listings and rankings of more than 1,000 franchisors by *Entrepreneur* magazine for 1987 and 1992. It found that "almost 70% of the franchising companies listed by Entrepreneur in 1987 no longer appeared in the 1992 rankings" (*The Franchisee Voice*). While all the missing franchisors may not have been financial failures, a significant percentage are presumed to have ceased operation or ceased franchising.

A more detailed analysis of various sources of information on franchise opportunities, including the annual *Entrepreneur* magazine listings, was published in 1993 by a University of Michigan business professor. The study found that while all published information on franchises using survey data from franchisors "suffer from selection bias" and should not be used "to infer general patterns in franchising practices," the *Entrepreneur* listings at least provided "the most detailed longitudinal data on individual franchisors" and on franchisor entry into franchising (Lafontaine 3/93).

Analyzing the *Entrepreneur* surveys between 1980 and 1990, the study identified significant attrition among franchisors listed the surveys that could not be explained by any limitation or selection criteria imposed by the magazine editors (Lafontaine 1/93). Of the 3743 franchisors listed in the surveys, nearly one-third (1226) appeared only once. Another third (1252) appeared in only two or three of the eleven annual listings. Less than 17 percent of all franchisors listed appeared in more than half of these annual listings. While the study can be said to confirm claims of significant franchisor entry into franchising during the 1980s, it also raises serious questions as to what happened to the "vast majority" of franchise systems that disappear from franchise listings.

Additional questions are raised by a survey of franchisors conducted in the fall of 1991 by the accounting firm of Arthur Andersen & Co. for the International Franchise Association. The accounting firm compiled a list of all known franchisors using lists supplied by the IFA, trade journals, company releases and other sources. After several mailings, the firm reported being able to "positively" identify only 2022 "active" franchising companies (Franchising in the Economy, 1992). This figure for "known active" franchisors is significant, since it is less than the total number of operating franchisors (2,177) found by the Commerce Department five years earlier. It was also reported that Arthur Andersen raised serious "methodological questions" with the base data on franchisors and franchisees used by the IFA, to the extent that the company would not include a figure for the total number of franchise outlets in its report (Tannenbaum, 1992).

A broader assessment of recent franchise failures has been provided by the publisher of *The Info Franchise Newsletter*, whose company also publishes the largest directory of U.S. and foreign franchise opportunities. The newsletter took issue with IFA claims of 15% growth in the number of franchise establishments during 1992, on grounds that "there has never really been an accurate survey of franchising in North America," and that its own listings have shown significant losses of franchisors (Dixon).

Since early 1991, according to the newsletter, 852 franchisors had disappeared from the company's annual listing of franchisors. "We just couldn't find them," it explained, "so we assume they've gone out of business." The newsletter also observed, "these franchise failures do not appear in the statistics." Since 1983, a total of 4,390 franchisors were reported to have disappeared from the company's franchise listings, with 3036 franchisors "lost" since 1989. The newsletter reported a total of 5,045 operating U.S., Canadian and "overseas" franchisors at the end of 1992.

Evidence exists to support the newsletter's assumption that most of the missing franchisors were financial failures. From its study of the financial statements of the "top 10" franchisors in a variety of business categories, business consultants Rubinoff-Rager Inc. estimated that "25% of the franchisors analyzed...are technically insolvent from a financial standpoint" (Rager). The franchise regulator for the State of Illinois, in testimony submitted to the Committee in 1991, observed that the "overall financial condition" of franchisors registering to sell franchises in the state had "deteriorated" during 1990 and that 38% of these franchisors had been required to provide some form of financial guarantee due to findings of "inadequate financial capability" to fulfill obligations to franchisees (Saunderson).

In the absence of reliable data, it is only possible to raise questions as to what happened to the large number of franchisors that have disappeared from these franchise listings? How many of these companies have failed or simply stopped franchising? And, as Ozanne and Hunt asked twenty years ago, "how many franchisees have been left stranded as a result of these franchisor failures?" (Ozanne & Hunt)

V. Estimates of Franchise Failure Rates

The large numbers of franchisors that have failed or stopped franchising raise serious questions regarding the accuracy of inflated claims of franchise success. When the number of franchises affiliated with failed franchise systems is combined with those reported as "discontinued" by franchisors, with those that are terminated, taken back or repurchased by franchisors, with those that never open or are later abandoned by franchisees and with those that are resold by franchisees at a loss, the total number of failed franchises is likely to be considerable. Clearly, the number would be significantly larger than the 5 percent annual "failure" rates routinely touted by the franchising industry.

From their research on failures rates for franchises of major franchise companies Rubinoff-Rager found a failure rate of between 30 percent and 40 percent for the three-year period of the disclosure documents they studied (Rager). This is not substantially different than the combined annual rates of failure and turnover reported by Walker and Cross in 1988. And it is only slightly higher (on an annualized basis) than estimates by Patrick Boroian, president of the franchise consulting firm, Francorp Inc., who commented in 1990 that "the real number of failures every year is probably 10%" (Boroian).

In his analysis of Census Bureau data on independent businesses, Bates tracks the performance of franchises over five years (1987 to 1991) to find franchise failure rates roughly comparable to those reported by Rubinoff-Rager. Of the computer sampling of 431 franchises operating during this period, Bates found that more than one-third (34.0 percent) went out of business. The "youngest" franchise businesses, those beginning operations in 1987, were found to be "the least likely to remain in operation" over the 1987-1991 period, with failure rates of more than 43 percent. Businesses already operating several years before the study period exhibited a lower 29 percent failure rate (Bates).

Other analysts have used a "slice-in-time" approach to arrive at somewhat comparable estimates of franchise success rates. Rupert Barkoff, chairman of the American Bar Association's Franchise Forum has estimated that for the typical franchise chain "probably at best a third are doing very well, a third are in definite financial trouble and a third maybe break even" (Barkoff). A 1991 survey of franchisees in the Pak Mail franchise system by an independent firm, Franchise Analysis, Inc., found nearly identical percentages as those noted by Barkoff for franchisees who where either making money, breaking even or failing, except that less than a quarter of the Pak Mail franchisees appear to have been able to draw more than minimal income from the business (Hadder).

A somewhat broader measure of franchise success is used by franchise guidebook publisher Robert Bond in assessing potential levels of success and failure among franchises generally. While noting that "the prospect for failure may be substantially reduced" with a franchise, he adds, "my sense is that success, defined in terms of meeting the franchisee's realistic expectations, is probably no greater than 40% (not 95%) over five years--still far above the success rate of the sole entrepreneur" (Bond).

The lack of independent, comprehensive data on franchise failures has helped perpetuate what the Federal Trade Commission termed "the most widespread myth" of franchising--the idea "that franchises are a safe investment because they have a much lower failure rate than independent business" (Cutler). In the absence of comprehensive studies of franchise performance, only anecdotal analyses of franchise failures exist with which to judge the truthfulness of industry claims of franchise success. The "void of reliable statistics" that Walker and Cross noted in 1988 still exists in franchising and continues to permit statistics on franchise success to be "created, misused, abused and/or misrepresented." From the perspective of public policy, the deficiencies of current research on franchising and franchise performance must be viewed, as one paper observed, "as inexcusable given the vast and growing significance of franchising" in the nation's economy (Elango & Fried).

References

Atkinson, J.F. (1968), *Franchising: The Odds-on Favorite*, International Franchise Association.

Balkin, Steven, "Self-Employment Training Programs For the Poor," *Journal of Small Business Strategy*, October 1990, p. 47.

Barkoff, Rupert (1991), cited in Moore, Lisa J. (1991), "The Flight to Franchising," *U.S. News & World Report*, June 10, p. 68.

Barkoff, Rupert (1992), statement, Hearing on "New Developments in Franchise Law", July 21, 1992, in *New Developments in Franchising*, Committee on Small Business, U.S. House of Representatives, Government Printing Office, Washington, D.C., 1992.

Bates, Timothy (1993), "Franchise Startups: Low Profitability and High Failure Rates," *EGII News*, Winter, 1993, Entrepreneurial Growth and Investment Institute, Washington, D.C.

Boe, Kathryn L. (1988), statement, Hearing on "Unfair Franchise Practices," Subcommittee on Antitrust, Impact of Deregulation, and Privatization, Committee on Small Business, U.S. House of Representatives, August 4, 1988, U.S. Government Printing Office, Washington, D.C.

Bond, Robert E. (1992), Letter to the Committee on Small Business, U.S. House of Representatives, January 24, 1992.

Boroian, Patrick (1990), interviewed in Tannenbaum, Jeffrey, "Franchising's Prospects Appear Bright, Specialist Says," *The Wall Street Journal*, September 27, B2.

Brown, Harold (1993), *Franchising Realities and Remedies*, Law Journal Seminar Press.

Cooper, A., C. Dunkelberg, C. Woo and W. Dennis (1990), *New Business In America: The Firms and Their Owners*, National Federation of Independent Business.

Cutler, Barry (1991), statement, Hearing on "Franchising in Hard Times," Committee on Small Business, U.S. House of Representatives, March 20, U.S. Government Printing Office, Washington, D.C.

Dixon, Ted, ed. (1992), *The Info Franchise Newsletter*, Vol, 16, No. 12, December.

Elango, B. and Vance H. Fried (1992), "Franchising Research: Towards A Holistic Approach," unpublished manuscript.

English, Wilke & Jo Willems (1992), "Franchise vs. Non Franchise Restaurant Attrition: Year-Two of a Yellow Pages Longitudinal Analysis," Unpublished manuscript.

"Entrepreneur's Annual Franchise 500", *Entrepreneur*, January 1987; January 1992.

Eschwege, Henry (1981), Statement, Hearing on "Problems With Small Business Administration Financial Assistance to Franchises," Subcommittee on Commerce, consumer and Monetary Affairs, Committee on Government Operations, U.S. House of Representatives, May 19, 1981, U.S. Government Printing Office, Washington, D.C.

Franchising in the Economy (1986, 1988), U.S. Department of Commerce, Industry and Trade Administration, U.S. Government Printing Office, Washington, D.C.

Franchising in the Economy, 1989-1992 (1992), International Franchise Association/Arthur Andersen & Co., Washington, D.C.

Franchising World (1988), International Franchise Association, January/February, p. 56.

Hadder, Jack (1992), *The Franchisee Survey Report*, Franchise Analysis, Inc., May 1992.

Hadfield, Gillian K. (1990), "Problematic Relations: Franchising and the Law of Incomplete Contracts," *Stanford Law Review*, April 1990, p. 927.

Kreisman, Richard (1986), "How Start-Up Franchisors Fail," *Inc.*, September, p. 106, 108.

Lafontaine, Francine (1993), "The Evolution and Characteristics of Franchising in the 1980's", Society of Franchising, 1993 Proceedings, Seventh Annual Conference, February 1993, Rajiv P. Dant, ed.

Lafontaine, Francine (1993), "A Critical Appraisal of Data Sources on Franchising," April 1993, Unpublished manuscript.

Levy, Robert (1969), "So You Want to Run A Franchise," *Dun's Review*, January. p. 36.

255

O'Donnell, Thomas (1984), "No Entrepreneurs Need Apply," *Forbes*, December 3, 1984.

Ozanne, Urban B. and Shelby D. Hunt (1971), "The Economic Effects of Franchising", Report prepared for the U.S. Small Business Administration, printed by the Select Committee on Small Business, United States Senate, September 8, U.S. Government Printing Office.

Padmanabhan, K.H., (1986), "Are the Franchised Businesses Less Risky Than the Non-Franchised Businesses?", Society of Franchising, 1986 Proceedings, *First Annual Conference*, R. Mittlestaedt, ed.

Rager, Les, (1992), Letter to John J. LaFalce, Chairman, Committee on Small Business, March 12, 1992.

Reynolds, John (1991), quoted in Narum, Beverly, "Franchise Row," *The Houston Post*, January 21, E1.

Saiki, Patricia (1992), Letter to Carl Levin, Chairman, Subcommittee on Oversight of Government Management, Committee on Government Affairs, United States Senate, April 6, 1992.

Saunderson, Christina M. (1991), letter of the Committee on Small Business, April 10, included in "Franchising In Hard Times," Committee on Small Business, U.S. House of Representatives, March 20, U.S. Government Printing Office, Washington, D.C.

Small Business Administration (1991), SBA Loan Experience By Franchise, computer listing provided to Small Business Committee, U.S. House of Representatives, October 2, 1991.

Solomon, Gabrielle (1993), "Sifting Through the Hype", in "Is Franchising Really Safe?", *National Business Employment Weekly*, Dow Jones & Company, April 23-29, 1993.

Tannenbaum, Jeffrey A. (1992), "It's growing, To Be Sure, But Just How Big Is The Franchising Industry?", in "Franchisees Weigh Joint Actions to Gain Protections", *Wall Street Journal*, September 28, B2.

Tannenbaum, Jeffrey A. (1993), "Are Franchisees Really As Successful As A Gallup Study Found?", in "Disclosure Guidelines Advance," *Wall Street Journal*, March 31, 1993, B2.

The Franchisee Voice (1993), American Association of Franchisees and Dealers, Winter.

The Future of Small Business in America (1978), Hearings of the Subcommittee on Antitrust, Consumers and Employment, U.S. House of Representatives, March/April 1978, Part I, U.S. Government Printing Office, Washington, D.C.

The Subway Concept (undated), promotional brochure, Doctor's Associates, Inc., Milford, Connecticutt *(1992)*.

Walker, Bruce J. and James Cross (1988), "Franchise Failures: More Questions Than Answers," Society of Franchising, 1988 Proceedings, *Forging Partnerships for Competitive Advantage*, R. Dwyer, ed.

Webb, Margaret K. (1989), "New Companies Not Necessarily Risky Businesses," *Wall Street Journal*, October 16, 1989.

Endnotes

CHAPTER 1

1. Page B6 (Franchise Advertising) of the August 27, 1992, edition of *The Wall Street Journal* includes the following teasers: "Don't blink? Or The Franchise You Want Will Be Gone"; "A Franchise Opportunity You Can Profit From"; "A Solid Growth Business"; "Build a Secure and Rewarding Future"; "Looking for an Individual Interested In: Being Self-employed, Controlling His/Her Own Financial Growth Enjoying Freedom and Prestige"; "Be Boss"; "Become a part of the Biggest, Best, and Fastest Growing Steakhouse Chain in America . . ."; "Many of the Owners Quit Their Careers at Such Corporate Giants as IBM, Chemical Bank, and Ford to Obtain Financial Security, Job Satisfaction, and a Better Life Style"; "You can enjoy the comfort of a solid customer base and choice locations. Don't wait . . ."; "Former Executives from Fortune 500 Companies and Professionals from Businesses Nationwide Are Taking Charge of Their Lives and Starting Exciting and New Careers as . . . Franchisees"; "Now's the time to join the exciting and wonderful world of . . !"; "Seven Additional Revenue/Profit Centers with Unlimited Income Potential"; "Excellent opportunity with an affordable investment"; "One big opportunity."
2. Erika Kotite, "A World of Opportunities," *Entrepreneur*, January 1992, 86.
3. *San Diego Union Tribune*, March 23, 1993.
4. From an advertisement appearing in the March issue of *Success* magazine. The author requested permission from the IFA to reproduce the advertisement in full, but received no response.
5. The Summer 1992 Edition of *IFA's Franchise Opportunities Guide*, p. 22 (published annually by the International Franchise Association), put it this way:

Why Buy a Franchise?

Franchising is an excellent way to be in business for yourself, but not by yourself, because the franchisor is always there to help. The franchisor provides a method of doing business that has been tested over time in the marketplace. The franchisor provides its expertise, experience and continuous advertising and market support.

6. Rubinoff Rager Incorporated. 1992.
7. The marketing brochure for A&W Root Beer Franchises extols the partnership aspects of the franchise relationship. The brochure opens with the claim "Strong Partnerships Are the Foundation of Our Chain," and concludes:

A&W Restaurants' Mission

We, at A&W, believe the success of our operation depends on the mutual trust and respect of partnerships that are formed. We invite those who will share in our mission to deliver the best possible dining experience to our customers, to become a partner with A&W Restaurants, Inc.

Compare the language in Section 11 of A&W's franchise agreement:

11.0 The Licensee is not, and shall not represent or hold itself out as, an agent, legal representative, joint venturer, **partner,** employee or servant of the Company for any purposes whatsoever . . .

It happens that A&W has one of the fairest franchise agreements around; nevertheless, the promise of the marketing materials presents a strong contrast to the reality of the contract language. As will be seen, U.S. courts have forgiven such inconsistencies as permissible "salesman *puffing.*"

8. See Appendix A, "Reprint of a Staff Memorandum on franchising failure rates addressed to Hon. John J. LaFalce, Chairman of the House Committee on Small Business" (U.S. House of Representatives).
9. From *IFA's Franchise Opportunities Guide,* Summer 1992, 38.
10. See Appendix A, and see Dr. Timothy Bates, "Franchise Startups: Low Profitability and High Failure Rates" *EGII News* (Dec. 1993).
11. The American Association of Franchisees and Dealers, *The Franchisee Voice,* (Winter 1993).
12. *The Info Franchise Newsletter, 16,* no. 12 (December, 1992).
13. See Appendix A.
14. Goodwill refers to the appreciated value of the business as a going concern as opposed to the market value of the hard assets of the business.

CHAPTER 2

1. Frequently, the exact reverse is true. The franchisor may negotiate a favorable lease for the premises and then "mark-up" the rent to its franchisees.
2. The name was later changed from Mac to Mc.

CHAPTER 3

1. Luxemberg, *The Roadside Empires: How the Chains Franchised America.* New York: Viking, 1985.
2. *The Roadside Empires* also dates franchising to the tithing practices of the Catholic Church in the twelfth century.
3. John F. Love, *McDonald's: Behind the Arches,* New York: Bantom Books, 1986, 51.
4. International Franchise Association, *IFA's Franchise Opportunities Guide,* Summer 1992, 39.

CHAPTER 4

1. From the Department of Commerce, *Franchise Opportunities Handbook* (1988).
2. From an advertising brochure produced and published by Chick's Natural, Encinitas, California in 1991. The company did not respond to the author's request to reprint the page of the brochure which included the quoted passage.
3. From an interview with a staff member at the House Committee on Small Business. It is most interesting to note that the 1980 White House Conference on Small Business concluded there was insufficient data available to determine how many small businesses exist in the United States, let alone predict reliable failure rates.
4. Dr. Timothy Bates, "Franchise Startups: Low Profitability and High Failure Rates," *EGII News* (December 1993).
5. Ibid. p. 1.
6. Ibid. p. 9.
7. When the Department of Commerce ceased publishing its annual update of franchising in the U.S. economy, the IFA *volunteered* to continue the publication for the Department of Commerce.
8. Dr. Timothy Bates, "Franchise Startups: Low Profitability and High Failure Rates," *EGII News* (December 1993), p. 9.
9. From a memo from A. W. (Tony) De Sio to "All Franchise Owners," dated November 17, 1993.
10. See Appendix A.
11. As recently as its January 1993 "Franchise Forecast," *Entrepreneur* magazine reported:

> According to U.S. Department of Commerce studies, less than 5 percent of franchised businesses have been discontinued in any given year since 1974. This statistic is especially impressive when compared to estimates of small-business failure rates in general, which range from as low as 30 percent to as high as 65 percent, depending on whom you ask.

12. *Entrepreneur,* January 1992.
13. *Entrepreneur,* January 1993.
14. The Contacts Influential trade name, which is respected for business to business mailing lists, was sold after all the franchisees had gone out of business. Nutri-System declared bankruptcy in 1993, but many former franchisees continue to use the name.
15. The Franchisee Bill of Rights set forth in Chapter 13 was first promulgated by the American Association of Franchisees and Dealers in September 1992. Although there has been no formal response by the franchise industry to these claimed rights, the International Franchise Association completely revised its own Code of Ethics in early 1993 and moved several important steps closer to recognizing some of the rights claimed by franchise owners.
16. *IFA's Franchise Opportunities Guide,* Summer 1992, pp. 35–59.
17. *Entrepreneur,* January 1992, pp. 130–131, explains its grading system as follows:

> Numerous factors, including length of time in business and number of years franchising, number of franchised units and company-owned operating units, start-up costs, growth rate, percentage of terminations, and financial stability of the company, are weighed according to our exclusive formula. These factors are objective, quantifiable measures of a franchise operation. We do not measure subjective elements such as franchisee satisfaction or management style, since these are judgments only you can make based on your own needs and experiences. All companies, regardless of size, are judged by the same criteria.

18. As noted in Chapter 1, 70 percent of the companies listed and ranked by *Entrepreneur* in 1987 do not even appear in the 1992 ratings.
19. American Association of Franchisees and Dealers, Analysis of the 1992 *Entrepreneur* Franchise 500©, September 1992.
20. The AAFD has also performed an analysis of the 1993 rankings which disclosed similar results: In 1993 *Entrepreneur* listed only 1018 franchise companies. Subway achieved the highest ranking with 5,207.51 points. The number 500 ranked franchising company was Pour la France, Cafe and Bakery, a Colorado company in business since 1980 with 8 total stores, six of which are franchised. Pour la France received just 64.13 total points in *Entrepreneur's* rating system. In 1993, only 195 companies received scores of 250 or better, although 50 companies got scores of better than 1,000 (a 20 percent improvement over 1992). Curiously, in 1994 *Entrepreneur* no longer shows the actual weighted rankings of listed franchisors!
21. Janine Huber, "Franchise Forecast," *Entrepreneur,* January 1993, 72.
22. Love, *McDonald's: Behind the Arches,* 240.
23. *Id.,* 172–173.

CHAPTER 5

1. Comments made by Phillip Zeidman before the American Bar Association Section on Anti-Trust Law "Franchise Terminations: Issues & Strategies," 4-20-91.
2. IRS Revenue Ruling 87-41, 1987-1 C.B. 296.

CHAPTER 6

1. Brochure produced by Women in Franchising, Chicago, Il., 1990.
2. Janean Huber, "R-E-S-P-E-C-T," *Entrepreneur, 20*, no. 1 (January 1992), 116.
3. See note 7, Chapter 1 regarding A&W, and pages 53–54 regarding Chick's Natural.

CHAPTER 7

1. Usually, the contract is completely silent as to the franchisee's right to terminate. Increasingly, however, the franchise agreement and disclosure documents blatantly and specifically provide that franchisees have *no right to terminate* under the agreement.
2. The author does not claim Coca-Cola® uses such noncompete covenants. This example is used to graphically illustrate the point.
3. John F. Love, *McDonald's: Behind the Arches,* New York: Bantam Books, 1986, 151–187.

CHAPTER 8

1. John F. Love, *McDonald's: Behind the Arches,* New York: Bantam Books, 1986, 70–80.

CHAPTER 10

1. *2 Henry VI*, 4.2.76.
2. *Nation's Restaurant News,* March 7, 1988.

CHAPTER 11

1. Although no federal statute applies to franchisees generally, in 1956 Congress passed the Federal Automobile Dealer Suits Against Manufactures Act (relating

to automobile dealerships) and in 1978 passed the "Petroleum Marketing Practices Act" (relating to gasoline service station dealers).

2. The Department of Commerce published several publications, including its annual *Franchise Opportunities Handbook* and biannual *Franchising in the Economy*, which tabulates franchise statistics generated from the DOC's annual surveys. The Small Business Administration and other governmental agencies have published brochures as well. To the author's knowledge, no other publication has critically examined the pluses and minuses of franchising.

3. The Federal Trade Act was originally enacted in 1916 and was substantially amended in the 1960s. The law created the Federal Trade Commission and gave the FTC broad authority to stem all kinds of unfair competition and fraudulent business activities.

4. As of this writing, bills similar to the Iowa law were pending in Kentucky, New York, Texas, and South Dakota. Other states reportedly were looking into increased franchise regulation.

5. Ibid.

CHAPTER 12

1. Conversely, a 1992 case against Burger King sent shock waves through the franchising community when a Florida District Court judge ruled that building a new restaurant too close to an existing restaurant may be a breach of good faith even if allowed under the contract. While the judge did not decide whether there had been a breach of faith, the issue was seen as a revolutionary development by franchisee advocates. *Sheck v. Burger King Corp.*, 756 F. Supp. 543 (S.D. Fla. 1991).

2. These numbers are based on the roster of the American Bar Association Forum on Franchising, which has approximately 2000 members. Within the organization, there is an informal group of lawyers interested in representing franchisees. The current roster of this group, affectionately called the Breakfast Club, stands at about 35, but that number includes some franchisor counsel who hang around to keep the pulse of what the franchisees are up to.

3. Saddler, "Franchise Pacts End in Suits over Contracts," *The Wall Street Journal*, Jan. 15, 1991, p. B-1.

4. *Sheck v. Burger King Corp.*, 756 F. Supp. 543 (S.D. Fla. 1991).

CHAPTER 13

1. Reprinted from Chick's Natural Franchise Offering circular, dated March 1991.
2. Steven S. Raab, *Blueprint for Franchising a Business,* New York: John Wiley & Sons, 1987, p. 81.

CHAPTER 14

1. Originally published in 1981 by Law Journal Seminar Press. Has since been re-published as *Franchising: Realities and Remedies,* most recently updated in 1993.

Index

Special FREE Introductory Membership to
The American Association of Franchisees and Dealers
for purchasers of

THE FRANCHISE FRAUD:
HOW TO PROTECT YOURSELF
BEFORE AND AFTER YOU INVEST

Mail your proof of purchase to the AAFD to receive a FREE six-month franchisee or associate membership. Mail or fax the application below to:

AAFD Membership Department
P.O. Box 81887
San Diego, CA 92138-1887

Name:_____

Address:_____

Phone:_____ Fax Number:_____

I am/am not (circle correct response) currently the owner of a franchised business.
Name of franchise system: (if applicable)

Please enroll me as a special six-month introductory member of the AAFD. Enclosed is my receipt for the purchase of *The Franchise Fraud: How to Protect Yourself Before and After You Invest.* I understand that I am under no obligation to extend my membership.

_____
Signature of Applicant

A $60.00 VALUE!